Without God

Science, Belief, Morality, and The Meaning of Life

Zachary Broom

Copyright © 2019

Without God: Science, Belief, Morality, and the Meaning of Life

Zachary Broom

All rights reserved.

To Mike
And Those Who Doubt

Contents

Preface   1

Introduction
Ideas Have Consequences   3

Chapter One
The Keys to Knowledge   17

Chapter Two
Science and Religion   39

Chapter Three
Right and Wrong   63

Chapter Four
Human Rights   81

Chapter Five
The Moral Lawgiver   97

Chapter Six
The Science of Good and Evil   125

Chapter Seven The Evolution of Morality	145
Chapter Eight The Meaning of Life	169
Chapter Nine A New Hope	189
Chapter Ten Evil and Suffering	221
Chapter Eleven The Evidence for God	251
Chapter Twelve Believe the Better Story	271
Acknowledgements	299
Notes	301

"THE EMPIRES OF THE FUTURE WILL BE EMPIRES OF THE MIND."

—Winston Churchill

Preface

From a very early age, I was a doubter. Beginning around the age of seven, I found myself regularly doubting whether I was really a Christian. "Had my salvation prayer worked? Did I really mean it? I'd better do it again to make sure," I thought to myself. As I grew older, my doubts began to shift. It was a few years later that I remember riding with my father in the car and asking him about the problem of evil. If God knew Adam and Eve would choose to sin, I wondered, why would He create them anyway?

Many years later while attending graduate school, I worked a job doing overnight security. My boss was an agnostic who seemed to know more about Christianity than most of the Christians I knew, and it wasn't long before we began discussing theology, philosophy, science, politics, and everything and anything else. During our many conversations, he raised several skeptical questions that I didn't have answers to. This compelled me to learn more about my faith and his skepticism, and so I began to read. We ended up sharing each other's favorite books on atheism and Christianity, which sparked many conversations. This precious experience forged my faith in a way that couldn't have happened inside the walls of a church or seminary. In the end, I walked away from these conversations with a respect for those who doubt Christianity, while also having three foundational reasons for my faith: the experiential, the historical, and the philosophical.

The first reason is the *experiential*, and if I am honest, it is probably the least compelling of the three for me. Even so, the power of the Gospel to radically change and shape people's lives is strong evidence for God's existence. The second reason is the *historical*. When I read C. S. Lewis's trilemma on determining who Jesus was, I found it compelling. We must all answer the question, "Who was Jesus?" Was He a *liar* who blatantly made false claims in an attempt to gain power and influence? Or was He a *lunatic* who just thought He was the Son of God? The third option is *Lord*—Jesus was who He claimed to be, and this explanation fits best with the historical records about Jesus and the rise of the church. Some have suggested that Jesus was merely a good teacher, but, as Lewis points out, this is the only conclusion we can't come to since a good teacher wouldn't say the sort of things Jesus said unless they were true—many of His followers suffered and died for His teachings. There is another view that Lewis left out, the *legend* view, which holds that Jesus' life story was embellished over time. However, I found this option to have too many insurmountable problems, so it didn't persuade me.

The last reason is the *philosophical*. When it comes to life's big questions, I believe that theism, specifically Christianity, offers the most explanatory power of all the worldviews. On issues such as basic human intuition, the meaning of life, morality, human rights, and evil and suffering, Christianity is unparalleled. This book is primarily an attempt to examine and defend this last reason, the philosophical argument for God's existence.

Introduction

Ideas Have Consequences

> *"Suffer the little children to come unto Me."*
> — Matthew 19:14

As a boy growing up in Minnesota, the name Jacob Wetterling was all too familiar. He was the kid whose picture was on the back of our milk cartons at school. Why? Because on October 22, 1989, Jacob went missing. That Sunday evening Jacob, his brother Trevor, and best friend Aaron had biked to a nearby Tom Thumb convenience store to rent a movie, but little did they know, Jacob's abductor, Danny Heinrich, had passed the boys on the road and was lying in wait for their return. Heinrich parked his car in a driveway and faced the direction of the road he knew they'd be coming back on. As the boys returned twenty minutes later, Heinrich got out of his car and approached them, wearing a mask and wielding a revolver. He ordered the boys to get into the ditch with their bicycles, and then asked them their names and ages. The boys offered Heinrich the movie they had just rented, but he knocked it down, told Trevor and Aaron to run away, and that if they looked back, they'd be shot.

Heinrich then forced Jacob into his car, handcuffed him behind his back, and drove to the next county while listening to a police scanner that was crackling with news of the abduction.[1] There, on the outskirts of town, Heinrich pulled the car over near a gravel pit, then walked Jacob to a grove of trees, uncuffed him, removed his clothes, and sexually assaulted him. Twenty minutes later, Jacob complained of being cold, so Heinrich allowed him to get dressed. "What did I do wrong?" Jacob asked. After not answering his question, the 11-year-old boy began to cry. Heinrich began to panic and pulled out his revolver. He told Jacob to turn away from him because he had to go to the bathroom, but then raised the revolver to the boy's head. Looking away, he pulled the trigger, but the gun only clicked. He pulled the trigger again, and this time it went off. Looking back, he saw Jacob was still standing, so he raised the revolver and shot him again, causing the boy to fall to the ground. He then buried Jacob's body in a shallow grave, covered it with grass and brush, and went back home. A year later, he returned under the cover of darkness to find Jacob's red jacket sticking out of the shallow grave, so he gathered as much of Jacob's remains as he could into a bag and re-buried him at a farm. Heinrich guarded his secret from authorities for nearly twenty-seven years until he was arrested for child pornography, which eventually led to the discovery that Jacob was not his first victim.[2]

Introduction

The story of Jacob Wetterling is evil beyond imagination. Is there anything more horrific than the violent murder and sexual assault of children? Evidently not everyone thinks so, as it is estimated that nearly ten million children worldwide are living an unimaginable nightmare as sex slaves in the illegal, multi-billion-dollar industry known as human trafficking. This plague upon our world isn't just overseas—it is happening in our very backyards, with estimates of up to 300,000 children in the United States alone.[3] In 2017, law enforcement busted a massive online pedophile ring, which had upwards of 70,000 members, including teachers, police officers, and scout leaders. Police rescued 230 children between the ages of seven and fourteen.[4] The market for human trafficking is booming, with profits increasing every year and no sign of decline. These startling truths should make us pause to wonder—how could so many people engage in such heinous evil?

But what is evil? We live in a world where the very definition of good and evil is being challenged. It was once nearly universally accepted that people had basic human rights that came from God Himself, and to trample on those rights was wrong, regardless of what anyone thought. Our society used to hold that everyone was born with a conscience that would caution them to the peril of committing moral evil or accuse them with guilt when they had. While our conscience could never inform us of moral truth, it did motivate us to live by it once moral truth was recognized.[5] Not so anymore. In 2017, a Barna survey showed that two-thirds of American adults believe that "every culture must determine what is acceptable morality for its people." Three-quarters of millennials strongly or somewhat agree with the statement, "Whatever is right for your life or works best for you is the only truth you can know," whereas only 39% of those born prior to 1945 strongly or somewhat agreed. David Kinnaman, president of the Barna Group, explains that the research shows, "The highest good, according to our society, is 'finding yourself' and then living by 'what's right for you.'[6]"

But even with such a massive change in moral perspective, isn't it simply obvious that child sex trafficking is wrong? Isn't it just common sense? In one way, yes. The great Christian writer C. S. Lewis, author of *The Chronicles of Narnia, Mere Christianity,* and a host of other theological works, believed that everyone has a basic sense of right and wrong, what he called "the law of human nature." We all continually appeal to some standard of behavior that we expect everyone else to follow. For instance, when we expect others to keep their promises, not budge in line, return favors, and not harm innocent people, we are appealing to a standard of behavior to measure a person's actions by. When people break this standard, it is not just a matter of their behavior displeasing us; rather, we respond as if they've broken a law they ought to have known about.

Though we quickly recognize when others break the law of human nature, Lewis noticed that we rarely admit when we break it ourselves. Instead, we come up with reasons why our circumstances are unique in order to justify our actions. We blame our bad actions on special circumstances, like being tired, frustrated, or hungry, while we credit our good actions to our good nature. But if the law of human nature doesn't exist, why are we so anxious to make excuses when we break it? The reality is that we all believe in the law of human nature so firmly that we cannot bear to face the fact that we are breaking it, so we strive to shift the blame in an attempt to justify our actions.[7]

Lewis believed that the law of human nature provides us with two moral truths. The first is that everyone has knowledge of a moral law that we did not create, but feels obligated to follow. The second truth is the realization that we all fail to keep this moral law. So even though we are experts at making excuses when we break it, we still know better. Popular New Atheist author Sam Harris alludes to Lewis's second truth when he writes:

I have no doubt that I am less good than I could be . . . I know that helping people who are starving is far more important than most of what I do. I strongly believe that I would be happier if I wanted to help the starving more—and I have no doubt that they would be happier if I spent more time and money helping them—but these beliefs are not sufficient to change me . . . I am, therefore, virtually certain that I am neither as moral, nor as happy, as I could be.[8]

Atheist philosopher Michael Ruse seemingly agrees with Sam Harris when he writes: "I believe I think along with most people that I have obligations to all human beings, although I would be the first to admit that I infrequently, if ever, live up to what I sometimes proclaim."[9] The words of the apostle Paul seem to echo in their thoughts; "For I do not understand my own actions. For I do not do what I want, but I do the very thing I hate."[10]

It is an inescapable truth that we are all breaking the law of human nature. Even though we might disagree on what is and is not a part of the law of human nature, we all know that we break it in at least some way. If you still disagree, I'd like you to try something. Write down a list of all of the things that you believe are wrong in this world—things that a person just shouldn't do. Now, if you're honest, when you compare yourself with your list, you will likely see that even you have failed to follow your own moral standard of right and wrong. Forget about following God's laws—we can't even follow our own.

Maybe your response to moral failure is something like the following: "Well, yes, we all break our own standards that we set up, but that doesn't prove there is any such thing as a law of human nature. Societies have always disagreed on what actions are right and wrong, and in fact, it has changed over time." Lewis would disagree. He pointed out that we must distinguish between differences of morality and differences of belief about facts. For instance, one argument against Lewis's view of a common morality was that three hundred years ago people were burning witches alive for selling their soul to the devil; however, today we know better, and so we have progressed morally. Lewis saw it differently:

> *But surely the reason we do not execute witches is that we do not believe there are such things. If we did—if we really thought that there were people going about who had sold themselves to the devil and received supernatural powers from him in return and were using these powers to kill their neighbors or drive them mad or bring bad weather, surely we would all agree that if anyone deserved the death penalty, then these filthy quislings did. There is no difference of moral principle here: the difference is simply about matter of fact. It may be a great advance in knowledge not to believe in witches: there is no moral advance in not executing them when you do not think they are there. You would not call a man humane for ceasing to set mousetraps if he did so because he believed there were no mice in the house.*[11]

Lewis's point is compelling. The different moral systems we find in cultures around the world are not actually different moralities, but the same law of human nature operating under different beliefs about facts, which results in different worldviews. However, even among the different worldviews you will still find the same common moral qualities in effect, though often applied differently (and sometimes horrifically). No country or people have ever admired men for being cowards or for double-crossing everyone that was kind to them.[12] Even radically corrupt cultures like Hitler's Nazi Germany still had the same law of human nature operating within its twisted moral system.

During Adolph Hitler's Third Reich, the Nazi killing machine murdered a total of eleven million people: one out of every three Jews on the planet (six million), and five million non-Jews, which included: Poles, Czechs, gypsies, homosexuals, religious deviants, and many others.[13] Eleven million people's lives were suddenly ripped away from them by the Nazis, who were barbaric and cruel to an unimaginable degree. Holocaust survivors have testified to the Nazis' brutality of how Jewish babies were thrown into crematorium furnaces alive, and their death cries could be heard all throughout the camp.[14] In the face of such horrific evil, how can we possibly reconcile these terrible actions with Lewis's law of human nature?

Viktor Frankl, an inmate at Auschwitz, saw firsthand the cruelty displayed by the Nazis' moral system. However, Frankl would have agreed with Lewis's view, since he believed that the Nazis' terrible cruelty was attributed to one thing: alternate beliefs about reality that shaped their moral system. Frankl wrote:

If we present a man with a concept of man which is not true, we may well corrupt him. When we present man as an automaton of reflexes, as a mind-machine, as a bundle of instincts, as a pawn of drives and reactions, as a mere product of instinct, heredity, and environment, we feed the nihilism to which modern man is, in any case, prone. I became acquainted with the last stage of that corruption in my second concentration camp, Auschwitz. The gas chambers of Auschwitz were the ultimate consequence of the theory that man is nothing but the product of heredity and environment—or, as the Nazi liked to say, "of Blood and Soil." I am absolutely convinced that the gas chambers of Auschwitz, Treblinka, and Maidanek were ultimately prepared not in some Ministry or other in Berlin, but rather at the desks and in the lecture halls of nihilistic scientists and philosophers.[15]

Do you see what Frankl is saying? The Nazis were not operating on an alternative moral system, but under the same moral system as everyone else. The difference is that they operated on dangerous alternative views of reality. The American scholar Richard Weaver had it right when he said that ideas have consequences. Ideas not only shape other ideas, but they drive our world and create our history.[16]

The Nazis believed in eugenics, a cruel and extremist version of Darwinian Theory, which strived to improve the human race by discouraging the reproduction of those with genetic defects or presumed undesirable traits, and then encouraging the reproduction of those with desirable traits. Essentially, the Nazis believed in the superiority and inferiority of races. However, this view didn't actually originate in Germany, but in the United States. From the early 1900s to the 1970s, over 60,000 individuals were deemed genetically inferior and were forcibly sterilized under eugenics legislation in the United States.[17] Popular eugenics books taught that only blonde-haired, blue-eyed whites were worthy of reproducing, while the inferior races should have their reproductive abilities destroyed. An *Applied Eugenics* textbook published in 1918 went as far as recommending the execution of the radically unfit by making use of gas chambers.[18] In a 1911 report sponsored by the Carnegie Foundation, several methods were advocated for "cutting off the defective germplasm in the human population," which included euthanasia. It was the writings of Californian eugenicists that first introduced the German officials and scientists to eugenics, which greatly influenced Hitler himself.[19] The Nazis' final solution did not spring up at random, but was the natural culmination of the ideas propagated by the eugenics movement.

The Nazis' crimes against humanity were certainly despicable, but even amidst such unbearable cruelty, they still believed it was absolutely wrong to kill another German in cold blood; it was only towards the inferior races that killing was morally permissible. The moral principle to not arbitrarily kill another human being was still in effect, if only in part. Think about it—if there were truly subhuman races living among us, corrupting our societies, and poisoning the human genetic pool, then it's not too far of a stretch to see how the Nazis came up with their final solution. It was the Nazis' wrong beliefs about facts that twisted their understanding of the law of human nature into a hideous nightmare.[20]

Returning once again to the issues of sexual assault and human trafficking, how can one's worldview lead to such horrific actions? As mentioned before, Christianity teaches that human rights really do exist, since all humans are created in the image of God and therefore have certain inalienable rights. But if you drop that belief, then what remains? Atheist writer Richard Dawkins offers us his answer that originates from within his worldview when he writes:

> *In a universe of electrons and selfish genes, blind physical forces and genetic replication, some people are going to get hurt, other people are going to get lucky, and you won't find any rhyme or reason in it, nor any justice. The universe that we observe has*

precisely the properties we should expect if there is, at bottom, no design, no purpose, no evil, no good, nothing but pitiless indifference.[21]

Whatever your worldview happens to be, it *will* affect your moral understanding, as a worldview is nothing but a collection of beliefs about reality.[22] When a society removes one moral foundation, it must and will be replaced with another. If a society drops its belief in God as its source for morality, then it must be replaced with something *else*, and whatever that *else* is will come with certain inevitable consequences.

On February 24, 2005, Mark Lunsford's alarm went off at 5:00 a.m. for his usual workday. As he lay there in bed, he could hear his nine-year-old daughter Jessica's alarm going off in her room. She was a very affectionate daughter. Her grandmother recounts how just the night before Jessica had told her father, "In case that you're not here when I get done with my bath, I just want to give you a hug and tell you I love you." As Mark was getting ready for work, he noticed that Jessica's alarm was still going off, and so he went into her room to wake her, expecting to find her fast asleep holding the stuffed animal she always slept with, but Jessica was nowhere to be found.

The police would soon discover that on the previous night, John Couey had snuck into little Jessica's room and taken her to his nearby trailer, where she was raped repeatedly and forced to remain in a closet without food for three days. Couey then tricked Jessica into getting into two garbage bags by assuring her that he was going to take her home, but instead, he buried her alive. On March 18, 2005, police found Jessica's body buried in a shallow grave under the back porch of a mobile home less than 150 yards from her house. She was found clutching her stuffed dolphin, which her father won for her at a state fair.[23]

Are we really ready to say that there is no such thing as absolute evil in this universe? Nothing but pitiless indifference? Though Dawkins would agree that crimes against children are wrong, how does his worldview allow him to say that? Atheist philosophers of the past, including Voltaire, Sartre, and Nietzsche, were honest enough to realize the ridiculousness of life and the pointlessness of everything in an atheistic universe. Sartre even eventually went as far as to denounce atheism on his deathbed as being philosophically unlivable.[24] Though many disagree with Sartre's conclusion, the question logically remains: how can we make sense of good and evil without God?

Philosophers have long wrestled over the question, "If God is dead, is everything permitted?" Non-theists assure us that God is not necessary for establishing a moral system, and they are often deeply offended when they hear theists argue otherwise; however, this misses the point. Theists are not saying that if you do not believe in God you are automatically going to be a terrible person; they are saying that logically justifying morality requires God's existence. An atheist could live a very moral life, and this wouldn't disprove the theist's claim that God is necessary for justifying morality. In order to disprove this claim, atheists would have to logically ground morality within their own naturalistic worldview.

But haven't Christians also committed terrible acts of violence? Doesn't this prove that belief in God is not necessary for grounding morality? I don't think so. The Christian apologist Ravi Zacharias explains why:

The difference between someone who calls himself or herself a Christian and yet kills and slaughters and an atheist who does the same thing is that the Christian is acting in violation of his or her own belief, while the atheist's action is the legitimate outworking of his or her belief.[25]

Zacharias insists that Christians who commit terrible acts of violence are acting contrary to their worldview, while atheists who live moral lives are acting contrary to theirs. Though Christians and atheists can both live moral lives, it is under the worldview of the Christian that there is a logical foundation for doing so, while under atheism, there isn't. Essentially, the claim is if God does not exist, then everything is morally permissible and life has no meaning. But if that's true, and God doesn't exist, then that would mean men like Danny Heinrich, John Couey, and Adolph Hitler did nothing wrong, since after all, our universe is one of "no design, no purpose, no evil, no good, nothing but pitiless indifference."[26] This is a bold conclusion that does not sit well with most atheists, but nevertheless, we must ask ourselves, is it true? But in order to determine if it is true, we must first establish how we determine truth.

CHAPTER ONE
The Keys to Knowledge

> *"Pilate said to Him, 'What is truth?'"*
> — John 18:38

> *"The greatest enemy of knowledge is not ignorance,*
> *it is the illusion of knowledge."*
> — Daniel J. Boorstin

In Western society, it is a commonly held belief that science is all that is necessary to determine truth. In the past, humanity used superstitious belief to explain natural phenomena, such as lightning being the result of the god Zeus hurling bolts from Heaven, or thunder being the result of the mighty god Thor beating his hammer. Today, however, we know better because of science and its rational explanations, which means superstitious religious belief should be discarded. While this narrative is appealing to many, it's misguided as both science and religion ultimately rest upon belief-based philosophical assumptions.

What Is Science?

Albert Einstein described a scientist as a "real seeker after truth."[1] But what about philosophy and other branches of knowledge? What is the difference between science and philosophy? Philosopher Alvin Plantinga defines science as the search for truth in an *empirical* (observable) way. He argues that even though it is difficult to nail down what exactly is required for something to be labeled as *science*, there must be some sort of observable element for it to qualify, which is what distinguishes science from philosophy.[2]

Popular atheist author Sam Harris argues that science is often defined with too narrow of terms. Advocating for a broader view, he writes:

Some people maintain this view by defining "science" in exceedingly narrow terms, as though it were synonymous with mathematical modeling or immediate access to experimental data. However, this is to mistake science for a few of its tools. Science simply represents our best effort to understand what is going on in this universe, and the boundary between it and the rest of rational thought cannot always be drawn. There are many tools one must get in hand to think scientifically—ideas about cause and effect, respect for evidence and logical coherence, a dash of curiosity and intellectual honesty, the inclination to make falsifiable predictions, etc.—and these must be put to use long before one starts worrying about mathematical models or specific data.[3]

Though Harris and Plantinga agree that it is difficult to give a precise definition of science, Harris's idea of science as "thinking scientifically" and "our best effort to understand what is going on in this universe" muddies the water in an effort to broaden science as the all-encompassing detector of truth.

Atheist philosopher Massimo Pigliucci strongly disagrees with Harris and the New Atheists' broad definition of science, saying:

What I do object to is the tendency, found among many New Atheists, to expand the definition of science to pretty much encompassing anything that deals with "facts," loosely conceived. So broadened, the concept of science loses meaning and it becomes indistinguishable from just about any other human activity. One might as well define "philosophy" as the discipline that deals with thinking and then claim that everything we do, including of course science itself, properly belongs to philosophy. It would be a puerile and useless exercise, and yet it is not far from the attitude prevalent among the New Atheists.[4]

Pigliucci is right. If we simply define science as "truth" or "facts," then it becomes so broad that it loses its meaning. A more balanced view of science would come closer to the Oxford dictionary's definition of the scientific method: "Science: a method of procedure that has characterized natural science since the 17th century, consisting in systematic observation, measurement, and experiment, and the formulation, testing, and modification of hypotheses."[5] However, this definition isn't perfect either, since few scientists limit their science strictly to the scientific method, as it would greatly limit their ability to make new discoveries. There are many scientific theories that go well beyond the scientific method, as they are not directly observable nor testable. For example, the theory of electrons is a scientific assertion; however, by itself it isn't observable or directly testable.[6] Compare this unobservable theory with another —there are invisible fairies that live in my garden who are responsible for its growth. Both theories are unobservable, but we regard one as scientific and the other as fantasy.

As Plantinga argues, we simply cannot take assertions one by one and declare them to be scientific or unscientific, depending solely upon whether they are empirically testable.[7] While the scientific method certainly is a good baseline for determining what is and is not scientific, science should not be strictly limited to this. Even though there isn't universal agreement on what is considered science, caution is needed the further we move away from the scientific method when defining it.[8] If we move too far away from the scientific method, and declare science as "anything that deals with facts," we venture into a philosophical belief system called *scientism*.[9] Pigliucci defines scientism as, "a totalizing attitude that regards science as the ultimate standard and arbiter of all interesting questions . . . human knowledge and understanding."[10] In the next chapter, we will take time to look at scientism more closely, but Pigliucci is right—scientism is the result of overstating the power of science while failing to recognize that science ultimately rests upon non-observable, philosophical assumptions.[11] So, what are those assumptions?

The Foundation of Science

Just as there are physical laws in the universe, there are also logical laws that ground reality and truth. The first of the three logical laws is *the law of identity*, which states that something is what it is, and isn't what it isn't. For example, a cat is a cat and that is that; it is not a dog, tree, zebra, or sunset. The second law of logic is *the law of noncontradiction*, which states that something cannot be both true and false at the same time and in the same way. For example, it would be a contradiction if you said that you went to the baseball game yesterday and that you did not go to the baseball game yesterday. The third law of logic is *the law of the excluded middle*, which helps us make absolute truth statements. The statement, "I am a father," is either true or false. I can't *sort of* be a father; either I am, or I am not.

The laws of logic only apply to objective truth, and are not affected by our personal opinions or feelings. On the contrary, subjective truth is not bound by the laws of logic, since it is based on our personal preferences, feelings, and experiences, which can change according to our whims and fancies. For example, I believe that blue is the prettiest color out of all the colors, and I find red to be slightly obnoxious. This is clearly a subjective truth based upon my personal opinion, and so logic has no authority over it. However, if I claim that two plus two equals four, this claim is either true or false, regardless of anyone's opinion. Since it is an objective claim about the nature of reality, the laws of logic then apply.

The laws of logic also give us three forms of thought: *deductive*, *inductive*, and *abductive* reasoning. Deductive reasoning is the most reliable form of logical reasoning that we have, but it has serious limits since it only works in certain circumstances. With a deductive argument, if all of the premises are true, then the conclusion absolutely follows logically.[12] For instance:

> *Premise 1: Everyone who lives in Manhattan lives in New York City.*
> *Premise 2: Everyone who lives in New York City lives in New York State*
> *Conclusion: Therefore, everyone who lives in Manhattan lives in New York State.*

The strength of this kind of argument is that it proves the conclusion absolutely so long as the premises are all true, and the argument has good logical structure. You may then perhaps be thinking, "Great, so let's only use deductive reasoning!" But there is just one problem—if we only used deductive arguments to determine truth, we wouldn't know much of anything since we couldn't even rely on our memories. This is where inductive reasoning steps in to help us out.

Inductive reasoning is all about probability and drawing conclusions based off past experiences. For example:

> *Premise 1: Swan 1 is white.*
> *Premise 2: Swan 2 is white.*
> *Premise 3: Swan 3 is white…*
> *Premise 1000: Swan 1000 is also white.*
> *Conclusion: All swans are white.*

Notice this conclusion isn't certain because we haven't been able to verify that every single swan that exists or has existed is white—but we conclude they all are anyway. An inductive argument differs from a deductive argument in that even if all of the premises are true, we cannot be certain that the conclusion is true. This doesn't mean an inductive argument is bad, it just means it's not a for-sure thing since it deals with past experience and probability, which is what we need to do science.

Playing the Odds

All of the objective facts in the entire universe represent *ontological truth*, while what we know and how we know things represent *epistemological truth*. Philosophers use these terms to distinguish between "what we think we currently know" and "what there is to know." For example: If all existing truth (ontology) were represented by a jigsaw puzzle, what we know (epistemology) would only be a few pieces from the puzzle. This means that what we know can only be known in varying degrees of probability, since after all, we only have a small portion of the entire puzzle—we are always drawing conclusions based off of partial information. So then, what would it take to overturn a scientific theory that is considered a near certainty? It's actually quite simple—more pieces from the puzzle.

Once we come to realize that we are working with only a small segment of the puzzle when we draw conclusions, we can easily see how what we consider scientific truth comes nowhere near one-hundred percent fact. How could it? At any moment, another piece or two of the puzzle could be discovered that might drastically reshape our understanding of what was previously considered a near scientific certainty. Journalist and atheist author Robert Wright recognizes this concept in his book *The Moral Animal*, where he writes:

> *Still, it is always good to have more evidence. Though absolute "proof" may not be possible in science, varying degrees of confidence are. And while evolutionary explanations rarely attain the 99.99 percent confidence sometimes found in physics or chemistry, it's always nice to raise the level from, say, 70 to 97 percent.*[13]

Consequently, the small total of what we know is different from what there is to know, and what we currently know is based upon varying degrees of probability. The reality is, when it comes to scientific certainty, we are only working with a small portion of the puzzle pieces.

Occam's Razor

One day after work, John arrives home to find a note from his wife that says, "Ran out of milk, went to the store." After seeing no milk in the fridge, John concludes that his wife left him the note, and must have gone to the store to get milk. But how can John know this? He didn't observe any of it. Isn't it possible that someone took his wife captive, drank the milk in the fridge, and left the note so that John wouldn't come looking for her right away? How can John confidently conclude that it was his wife who left the note and not an abductor?

The reason John doesn't jump to wild conclusions is because of abductive reasoning, which is the third form of logical reasoning. This form of reasoning is similar to inductive reasoning, and is sometimes called an educated guess, or inference to the best explanation. For example, when a baby cries and you smell something unpleasant, you use abduction to conclude that the baby's diaper needs to be changed, while you use induction to further support it since this has happened in the past. Without inductive reasoning John could not draw conclusions based off past events, and without abductive reasoning he might come up with all sorts of extravagant explanations when there aren't enough regular past occurrences to make use of inductive reasoning. Abductive reasoning is often called *Occam's razor*, which comes from the medieval philosopher William of Occam. The idea is to *shave off* unnecessarily complex explanations when a simpler one suffices. Therefore, by using Occam's razor (abductive reasoning), along with inductive reasoning, we prevent ourselves from rushing to wild explanations.

The Inductivist Turkey

Bill and Ned are turkeys who have been fed at 8:30 am every day for the past 364 days. On the 365th day, no food arrives. It's now 9:30 am, and Ned is getting paranoid since he's heard rumors about turkeys being cooked and eaten for some sort of human festivity. Bill, the rational and enlightened inductivist turkey, calmly explains to Ned why he is being irrational. "Ned, we've been fed at roughly the same time every day for nearly a year, so we can easily conclude that the farmer is just behind schedule and will be here shortly." Ned listens to Bill's rational and carefully thought-out reasoning, but he doesn't care. He trusts his intuition and heads for the woods. Bill laughs at Ned for being so paranoid and superstitious, and for not trusting in the powers of induction and abduction to arrive at rational and scientific conclusions. Fifteen minutes later, the farmer arrives just as Bill predicted, but for some reason he is carrying a sharp axe instead of a bag of food.[14]

The sad story of the inductivist turkey demonstrates the limits of inductive and abductive reasoning. While they are both useful and necessary tools, they have and will fail us from time to time. At the start of this chapter I said that science ultimately relies on philosophical assumptions to even get started. The idea that the future will resemble the past, often called the uniformity of nature, is one of those assumptions that comes from inductive reasoning. But as we have seen, inductive reasoning is anything but guaranteed. Still, we must rely on it if we want to do things like build a house, use language, rely on our memories, design and manufacture cars, cure strep throat, or farm crops. If we didn't assume the uniformity of nature (inductive reasoning), we would be unable to do much of anything, and science would not be possible.[15] Even though this assumption doesn't bother most people, philosophers are deeply troubled by it.

Massimo Pigliucci explains how the great philosopher David Hume was deeply troubled by his discovery that inductive reasoning is ultimately a form of circular reasoning. He writes:

> *[Hume] pointed out that the only reason we think that induction is a good way to proceed about making inferences concerning the world is because it has worked in the past . . . Hume was saying that our endorsement of induction is in itself a form of induction: we argue that induction works because it has worked in the past, thereby applying inductive reasoning to justify induction. This, Hume observed, is an instance of circular reasoning, one of the most elementary logical fallacies. Let me put it clearly: Hume's critique amounts to saying that there is no rigorously logical foundation for the entire enterprise of science!*[16]

Is Hume right? If science rests upon inductive reasoning, and we can't prove inductive reasoning without appealing to it, then is science dependent upon a circular argument?

Stepping Out of the Darkness

When I was in high school, a classmate of mine explained that he believed everyone and everything was part of a dream world in which he was the only actual real person, and everyone else was just a figment of his imagination. Whether he truly believed this, I don't know, but I remember some of the arguments other classmates would use against his view of reality. While we all thought he was a little bit crazy, interestingly enough, every argument in favor of our view of reality also fit with his.[17]

Alvin Plantinga explains that the history of modern philosophy, from Descartes through Hume, reveals that there doesn't appear to be any good arguments for the existence of other minds, the past, or even an external world, but we go on believing in them anyway.[18] Famous atheist writer Bertrand Russell agreed, when he pointed out that for all we know, the world popped into existence five minutes ago and all of our memories are fabricated, and we really have no good evidence to prove one view over the other.[19] The question must then be asked, why do we continue to believe in the past, other minds, and the external world if we cannot empirically prove their existence?

When we begin to build our collection of knowledge, we must start with a few basic beliefs, or self-evident truths. In order to know anything, we must know something already, or we won't have any equipment for the investigation. There must be some truths that are not derived from other truths, some first knowledge that does not come from other knowledge or past investigation. These self-evident truths are the foundation from which all truths are built.[20] This is easily understood by asking questions like, "How do we know that we really exist?" You might say, "I think, therefore I exist." But how do you know that you think and that your thoughts are really your own? What evidence could prove the value of evidence? What logic could show the importance of logic?[21] Philosophers understand that these fundamental questions and answers reach a point where no further progress can be made; eventually, some things just are the way they are.

The laws of logic are self-evident truths. Instead of being discovered through observation and the accumulation of evidence, we intuitively recognize these truths. We simply perceive its truth upon reflection, and therefore it needs no further justification. Are you unconvinced? If so, ask yourself how you know that a square circle doesn't exist. You might say, "Well, it's just obvious that it's not possible," and you'd be right. We know that this idea is nonsense since it breaks the laws of logic. Any attempts to disprove the laws of logic can't work since they would depend on logic to do so, and thus are self-defeating.

The existence of self-evident truth doesn't sit well with many, especially those living in a scientific culture who would rather not believe that science rests upon belief, nor that some beliefs do not require evidences to be true.[22] In *The God Argument*, philosopher A. C. Grayling rejects the existence of basic beliefs (self-evident truths), when he writes:

> *The main problem is that calling a belief 'basic,' so that you do not have to argue for it or provide evidence for it, is gratuitous: you can help yourself to anything you like, and of course anything follows. Choose a convenient belief, give it the most convenient content for what else you wish to believe, and then claim that it is 'basic' and therefore in no need of justification. This is too obviously unacceptable to need much comment.*[23]

If you look closely at Grayling's argument, he is essentially saying that it is wrong to call a belief "basic" because it is "too obviously unacceptable." But did you notice the problem? By arguing that we can't appeal to basic arguments because it is a basic truth that we shouldn't, he appeals to a self-evident truth to deny self-evident truths, which is illogical and self-defeating. As C. S. Lewis would say, his argument slits its own throat.

In *The End of Faith*, Sam Harris agrees that some facts are self-evident truths. He writes:

> *The question of why physical events have causes, say, is not one that scientists feel the slightest temptation to ponder. It is just so. To demand an accounting of so basic a fact is like asking how we know that two plus two equals four. Scientists presuppose the validity of such brutishness [self-evident truth]—as, indeed, they must. The point, I trust, is obvious: we cannot step out of the darkness without taking a first step.*[24]

Harris is right. We all start with some brute facts (self-evident truths), and so a person is mistaken if they claim they hold no unprovable beliefs; we all have them, but we differ over which ones we accept. As an evidentialist, Grayling is concerned that if we accept some beliefs as self-evident, then we will open the door to those who claim all sorts of wild beliefs as self-evident, such as belief in God. In philosophy, this is sometimes called the Great Pumpkin Objection.

In the comic strip *Peanuts*, Linus believes in the existence of the Great Pumpkin that rises from the pumpkin patch every year on Halloween to reward good children with presents. Now, if theists can claim God exists without requiring evidence, then what prevents belief in the Great Pumpkin (or the Flying Spaghetti Monster for that matter) without requiring evidence? This question is certainly worth asking; however, it stems from a misunderstanding of the nature of self-evident truths. Self-evident truths are not self-evidently true because they have no evidence, they are self-evident because they do not begin with evidence. For example, if you ask a child how they know they went to the park the other day, they'll likely be confused, and probably say something like, "Because I went there." Notice that the child isn't listing off all of the reasons for why their belief in the past is justified (evidentialism); instead, they naturally presuppose the past's existence because it is self-evident.

Now, contrast this with the recent graduate of a bad Philosophy 101 course, who instead builds a logical and reasoned case for believing in the existence of the past, an external world, and other minds. Alvin Plantinga rightly argues that what they are doing is actually perverse, since they are questioning truths that we were never meant to question.[25] Even though we can come up with reasons that support a self-evident truth, ultimately, empirical evidence-based arguments are inappropriate as the starting point for them. How could you use reason to prove that the real world isn't a dream world and our dream world is the real world? How could you attempt to prove that your memories of the past exist because the past really happened, instead of them existing because the universe popped into existence five seconds ago and all of your memories are fabricated? Any evidence that you might use is a form of inductive reasoning, and so you are relying on inductive reasoning to prove inductive reasoning, which is a circular argument. Therefore, belief in the past, other minds, an external world, self-existence, mathematics, and logic are all self-evident truths that are derived from our intuition, not argument and evidence.

Some worry that accepting a single self-evident truth opens the door for any belief to be justified on the same grounds. However, as we've seen, everyone holds to at least some self-evident truths, and so we all face this problem of opening and closing the door on which beliefs are truly self-evident. Also, just because a belief is self-evidently true doesn't mean it can be chosen arbitrarily, as a belief can only be self-evident if it is *actually* true and foundational for understanding reality. Simply saying a belief is a self-evident truth does not make it so. When it comes to shutting down self-evident truth claims, we must do so by showing their blatant falsehood, identifying their incompatibility with their own worldview, or by dismantling the worldview.

So, what is the takeaway here? Eventually, all knowledge is pushed back to something foundational—something we seem to have direct awareness of and needs no further evidence. Without at least some self-evident truths, we'd be in an infinite regress and incapable of knowing anything at all.[26] Or, as C. S. Lewis famously put it, "If nothing is self-evident, nothing can be proved."[27] Once our first principles (self-evident truths) have been established, we have a foundation for embracing and applying the laws of logic and thinking rationally—this then allows us to rely on inductive reasoning, which is the foundation for all science.

I am sure that this notion that science ultimately rests upon unprovable beliefs will not sit well with many, but it is undeniably true. Both atheist and theist philosophers alike have recognized this truth for thousands of years, and only recently has our culture forgotten it, since it does not fit well with the warfare model of science and religion.[28] As Aristotle bluntly put it, "it shows lack of education not to know of what we should require proof, and of what we should not. For it is quite impossible that everything should have a proof; the process would go on to infinity."[29]

All Belief Is Biased

Not only does all truth rest upon unprovable beliefs, but we are biased towards certain beliefs. C. S. Lewis once said that we cling to belief in the uniformity of nature (inductive reasoning) because a universe without uniformity is repugnant to us; we refuse to accept such a universe as it is utterly detestable and shocks our senses.[30] We are inclined, or even biased, towards believing in uniformity and inductive reasoning. We all naturally begin with unprovable beliefs to build our knowledge base and there is simply no alternative. Without first principles (self-evident truth) we can't even get started, let alone think about doing science. It is from these unprovable beliefs that a person builds their worldview. This is why Massimo Pigliucci critiques his fellow atheists when they claim that they have no beliefs at all and rely solely upon science to form their worldview; it's simply not possible. While Pigliucci is a serious critic of religion, he realizes that many atheists have a wrong understanding of the difference between belief and knowledge, and so he writes:

> *Atheists need to seriously reconsider how they think of human knowledge in general . . . [They need] a more nuanced, comprehensive embracing of all the varied ways—intellectual as well as experiential—in which human beings acquire knowledge and develop understanding of their world.*[31]

Pigliucci is right; the way we acquire knowledge is more complex than atheists often admit. No matter our worldview, we all rely on belief as the foundation of knowledge. Still, atheists do not consider God's existence to be self-evidently true, and often argue that it is really a form of biased wish fulfillment.

Belief in God Is Wish Fulfillment

The great German philosopher Friedrich Nietzsche once argued that alcohol and Christianity were the two greatest narcotics in all of Europe.[32] Nietzsche said this because he believed that all religious belief is a form of wish fulfillment and is therefore a different kind of belief entirely. Nineteenth-century British mathematician W. K. Clifford firmly declared, "It is wrong, always, everywhere, and for anyone, to believe anything upon insufficient evidence."[33] One could question what evidence Clifford had for this belief, but his point is that religious belief is wrong because it is based upon insufficient evidence. Similarly, the psychologist Sigmund Freud agreed that religious belief was a form of wish fulfillment—a sort of evolutionary illusion that had indirect survival benefits.[34] Bertrand Russell agreed, and saw religion as an attempt to satiate our fear of death. He believed that the function of belief in God is to "humanize the world of nature and to make men feel that physical forces are really their allies."[35] While I disagree with this as a total explanation for religious belief, I do think critics of religion are partly right when they claim that religion is a form of wish fulfillment. However, if we say that religion is a form of wish fulfillment, then we must also admit that atheism is equally its own form of wish fulfillment.

Atheist philosopher Thomas Nagel confesses that his atheism is, without a doubt, influenced by his desires and fear of religion. In his book *The Last Word*, he writes:

> *I want atheism to be true and am made uneasy by the fact that some of the most intelligent and well-informed people I know are religious believers. It isn't just that I don't believe in God and, naturally, hope that I'm right in my belief. It's that I hope there is no God! I don't want there to be a God; I don't want the universe to be like that.*[36]

If we say that theism is a crutch, then so is atheism. If belief in God is a response to the desire to avoid death, could it not also be argued that atheism is a response to the human desire for autonomy and freedom?[37] Aldous Huxley, author of the dystopian classic *Brave New World*, admitted that much when he wrote:

I had motives for not wanting the world to have a meaning; consequently I assumed that it had none, and was able without any difficulty to find satisfying reasons for this assumption . . . For myself, as no doubt for most of my contemporaries, the philosophy of meaninglessness was essentially an instrument of liberation . . . [Liberation from] a certain political and economic system and liberation from a certain system of morality. We objected to the morality because it interfered with our sexual freedom.[38]

Marx and Lenin called religion "the opiate of the people" because of the promise of an afterlife. But it was the Polish poet Czeslaw Milosz who argued, "a true opium of the people is a belief in nothingness after death —the huge solace of thinking that our betrayals, greed, cowardice, murders are not going to be judged."[39] While religious belief is certainly a comfort for the fear of death and the unknown, there is undoubtedly a great liberation and comfort in thinking that we will not be judged for our wrongs. Therefore, if religion is an "opiate of the people," so is atheism.[40]

All belief is biased, complicated, and is never strictly rational across the board. We all bring our predispositions and cultural experiences to the table when we form our worldview, both atheist and theist alike. Another important factor is that beliefs seem more plausible to us if they are held by people whom we admire and desire approval from. For example, if we have known many thoughtful, loving, and kind Christians over the years, we will find the intellectual arguments for Christianity much more believable than if we have known Christians who were self-righteous hypocrites.[41] Though we often do not realize it, we are all deeply biased, which is problematic since determining truth is already difficult enough on its own. So, what should we do then? Should we throw up our hands and give up hope that truth is even possible to discover?

Determining Truth Is Hard

We are all heavily influenced by biased thinking to varying degrees. This is why in a 2001 column in the *National Post*, Robert Fulford wrote: "It is a melancholy truth that most of us are wrong most of the time about the way the world is going. We watch it, we hear about it, we experience it, and usually we don't know what it means."[42] Similarly, philosopher Jean-François Revel argued:

> *The fact is that we do not use our minds to seek out the truth or to establish particular facts with absolute certainty. Above all and in the great majority—if not in the totality—of cases, we use our intellectual faculties to protect convictions, interests, and interpretations that are especially dear to us.*[43]

Determining truth is extremely difficult, and there are no shortcuts or easy solutions. While science has provided us with amazing discoveries, it hasn't even come close to being able to answer our deepest questions, nor could it, since it is the wrong tool for the job. Even though determining truth is hard, we simply don't have any other choice.[44] We must participate in the difficult task of determining truth, while striving to examine our biases, and weigh truth responsibly, despite our preferential nature. When we begin to realize the nature of truth and how it is actually acquired, this should greatly humble us, while also giving us a great advantage in being able to avoid many of the philosophical sand traps that have befallen so many others.

CHAPTER TWO
Science and Religion

"Science flies you to the moon. Religion flies you into buildings."
— Victor Stenger

"Gods are fragile things; they may be killed by a whiff of science or a dose of common sense."
— Chapman Cohen

"In the beginning, God created the heavens and the earth."
— Genesis 1:1

Today's popular atheist writers have drawn their line in the sand: you're either with them or against them. You can either embrace rational scientific thinking, or you can reject it and embrace superstition and ignorance. Religion and science are simply incompatible; it's one or the other. In the past several years, I have had many conversations with atheists and agnostics who seemed to show genuine interest in religious belief, but shied away from it because of its incompatibility with science. Many popular, outspoken scientists tell us that even though God's existence is theoretically possible, it is extremely unlikely.

Modern science has spoken—the God hypothesis is completely unnecessary, since the universe can be explained by natural processes.

Modern atheist writers view religion as an evolutionary byproduct that originated from primitive man, who invented these supernatural explanations in order to make sense of our universe in a pre-scientific world. Popular New Atheist author Christopher Hitchens wrote:

Religion comes from the period of human prehistory where nobody had the smallest idea what was going on. It comes from the bawling and fearful infancy of our species, and is a babyish attempt to meet our inescapable demand for knowledge (as well as for comfort, reassurance and other infantile needs). Today the least educated of my children knows much more about the natural order than any of the founders of religion.[1]

Along the same lines, Bertrand Russell believed that science was the means by which we could throw off our childish ignorance of inventing imaginary friends in the sky, and move on to heal our world from all of the harm that religion has caused.[2] Their point is, science is based on reason, while religion is based on superstition.

Most religions believe that humanity is valuable and holds a position of some importance in the universe. However, modern atheist writers insist that the universe is not about us, and to think so is arrogant.[3] For instance, American paleontologist George Gaylord Simpson wrote, "Man is the result of a purposeless and natural process that did not have him in mind."[4] When the spacecraft

Voyager 1 passed the planet Saturn and sent back a picture of Earth, scientist Carl Sagan, who was a professing atheist, described our planet as "a mote of dust suspended in a sunbeam."[5] According to this thinking, our significance is evidently related to our size, which is comparably microscopic. As an individual, you are merely one person out of seven billion people, on one planet out of eight, located in one star system out of one-hundred billion star systems, inside of one galaxy out of one-hundred billion galaxies. While the old adage, "you are one in a million" might be true, mathematically, this would mean there are seven thousand other identical *yous* out there. We are then, according to this line of thinking, incredibly insignificant.

And yet, the belief that we are insignificant is directly incompatible with what many religions teach. While there are undoubtedly ideas held by scientists that really do conflict with religious belief, philosopher Alvin Plantinga argues that it is the philosophical beliefs that conflict, not the actual scientific evidence.[6] Why should we think that size determines our significance? Science is not a realm that establishes size as a basis for significance. The extensive study of the atom alone would contradict Sagan's size-to-significance argument. In fact, when this claim is examined closely, it doesn't even hold up philosophically, let alone scientifically. Is an eighty-pound child more significant than a forty-pound child? Why assume that size has any bearing at all on significance? And yet, because of unfounded philosophical beliefs such as this, there are many that continue to argue that science and religion are deeply irreconcilable. While the conflict between science and religion has arguably never been stronger than it is now, this wasn't always the case.

Religion Bred Science

The conflict model between science and religion can certainly lead a person to believe that science came along and vanquished the naïve religious beliefs of humanity's ignorant past; however, this couldn't be further from the truth. Nearly all of the great names of early Western science, including Nicholas Copernicus, Galileo Galilei, Isaac Newton, Robert Boyle, John Wilkins, and Roger Cotes, were serious believers in God.[7] The great scientist Isaac Newton once wrote: "This most beautiful system of the sun, planets and comets, could only proceed from the counsel and dominion of an intelligent and powerful Being . . . This Being governs all things, not as the soul of the world, but as Lord over all."[8]

Alvin Plantinga argues that the claim that Christianity is anti-science is a false one. The truth is, he writes, "Modern Western empirical science originated and flourished in the bosom of Christian theism and originated nowhere else."[9] The great twentieth-century physicist C. F. von Weizsäcker agreed, saying: "In this sense, I call modern science a legacy of Christianity."[10] It was their theistic worldview that led many of the great early scientists, such as Johannes Kepler, to expect the regularity of nature and believe that nature had laws that made sense, since they were put into place by a great intellect.[11] Paul Dirac, the physicist who contributed to the early development of quantum theory, said that God was a "mathematician of a very high order and He used advanced mathematics in constructing the universe."[12] Though atheists rightly point out that Albert Einstein didn't believe in a personal God, but in Spinoza's divine force god, Einstein nevertheless wrote: "Every one who is seriously involved in the pursuit of science becomes convinced that a spirit is manifest in the laws of the universe—a spirit vastly superior to that of man, and one in the face of which we with our modest powers must feel humble."[13] Many great scientists have firmly believed in a creator, and this belief drove their science, not hindered it. But if science and religion used to be hand in hand, why are prominent atheist writers declaring that the two are in deep and irreconcilable conflict?

The Conflict Model

In *The Reason for God*, Tim Keller explains how the conflict model between science and religion has been deliberately exaggerated by the media because of their need to report events with a protagonist and antagonist. Because controversy sells, the media gives wide publicity to the battles between secular and religious people over the teaching of evolution in schools, stem-cell research, in vitro fertilization, and many other controversial areas of medicine and science. It is the wide reporting of these battles that gives credibility to New Atheist writers' claim that you must choose between science and religious belief.[14] The conflict model was deliberately exaggerated by both scientists and educational leaders near the end of the nineteenth century in order to undermine the church's influence and cultural power.[15] Even though the conflict model between science and religion receives a lot of attention, no major historian of science takes this conflict seriously anymore.[16] Explaining how the conflict model is a myth, historian Alister McGrath writes:

> *One of the most remarkable developments of the nineteenth and early twentieth centuries has been the relentless advance of the perception that there exists a permanent, essential conflict between the natural sciences and religion . . . One of the last remaining bastions of atheism survives only at the popular level—namely, the myth that an atheistic, fact-based science is permanently at war with a faith-based religion. Not only is this caricature clearly untrue in the present day, but historical scholarship has now determined it to be misleading and inaccurate in the past. Yet the myth still lives on in popular atheist writings, undisturbed by the findings of scholars.*[17]

Modern scholarship has decisively come down against the notion that science is connected with atheism. Nevertheless, in his book *The God Delusion*, Richard Dawkins claims that nearly all prominent scientists disbelieve in God. However, critics have shown that there are flaws with the way Dawkins interpreted the data he relied on. For example, a survey he referenced was designed to only detect scientists with conservative beliefs in a personal God, so anyone with a more general deistic belief was ruled out entirely.[18] Also, Dawkins's conclusion assumes that the cause of atheism amongst scientists is on purely scientific grounds, but the study doesn't show this.[19] Many atheists reject belief in God not for scientific reasons, but for philosophical ones. For instance, it was the problem of evil that led Einstein to reject traditional belief in God.[20] Contrary to Dawkins's conclusion, a large number of scientists consider themselves deeply or moderately religious and those numbers have increased in recent decades.[21]

Miracles

At the center of the debate over science and religion is the question whether miracles can happen. The supposed problem is that science only detects and endorses natural laws, so if God acted miraculously in the world, He would have to break these laws, which is incompatible with science. Because science is limited to methodological naturalism (the study of natural causes), scientists can only search for naturalistic explanations for phenomena since those are the only types of causes it can detect. Therefore, science is by definition incompatible with supernatural belief.

While it is true that science can only detect natural causes, this doesn't mean that supernatural causes can't or don't happen; it just means that science is incapable of detecting them. For example, just because we can't mathematically prove that Abraham Lincoln was the President of the United States doesn't mean that math is unreliable; it just means that math isn't the right tool for the job. Similarly, science is a tool that only works with naturalistic causes, so attempting to use it for other tasks is a mistake. It was with this in mind that C. S. Lewis wrote:

> *What cannot be trusted to recur is not material for science: that is why history is not one of the sciences. You cannot find out what Napoleon did at the battle of Austerlitz by asking him to come and fight it again in a laboratory with the same combatants, the same terrain, the same weather, and in the same age. You have to go to the records. We have not, in fact, proved that science excludes miracles: we have only proved that the question of miracles, like innumerable other questions, excludes laboratory treatment.*[22]

The fact that science is incapable of detecting miracles should not alarm us, as classical science tells us how the laws of nature *typically* go, not how they *always* go. Science only tells us how things go when no outside agency interferes.[23]

Though the conflict model between science and religion tends to get the spotlight, the truth is that many leading scientists believe science is incapable of answering the God question as it lies beyond its power. There just isn't any logically airtight means of arguing for the existence or nonexistence of God based solely upon empirical observation of the world.[24] As Alister McGrath points out, the natural sciences have an interesting way of leading some people away from God and others towards Him. To argue that science must lead a person one way over the other is to move away from the scientific method and to smuggle in religious or antireligious claims under a pseudoscientific smokescreen.[25] It is with this in mind that Stephen Jay Gould and other scientists have argued that science and religion address completely separate realms of truth.

Non-overlapping Magisteria

Even though Stephen Jay Gould did not personally believe in God's existence, he fought against the conflict model by advocating for a position called *non-overlapping magisteria*. This view holds that science tells us how the heavens go, while religion tells us how to get to Heaven. This view has increased in popularity as of late, with both religious and non-religious advocates. However, many atheists strongly oppose this approach since so many religions clearly make claims about the natural world. For example, atheist philosopher of science Massimo Pigliucci writes:

> *It is not true that (most) religions do not make claims about the natural world. Besides the tens of millions of people who believe the Earth is 6,000 years old, the Bible was never meant as a book of metaphors. It is read that way by enlightened Christians today precisely because of the long battle between science and religion, with the latter constantly on the losing side.*[26]

Similarly, Richard Dawkins disagrees with Gould's view, arguing that the virgin birth, the resurrection of Jesus, and the afterlife, are all claims of a clearly scientific nature. Either Jesus had an earthly father or He didn't. This is a scientific question even if we do not have the evidence necessary to answer it.[27] Dawkins's point is that most religions break the non-overlapping magisterium by making claims about the natural order, which crosses over into the realm of science. Because of this, atheists conclude that science and religion are deeply incompatible. For instance, A. C. Grayling writes:

> *In fact religion and science are competitors for the truth about quite a number of things, including the origins of the universe, the nature of human beings, and the belief that the laws of nature can be locally and temporarily suspended—thus allowing for miracles. We can be confident that if tests were arranged to adjudicate between these competing claims, they would be won by science.*[28]

The idea of keeping science and religion in their separate corners is appealing to many, as it provides a simple solution to the conflict model by having something for everyone. However, I think Grayling, Dawkins, and Pigliucci are mostly right—religion, especially Christianity, does in fact make claims about the natural order. Another problem with the *non-overlapping magisteria* approach is that it ends up limiting religion to only the leftover questions that science isn't able to answer (at least, not yet), which pushes religion to the sidelines. This also creates a *god of the gaps* approach towards science and religion, which, as Grayling explains, operates by the following principle: "in the absence of having any clue as to what the explanation might be for something, just settle for saying 'a god did it.' This is the 'god of gaps' move."[29] According to this thinking, as science continues to progress, religion is needed less and less, and so it will eventually (if not already) be unnecessary.

Atheists are right that the *god of the gaps* approach to science and religion is lazy and should be avoided. However, they fail to recognize they are also guilty of committing their own kind of *god of the gaps* blunder. By claiming that science will one day be able to explain existence and the universe entirely, they are merely imposing their philosophical beliefs onto science. For instance, they aren't sure how matter came into existence, but nevertheless suggest that a naturalistic solution will one day be discovered. But how do they know that? Is that a scientific claim or a philosophical one? While it is true that science ought to look for naturalistic explanations, since these are the only kind it can detect, to say that because science cannot detect non-natural occurrences means no such occurrences exist, is not science but scientism. This belief that science will one day be able to answer all important questions could rightly be called *naturalism of the gaps,* as it makes a similar error to that of the *god of the gaps* approach.

Philosophy Masquerading as Science

The alleged conflict is not between science and religion, but between scientism and religion. The *god of the gaps* error exists in part because of incorrect interpretations of the Bible, as well as misunderstanding the nature of science. Though, as we discussed in the last chapter, defining the exact nature of science is difficult, it must involve empirical observation and naturalistic explanations. While science doesn't rule out the miraculous, it is incapable of detecting such explanations because of its naturalistic nature. However, notice that by this definition, science is fully compatible with belief in God. Still, many argue that because science can only detect naturalistic causes, no other causes can exist; this, however, is a philosophical belief, not a scientific one. To say that supernatural causes can't occur because science can't detect them is like saying diamonds don't exist because metal detectors can't detect them.[30]

Because of the failure to understand the difference between science and philosophy, it has become popular to look to scientists for answers to questions that are outside the realm of science, on matters in which they have no special expertise. The result is that scientists have been made into the new priestly class who frequently represent their own philosophical views as established scientific truth.[31] However, if we present our philosophy as science, we leave science well behind and venture into scientism. Those who believe in philosophical naturalism are frequently guilty of this error. Philosophical naturalism claims that *only* natural causes exist, while methodological naturalism (science) only works with natural causes once they have been discovered. The one is science; the other is philosophy.

Not only is philosophical naturalism not science, but it closely resembles religious belief. While it is not a religion per se, it clearly plays the same role as one. Alvin Plantinga believes it to be a pseudo-religion since, like religion, it explains our place in the universe, determines how we relate to other creatures, speaks to the existence of God, alludes to how we ought to live, and answers whether there is life after death.[32] This semi-religious belief was demonstrated by Sir Richard Gregory, one of Britain's leading scientists, when he suggested his grave inscription read: "My grandfather preached the gospel of Christ; my father preached the gospel of socialism; I preach the gospel of science."[33] While atheists are free to believe in philosophical naturalism, they make a serious error when they confuse their philosophical beliefs with science.

Philosophical Blunders

Philosophical naturalism's embrace of scientism carries with it several problems—one of which is an improper reverence for nature. In contrast, Christianity offers a deep and rich resource for both appreciating and respecting the environment, while not elevating it to an object of worship. The book of Genesis tells of how God gave humanity the unique responsibility of being stewards over the creation, while in Romans chapter one, we learn that humanity has corrupted the creation through sin, which results in our worshiping the creation rather than the creator. Though caring for the environment is a good thing, when we make good things into gods, we ruin them, since this is a weight they cannot bear. It is certainly true that some Christians have wrongly used and abused the creation; however, Christianity rejects both of these improper responses. The term *mother nature* demonstrates this improper view towards our environment. Instead, Christianity presents the proper attitude towards the creation being more like that of a younger sister than a mother—we are to respect her, look out for her, and treat her with dignity, but not revere her, since reverence is only appropriate for the Creator. While the creation certainly is marvelous, it was meant to give glory to God, not itself.

Philosophical naturalism also suffers from strong rationalism, which is the belief that individuals should rely on their own reasoning power when it comes to answering life's big questions. In Western culture, freedom to think for oneself and to not rely on authority is seen almost as a virtue. Relying on authority is considered repressive, ignorant, and irresponsible.[34] Modern atheist writers evaluate opposing arguments based upon the verification principle, which holds that no person should believe any claim unless it is confirmed by logical and observable experience.[35] But as we saw in the last chapter, all truth rests upon unprovable beliefs for its foundation. This means that strong rationalism is self-defeating, as it is impossible to prove that no one should believe something without proof. Strong rationalism wrongly assumes that it is possible to achieve "the view from nowhere," a position of almost complete objectivity.[36] Philosophers stand in nearly universal agreement that this is impossible, since we all hold unprovable beliefs that are greatly influenced by our preferences, experiences, and culture.

Strong rationalism leads to a zealously biased skepticism, which is precisely what atheists criticize religion for doing. For instance, A. C. Grayling writes: "It is a false view purveyed by monolithic ideologies—the ideologies that say there is one great truth and one right way to live, and everyone must conform, be the same, do the same, obey, submit—that there is only one kind of good life and that it is the same for all."[37] While Grayling's argument might sound reasonable, it does the exact thing that it forbids; it says that the one great truth is that there is no one great truth, and the one right way to live is embracing many right ways to live. Skeptics frequently claim that we should all think for ourselves and choose our own path based upon critical and rational thinking. We ought to refuse to accept dogma or any biased system of belief. But this is impossible since no one can avoid having a system of belief. If skeptics were as skeptical of their religious doubts as they are towards religious belief, then they wouldn't be a skeptic. How could they? Their skeptical assumptions are unable to pass their own standards. Therefore, it is no more narrow-minded to claim that one truth is right than it is to claim that one way to think about all truth is right. The truth is, the skeptic's position is just as exclusive and narrow as the religious positions they criticize.[38]

Belief Is a Product of Our Environment

I have often been told by skeptics of religion that if I had been born in the Middle East, I would most likely be a Muslim, and therefore my belief is merely a product of my cultural background and upbringing, and isn't rooted in objective truth. Grayling makes this particular argument when he writes:

In the great majority of cases, people belong to their religion because it is the religion of their parents, learned in childhood and thereafter constantly and in diverse ways reinforced by being present and observed in their communities. When a religion is adopted in later years the impulse for it is almost wholly emotional rather than rational; proselytising of teenagers and adults typically targets loneliness, confusion, failure, grief, anxiety, and depression as opportunities for conversion.[39]

Even if this is true, the argument doesn't bode well for the skeptic. Think about it—if the skeptic had been born in the Middle East, then they most likely wouldn't be a skeptic either, which means that the skeptic's beliefs are equally conditioned by their culture and where they were born as those of a particular religion. If we say that a person's belief is the result of their environment, then all worldviews must be held to this standard, whether religious or non-religious.[40]

Another problem with this criticism is that it doesn't actually address the truth claims of the actual belief. Even if a person's beliefs are largely determined by their culture, and even if proselytizing works best on the lonely, confused, failing, grieving, anxious, and depressed, this doesn't tell us whether the belief in question is true or not. Instead, this criticism merely proceeds from the assumption that these religious beliefs have already been proven wrong. But have they? While psychological motivations can tell us why a person might be drawn to a particular belief, it tells us nothing about whether the belief in question is true or not.[41] In the words of C. S. Lewis, "you must show that a man is wrong before you start explaining *why* he is wrong."[42]

Religion Is Child Abuse

Skeptics of religion argue that it is wrong for parents to teach their religious beliefs to their children. Richard Dawkins believes that faith is a dangerous thing and to implant it into the vulnerable mind of an innocent child is a grievous wrong.[43] While giving a lecture in Dublin, Dawkins was asked what he thought about the widely publicized cases of sexual abuse by Catholic priests in Ireland. He said that as horrible as sexual abuse no doubt is, the damage was arguably less than the long-term psychological damage inflicted by bringing the child up Catholic in the first place.[44] To teach children that there is a Heaven and Hell is child abuse.[45] Instead, children should be taught how to think, not what to think. Religious doctrines and systems should not be taught to anyone until they are old enough to weigh them responsibly.[46]

Though this position might appear to be neutral, it isn't. We all hold unprovable beliefs, and there is simply no such thing as a belief-free, neutral position. For example, as an atheist, A. C. Grayling believes in the Humanist worldview, which is the belief that humans are basically good and most of our problems can be solved through reason. But this is a highly controversial belief that is not rooted in science. Though Grayling believes that very few people would choose religion if they were raised without religious indoctrination, how is this any different from being raised under any other belief system, including Grayling's Humanistic worldview? Raising children in a religion-free environment simply exchanges one set of philosophical beliefs for another.[47]

Where the Conflict Lies

The conflict between science and religion is an illusion. Religion is fully compatible with methodological naturalism, and therefore it is compatible with science. However, what religion is incompatible with is philosophical naturalism, which is not science, but a philosophical worldview, or even a pseudo-religion. Interestingly enough, it turns out that philosophical naturalism is the one that actually conflicts with science.[48]

In *Where the Conflict Really Lies: Science, Religion, and Naturalism*, Alvin Plantinga argues that the conflict between science and theistic religion is superficial at best, since they actually share a great unity. Though we won't get into the specifics of evolution and free will until chapter seven, Plantinga calls into question whether our rational faculties can be trusted if philosophical naturalism and evolution are true.[49] Since Darwinian natural selection is only concerned about a belief's capacity to enable creatures to survive, whether a belief is actually true is of no importance. This is why many evolutionary psychologists see religion as something that once had a survival benefit, even though it is made up of false beliefs. In agreement with Nietzsche, Stroud,

Churchland, and even Darwin, atheist philosopher Thomas Nagel admits that if we came to believe that our capacity for true beliefs were the product natural selection, it would warrant serious skepticism about our capability to know truth.[50] Barry Stroud, Professor of Philosophy at Berkley, writes:

> *There is an embarrassing absurdity in this position that is revealed as soon as the naturalist reflects and acknowledges that he believes his naturalistic theory of the world . . . I mean he cannot say it and consistently regard it as true. In fact he cannot say anything and regard it as true.*[51]

Philosophical naturalism affirms that life in our universe came about from non-intelligent and purposeless processes: specifically, Darwinian natural selection. However, there is a serious problem here. If every event can be traced back to a prior cause, then the naturalist has a difficult time explaining the leap from unconscious and determined processes to free thoughts and actions, which is why many of them are now beginning to deny free will.[52] However, as C. S. Lewis points out, this doesn't actually save naturalism. He explains:

> *Whenever you know what the other man is saying is wholly due to his complexes or to a bit of bone pressing on his brain, you cease to attach any importance to it. But if naturalism were true, then all thoughts whatever would be wholly the result of irrational causes. Therefore, all thoughts would be equally worthless. Therefore, naturalism is worthless. If it is true, then we can know no truths. It cuts its own throat.*[53]

If philosophical naturalism is true, then all of our thoughts and actions are determined, and free will is merely an illusionary byproduct of evolution, which means that we don't have any good reasons to trust our thoughts. Both Plantinga and Lewis explain how this is a massive problem for philosophical naturalism, since it is a system of thought that claims all of our thoughts are mere events that originate from irrational causes. Since naturalism is itself a system of thought, it is discredited by its very own claims.[54] This would be comparable to an argument that proved no argument was sound, or a proof that there are no such things as proofs, which is nonsense.[55] This is why even if every religion is wrong, we still cannot believe in philosophical naturalism.

If there is no reason to trust our thoughts, then we have no reason to trust inductive reasoning nor the uniformity of nature, and therefore also science. This is why both Lewis and Plantinga conclude that it is not philosophical naturalism but Christianity that should be considered the scientific worldview, since Christianity has a sound basis for believing our reasoning capabilities are basically reliable, while philosophical naturalism doesn't.[56] Therefore, it is philosophical naturalism, not Christianity, that stands in conflict with science.

Evolving Scientific Certainty

Philosophical naturalism is founded upon total trust in the powers of inductive reasoning. However, thinking back to the last chapter, how do we know that we aren't in a situation similar to that of the inductivist turkey? What guarantee do we have that we aren't sitting upon the precipice of a Thanksgiving Day that will radically change our scientific conclusions? Perhaps you feel this is an overstatement, and that we can be confident in our scientific discoveries. While science has indeed made astonishing discoveries, the atheist who has embraced philosophical naturalism in order to debunk religion has a serious problem—science regularly gets things wrong.

Alvin Plantinga points out that science contradicts itself not only over time, but also at the same time. He explains: "Two of the most important and overarching contemporary scientific theories are general relativity and quantum mechanics. Both are highly confirmed and enormously impressive; unfortunately, they can't both be correct."[57] Based upon our current understanding, these two views are deeply incompatible with each other, and this isn't the only example of this sort of problem within science. Renowned scientist Stephen Hawking released a paper in which he radically altered his view on black holes, and considered his previous view to be his "biggest blunder."[58] If science often gets things wrong and some of our greatest scientific discoveries are in conflict, how much confidence should we place in science? If the history of science shows us anything, it shows a steady progression from one view that was considered scientific truth being replaced by the next.

Scientists frequently hold to ideas that fit with the current evidence, but ultimately cannot be proven and often end up being wrong. Darwin himself realized that his theory of natural selection was nowhere near a scientific certainty as it faced numerous obstacles. Nevertheless, he still believed it was true in spite of its difficulties, which is why he wrote:

A crowd of difficulties will have occurred to the reader. Some of them are so grave that to this day I can never reflect on them without being staggered; but, to the best of my judgement, the greater number are only apparent, and those that are real are not, I think, fatal to my theory.[59]

Atheists who claim that science "proves things" while religion takes things on "blind faith" greatly misunderstand both science and faith. Einstein's theory of relativity took fifty years to finally be confirmed. During this fifty-year timespan, scientists proceeded on the assumption that the theory was true and were prepared to live with its unresolved tension. They lived as though Einstein's theory was true, even though they knew they were not in a position to ultimately know.[60] If this is not faith, what is?

Atheist and evolutionary psychologist Steven Pinker admits that science offers no final answers. He writes: "There are no final answers in science, only varying degrees of probability. Even scientific 'facts' are just conclusions confirmed to such an extent that it would be reasonable to offer temporary agreement, but that assent is never final."[61] In agreement with Pinker, Massimo Pigliucci explains how science only offers provisional truth that is likely to be superseded (and occasionally overturned) by better methods. He explains: "we have the undeniable fact that scientific knowledge is always provisional, which implies that some, perhaps even most, of the specific scientific claims you have read about in this book may be out of date in a year, or a decade."[62] The point is clear: science is provisional truth.

The New Atheists' claim that science not only conflicts with religion, but also proves it wrong, is a profound misunderstanding of science, religion, and philosophy. When the New Atheists speak of religious belief as "blind" and "dogmatically opposed to science," they are mistaking their own philosophical beliefs for science and have fallen into scientism. For example, take the uniformity of nature, which assumes that the laws of the universe we observe today functioned the same way in the past. It is the principle that the present is the key to the past. While this form of inductive reasoning is certainly useful for doing science, Christians reject total uniformitarianism, instead believing in catastrophism, which holds that nature has been altered by certain supernatural events. Notice, if we assume that nature is completely uniform then our conclusions will be drastically off if miracles have really occurred. However, both views are philosophical assumptions that cannot be ultimately proven. To say that one is the scientific worldview and the other is not, is not a scientific conclusion; rather, it is an unprovable philosophical belief. It is a pseudo-religious belief.

My goal in this chapter was not to leave you in the dry and empty badlands of total skepticism, but to help clear up the erroneous idea that atheism, under the banner of philosophical naturalism, is the scientific worldview, and is therefore in conflict with religious belief. However, in order to understand this, we must recognize the difference between scientific truth and philosophical belief. Without a doubt, science is truly remarkable; however, when it comes to scientific certainty, instead of grasping onto it with both hands, we should let it rest openly and freely on our hand. Let it amuse us, even fascinate us, but realize its fragile and limited nature. This means that whether you are an atheist or theist, you shouldn't use scientific truth as an end-all argument for or against belief in God, since the great philosophical questions of life cannot be answered by the ever-changing scientific understanding—our world is much too complex, and human nature is far too limited. Science is truly one of the most incredible tools that humanity wields, but if we misuse this tool, we not only damage it, but anything else it comes into contact with.

CHAPTER THREE
Right and Wrong

> *"What, after all, compels us to keep our promises?"*
> — Heinrich Himmler

> *"Lying lips are an abomination to the Lord."*
> — Proverbs 12:22a

In 2002, the University of Massachusetts conducted a study on lying and discovered that sixty percent of people lied at least once during a ten-minute conversation, with an average of two to three lies told. Psychologist Robert Feldman commented on the study saying, "People tell a considerable number of lies in everyday conversation. It was a very surprising result. We didn't expect lying to be such a common part of daily life."[1] This brings up an interesting question: if most people lie so often, what leads us to believe that lying is wrong? And if we say it's wrong, what do we even mean by this? Is it intrinsically wrong, or is lying simply "bad for business"? Clearly, we live in a world where people lie all the time, so on what basis do we say we ought not lie?

Eighteenth-century philosopher David Hume once pointed out a great philosophical problem. He realized that there was a massive gap between how the world *is* and how people think the world *ought* to be, which is often called the *is-ought* problem, or Hume's Law. Hume recognized that nearly everyone agrees that certain acts are wrong and people *ought* not do them, regardless of their personal beliefs. However, not everyone agrees on what is right and wrong, so without God, how do we justify our moral preferences over another's? While some might look to science for such an answer, Hume saw this as a mistake, since he rightly understood that science is incapable of telling us what we should or shouldn't value, and therefore is unable to determine morality.

Without a moral foundation for determining right from wrong, moral statements merely serve to express emotions and commands.[2] For example, to say that promise keeping is morally right is to say something like, "Hooray for promise keeping!" It is simply cheerleading for the morals you prefer. But the problem with this approach is that we have no basis upon which to tell someone else they are wrong for the acts we deem horrific, such as female circumcision, human trafficking, or ethnic cleansing. Moral rightness instead comes down to which group can cheer the loudest. The point is, if you start with a non-moral premise, you must (and yet cannot) justify how you end with moral conclusions.

Phrased differently, you cannot get out what you haven't put in.

David Hume understood that science is *descriptive* not *prescriptive*; it can only tell us what the world *is* like and is incapable of telling us what the world *ought* to be like. When we make a moral statement, we assume a moral standard. When we assume a moral standard, we must justify not only its existence, but also its authority over us. Even if a moral standard exists, why should we bother following it? What reason is there to comply with the demands of morality except when it works in our favor? These kinds of questions belong to the branch of philosophy called metaethics, which attempts to explain how we ground our moral beliefs.[3]

Morality and Ethics

When discussing the foundation for moral thinking, we need to understand the difference between morality and ethics. With morality, we are trying to understand the nature of right and wrong. Is it created or discovered? Does it come from God, nature, or ourselves, and what makes us obligated to obey it? With ethics, we are trying to determine how to best apply moral standards in specific situations.[4] For example, while most people believe it is morally wrong to lie, what about in a situation where it will save another person's life? If God commands us not to lie, is it wrong to tell the German Gestapo there are no Jews in your attic when there really are? These kinds of problems are ethical in nature, not moral.

The difficulty with ethics can be easily demonstrated by what philosophers call *The Trolley Problem*. Imagine a runaway trolley barreling down the railroad tracks. As a bystander, you notice that there are five people tied up on the tracks some distance ahead of the trolley. Fortunately, you are near a lever that can divert the trolley onto a sidetrack, which will avoid the victims and save their lives. However, there happens to be one person tied up on the sidetrack, and so by pulling the lever to save the five, you will kill the one. These are the only two options —so, what do you do?

Perhaps you think the choice is easily solved with a consequentialist approach. "It comes down to simple numbers," you say. "Of course, you should sacrifice the one to save the five!" However, what if the one person is a child, or a great humanitarian leader, or a scientist who is on the verge of discovering a cure for a deadly disease? What if the other five are terminally ill cancer patients or convicted murderers? Does this change things? A strict consequentialist approach has enormous difficulties that prevent it from being a complete solution. For another example, imagine a doctor with five patients who all need a different organ transplant. Would it be ethically permissible for this doctor to sacrifice one patient by dividing up his healthy organs for the rest? Most people would agree that this is wrong. But what makes this situation different from the one with the trolley? Whatever your response is to these ethical dilemmas, it will be largely determined by your moral foundation, which comes from your worldview. Therefore, if we are going to argue ethics, we must first establish our moral foundation.

Today, it is common for many people to argue over ethical issues when they do not share the same moral foundation. Because of their differing moral foundations, they cannot hope to come to an agreement. For example, A. C. Grayling, an atheist advocate of moral subjectivism, argues that morality is "the responsibility of a social conversation, a discussion, even a negotiation."[5] However, most theists cannot agree with this view since they believe morality is objective—it is not based upon human consensus, but is derived from absolute and unchangeable laws that aren't up to us. Because of this difference, there are many issues these two camps will never agree on, unless one of them changes their moral foundation. However, this requires changing your entire worldview, which is something that rarely comes easily.

Many atheist authors argue that morality and ethics are basically the same thing. This is because they believe that morality is subjectively created based upon our values and moral feelings, and therefore no universal moral standard exists by which to judge actions right from wrong. If, however, you believe that morality is discovered rather than created, then it is not based upon our moral feelings, since it is woven into the very fabric of the universe.[6] This view sees morality as the basic "thou shalts" of a moral system, while ethics attempts to solve moral dilemmas when two "thou shalts" are in play, and the solution is not at all clear on how to follow them both simultaneously.

While there are many moral positions, the next several chapters will focus on the three most prevalent moral views held in our society today. As we will see, each of these moral views can be classified as being either theistic or naturalistic. But before we get to them, we need to briefly look at the worldview that is most commonly associated with naturalistic moral philosophies.

Atheism and Agnosticism

New Atheist author Sam Harris argues that atheism shouldn't even be considered a philosophical category. Similar to how no one describes himself as a "non-astrologer," no one should have to classify himself as a non-theist.[7] A common atheist expression goes, "Atheism is a religion just as bald is a hair color." From the atheist's point of view, talk of gods and goddesses is taken as seriously as talk of fairies, goblins, or Santa Claus. At first glance this might sound reasonable, however, philosophers know better. Atheism is a worldview that does not escape philosophical critique.

In *The God Argument*, A. C. Grayling responds to the claim that atheism is an alternate set of beliefs that simply differ in content from theistic beliefs. He disagrees, arguing that atheism is not a belief, but the absence of belief in the supernatural. He explains the difference by way of an analogy:

theists think they are in a kind of belief football match, with opposing sets of beliefs vying for our allegiance. What is happening is that the theists are rushing about the park kicking the ball, but the atheists are not playing. They are not even on the field; they are in the stands, arguing that this particular game should not be taking place at all. The correct characterisation of the opposition between theism and atheism is therefore this: the theist has existential beliefs, metaphysical beliefs, of a certain distinctive kind; and the atheist does not share them.[8]

Grayling believes that to call atheism a belief would be like saying that not collecting stamps is a hobby.[9] Atheists such as Harris and Grayling reject the accusation that atheism is a positive claim, and so they believe it does not require supporting evidence.

Christian apologist Ravi Zacharias disagrees with Harris and Grayling for believing that atheism is exempt from philosophical categorization. He writes:

But this is not atypical. Existentialists did not want to be classified; postmodernists do not want to be boxed in. They just want to be able to stigmatize others without attaching a name to themselves. They shun categorization of anything to which they hold (though they comfortably categorize others, including God). The reason is this: it does not hold. They look for a universal solvent to dissolve the notion of God. With predictable result, they end up only dissolving their own worldview.[10]

For this reason, Thomas Huxley created the term *agnostic* for those who claim to be hopelessly ignorant concerning worldview beliefs, such as God's existence. Huxley rightly realized that using the term atheist (the declaration that God does not exist) is a form of philosophical suicide. Huxley was hostile toward anyone who thundered dogmatic judgments without adequate grounds (both theists and atheists alike). To make a pronouncement one way or the other on the God issue was to move outside the possible realm of human knowledge.[11]

Understanding Huxley's point, Bertrand Russell described himself as an agnostic when speaking to philosophical audiences, but as an atheist when speaking popularly.[12] Though Russell felt "at one with the atheists," he felt bound by logic to classify himself philosophically as an agnostic, since he was unable to disprove the existence of God. The truth is, theists hold belief in God's existence, while atheists hold belief in God's nonexistence—both are positive, belief-based truth claims on the nature of reality, and therefore require support. It is only the agnostic who suspends judgment, believing there are not sufficient grounds to affirm or deny God's existence.

Several years ago, an atheist friend and I were discussing who bears the burden of proof for God's existence: atheists or theists. It was in this conversation that I was introduced to the *presumption of atheism*. The idea holds that in the absence of evidence for the existence of God, we should presume God does not exist. My friend's claim was that atheism was the natural and default position, so the burden of proof lies on theists to support their positive claim. But he didn't realize claiming "there is no God" is just as much a truth claim as "there is a God." Thinking back to Grayling's "belief football match" illustration, the atheists in the stands arguing that the game should not be taking place are making just as much of a truth claim as the theists on the field.

If you pay close attention to how atheists often use the term "atheist," you will notice how they have subtly redefined it to mean "non-theist," in an effort to avoid philosophical critique. By doing this, they can hold theists to a special burden of proof while sitting comfortably behind their positive proof claim that has been masked by the redefined term. When atheism is redefined into this softer form there becomes essentially no difference between an agnostic and an atheist. Atheism now includes everyone from babies to cats, and the college graduate who has suspended judgment on God's existence while they think it over.[13] Alister McGrath attributes this redefinition of atheism to the numerical decline and growing revolt against all forms of dogmatism, both theistic and nontheistic.[14] This new atheism has been expanded to include all those who are undecided about God's existence. He explains that although this was a smart public relations move, atheism has lost the cutting edge that it once had and is now dulled and grayed from its overextension.[15]

Atheism is simply not the proper term for the person who is unsure of God's existence; it is agnosticism. Philosopher and Christian apologist William Lane Craig criticizes this contemporary redefining of atheism, saying:

So why, you might wonder, would atheists be anxious to so trivialize their position? Here I agree with you that a deceptive game is being played by many atheists. If atheism is taken to be a view, namely the view that there is no God, then atheists must shoulder their share of the burden of proof to support this view. But many atheists admit freely that they cannot sustain such a burden of proof. So they try to shirk their epistemic responsibility by re-defining atheism so that it is no longer a view but just a psychological condition which as such makes no assertions. They are really closet agnostics who want to claim the mantle of atheism without shouldering its responsibilities. This is disingenuous and still leaves us asking, "So is there a God or not?"[16]

Even if atheists still disagree and believe atheism is exempt from philosophical categorization, they have other beliefs that stem from their atheism that are undeniably philosophical.

Humanism

Pure atheism never stands alone. Even if atheism equates to the rejection of theistic belief, an atheist is almost assuredly a naturalist, and a naturalist is likely a materialist, which is the belief that matter is all there is (there are no gods, ghosts, ghouls, or spirits). A. C. Grayling writes, "An atheist is of course going to be a secularist and, almost certainly, a Humanist."[17] This is because we cannot live a belief-free life.

In the past, atheists have been criticized for centering their identity on the denouncement of religion, but today many are tired of such negativity and instead want to hear what atheism has to offer our world. Greg Epstein, Humanist Chaplain of Harvard University, understands this concern, and so he writes:

> *When I first got involved in organized Humanism I was shocked that the groups I spent time visiting seemed to spend so much time and energy sponsoring debates about the existence of God or publishing magazines, journals, and newsletters, rather than staging poetry readings and concerts or going on hikes together.*[18]

Unlike pure atheism, Humanism strives to tell the story of a life worth living, instead of merely denouncing the ones it loathes. With this in mind, Epstein explains, "What is truly important is to assert, loudly and boldly, that we have a dramatically different way of understanding the world and human values. We are not simply atheists or agnostics or nonreligious—we are Humanists."[19]

Humanism holds that we don't need God to find our way through life. Instead, we are individually responsible for choosing our life's goals and values, while striving to be rational and considerate towards others.[20] Typically, Humanism prides itself on rejecting dogmas and creeds; yet to be a Humanist, you must embrace the dogma of philosophical naturalism and strong rationalism.[21] Though atheists tend to believe they have no faith whatsoever, Humanists such as Epstein know better, saying:

> *Call Humanism a faith if you like—we should have no particular allergy to that word—but recognize that it is a faith in our ability to live well based on conclusions and convictions reached by*

empirical testing and free, unfettered rational inquiry. In other words, we question everything, including our own questions, and we search for as many ways as we can to confirm or deny our intuitions. We have no holy books meant to be taken at face value or blindly obeyed. We are open to revising any conclusion we have made if new evidence appears to contradict it. However, we also recognize that there can and often is a point where sufficient evidence has been gathered on a certain subject to make a reversal of views extraordinarily unlikely, and where the explanation we have pieced together works extremely well. This is certainly the case with whether the sun will rise tomorrow, and it is equally true for evolution, and about our basic picture of the origins of the universe.[22]

While many do not consider Humanism a faith-based religion, it easily classifies as a pseudo-religion since it tells us where we came from, why we are here, and where we are going when we die. It is a belief-based worldview that answers life's most difficult questions, or at minimum tells us the correct way to go about trying to answer them. Therefore, whether you believe in God or not, your worldview has an element of belief, or faith.

It is true that an atheist technically doesn't have to be a Humanist; however, there is a natural and logical progression that results from our beliefs and ideas. Ideas have consequences, and our presuppositions have an enormous impact on our worldview. While no label will be able to accurately cover every aspect of atheism, or theism for that matter, the majority of atheists are Humanists, whether realized or not.[23] Therefore, for the remainder of this book we will treat Humanism as the default atheistic worldview. Humanism is certainly a complex worldview that consists of a multitude of diverging ideas and opinions; however, one thing that Humanists agree on is that God is not necessary for morality. We can be good without God.

The Golden Rule

In Matthew 7:12 Jesus spoke of what people commonly refer to as the Golden Rule, saying: *"So whatever you wish that others would do to you, do also to them, for this is the Law and the Prophets."*[24] While the Golden Rule is often attributed to Christianity, Humanists claim that it is not the product of any one religion but is a universally held belief by atheists and theists alike. Atheist author Victor Stenger argued that most people in our Christian-dominated society wrongly assume that the Golden Rule originated from Jesus' Sermon on the Mount, when in reality it was a widespread idea long before Jesus came along. For example, around 500 BC, Confucius said, "Do not do to others what you do not want them to do to you."[25] Around 375 BC, Isocrates said, "Do not do to others that which angers you when they do it to you."[26] Around 150 BC, the Hindu Mahabharata taught, "This is the sum of duty: do not do to others what would cause pain if done to you."[27] Stenger goes on to say that no original moral concept of any significance can be found in the New Testament, and any sentiments attributed to Christ are already found in the Old

Testament.[28] In other words, Jesus was a mere plagiarizer with no original thought of His own.

In agreement with Stenger, Richard Dawkins explains that Jesus' teaching to "love thy neighbor" didn't mean what we now think it means—it only meant to love another Jew.[29] The same principle applies to the sixth commandment; thou shalt not kill only meant thou shalt not kill another Jew—everyone else was fair game.[30] Dawkins goes so far as to suggest that Jesus would have turned over in His grave if He had known that Paul had taken His plan to the non-Jewish pigs.[31] If what Dawkins suggests is true, then Jesus was a bigot.

There are some problems with these arguments. First, Stenger failed to understand the difference between the Golden Rule's two forms: cautionary and directive. In its cautionary form, the rule states that we should not treat others in a way that we would not want to be treated—this form is often called The Silver Rule. However, in its directive form, as seen in Matthew 7:12, it not only states to do no harm, but also to treat others how we would like to be treated. While Stenger and the other Humanist critics are right that other religions teach a form of the Golden Rule, they only teach it in its cautionary form. Jesus' version of the Golden Rule, which was derived from the Old Testament, has a subtle difference that makes it truly unique from other world religions. Eastern religions hold to the Golden Rule in its cautionary form, which says, "Do not act unlovingly!" While Jesus' directive form says, "Act lovingly!" This is a significant difference. It's the difference between "feed the poor" and "do not steal food from the poor." The Golden Rule is an others-regarding ethic, while The Silver Rule is a self-regarding ethic. The second problem is that Jesus' source for His version of the Golden Rule predates Eastern Religions' Silver Rule by roughly one-thousand years. Jesus' version of the Golden Rule comes directly from Leviticus 19:18, which says: "You shall not take vengeance or bear a grudge against the sons of your own people, but you shall love your neighbor as yourself: I am the Lord."[32] To argue that Jesus merely copied the Old Testament fails to understand that Jesus was Jewish and so His teaching would naturally draw upon the Old Testament. Therefore, the Judeo-Christian imperative to love others as yourself makes it truly unique from other religions.

What about Dawkins's claim that the command to love your neighbor meant to only love another Jew? In the New Testament Matthew writes, "You have heard that it was said, 'You shall love your neighbor and hate your enemy.' But I say to you, love your enemies and pray for those who persecute you."[33] In the Old Testament, the book of Exodus says, "If you meet your enemy's ox or his donkey going astray, you shall bring it back to him. If you see the donkey of one who hates you lying down under its burden, you shall refrain from leaving him with it; you shall rescue it with him."[34] This concept is repeated again in more detail in the book of Leviticus, which says, "When a foreigner resides among you in your land, do not mistreat them. The foreigner residing among you must be treated as your native-born.

Love them as yourself, for you were foreigners in Egypt. I am the Lord your God."[35] Also, Jesus' parable of the Good Samaritan clearly taught that we are to love others regardless of their religion or race.[36]

The Old Testament clearly teaches Israel held a special blessing from God, however, God's plan was for all the nations of the Earth to be blessed through the Jewish people.[37] Israel was to act as a sort of intermediator between Yahweh and the rest of the nations. To simplify the concept, one could say the Old Testament teaches, "Love your neighbor, enemy or not, but especially if he is a fellow Jew." This principle is no different in the New Testament. Therefore, Dawkins's claim is mistaken.[38]

Most Humanists will agree that we should "love our neighbor." However, what Christianity means by "love your neighbor" is radically different from its Humanist counterpart. Christian theologian Francis Schaeffer explained the difference when he wrote:

One of the problems with humanists is that they tend to 'love' humanity as a whole—Man with a capital M, Man as an idea—but forget about man as an individual, as a person. Christianity is to be exactly the opposite. Christianity is not to love in abstraction, but to love the individual who stands before me in a person-to-person relationship. He must never be faceless to me, or I am denying everything I say I believe.[39]

Christ commands His followers to imitate Himself by loving the unlovable—from the micromanaging boss, to the backstabbing coworker, to the horrible neighbor, the command is to be followed across the board. Loving the lovable is easy, but under atheism, what reason is there to love the unlovable?

Humanists believe the Golden Rule is a self-evident truth that is available to us all. While many religions rely on God as their source for morality, atheists argue that we do not need God to live a moral life; we can be good without God.[40] Many atheists, such as Greg Epstein, find the theist's question, "How we can justify morality without God?" obnoxious.[41] Epstein believes that moral goodness is that which facilitates human dignity and the health of the natural world, while moral wrongness is that which creates needless human suffering.[42] Atheist philosopher Walter Sinnott-Armstrong agrees with Epstein, and finds it insulting to say that we need God to be moral. He writes:

Almost nothing turns people off more than telling them that they are immoral. That particular insult accuses them of being dishonest and of having perverse values, so it strikes at the essential basis of communication. Yet that is what theists tell atheists when they say that morality depends on religious belief.[43]

This argument states that by believing morality depends on God, you are saying that atheists are bad people, and to say that atheists are bad people is wrong. However, when you look closely at this argument, it basically amounts to saying it is immoral to tell someone they are immoral—which is not only a circular argument, but is the very thing that Sinnott-Armstrong is upset about in the first place.

Atheists also argue that God cannot possibly be the source of human morals and values, because nonbelievers show themselves to be no less virtuous than believers.[44] Victor Stenger, Richard Dawkins, and Sam Harris together claim there is no supporting evidence that nonbelievers commit crimes or other antisocial acts in greater numbers than believers, and that some studies even indicate the opposite to be true.[45] Therefore, we do not need God to be a good person.

Atheists are partly right; it is incorrect to claim that anyone who does not share belief in God is incapable of morally good behavior. However, they misunderstand the theist's question. The question is not, "Can we live moral lives without belief in God?" Nor is it, "Can we recognize the existence of moral values without belief in God?" Neither is it, "Can we formulate a system of ethics without belief in God?"[46] Rather, the question is, "What is the logical foundation on which atheism grounds moral truth and obligation." There is little doubt that atheism is capable of formulating a system of ethics—some atheists have even developed their own version of the Ten Commandments.[47] Even so, Hume's question from the beginning of the chapter lingers unsettlingly: on what authority does atheism derive its prescriptive moral behavior from its descriptive observations? What makes the atheist's version of the Ten Commandments any better, or any more "right," than anyone else's? What is the standard by which moral behavior is measured? Hume's question demands an answer: how do we derive an "ought" from an "is"?

CHAPTER FOUR
Human Rights

> *"What is mankind that you are mindful of them,*
> *human beings that you care for them?"*
> — Psalm 8:4

> *"So God created mankind in his own image, in the image of God*
> *he created them; male and female he created them."*
> — Genesis 1:27

Within the jungles of Papua New Guinea, there is a people known as the Korowai. When a member of the tribe dies unexpectedly, the Korowai people believe it is caused by an evil spirit known as the Kakua. What follows is a frightening witch-hunt to find the evil Kakua. Once the tribe decides whom the Kakua has possessed, that person is pitilessly murdered and then eaten: everything except the teeth, hair, and nails. Many Korowai people have killed and eaten their close friends and even family members. When one member of the tribe was asked about killing and eating one of his best friends, he responded, almost apathetically, "It's just normal. I don't feel sad or anything like that." The Korowai people believe this is their responsibility; it is the right and moral thing to do.[1]

As Westerners, we are horrified by the Korowai's cultural beliefs. We strongly believe that humans have an innate dignity and value, and to trample on another person's rights is wrong. In Western nations, this belief is historically rooted in theism, specifically Christianity.[2] God is our creator and moral lawgiver; therefore, we owe Him our allegiance and obedience. When we determine an action is evil, we assume there is such a thing as good; when we say there is such a thing as good, we assume there is a standard by which to differentiate good from evil.[3] So, if we believe things like rape, child molestation, murder, and cannibalism are wrong, then we must provide an objective standard by which to judge such actions as wrong. If God exists, we have a plausible foundation for the existence of objective moral values; however, if He doesn't, how can we justify their existence?

In Fyodor Dostoevsky's Russian novel, *The Brothers Karamazov,* atheism is questioned as a credible worldview. Through the novel's characters, Dostoevsky considers what kind of a world atheism would envision and sustain if its beliefs were carried out to their logical ends.[4] One of the brothers, Ivan Karamazov, claims that if God does not exist, every kind of action is morally permissible. If there is no God, then there are no moral rules or laws that humanity is bound to; we can do whatever we want. In agreement with Ivan, French philosopher Jean-Paul Sartre wrote: "Nowhere is it written that the Good exists, that we must be honest, that we must not lie . . . Dostoevsky said, "If God didn't exist, everything would be possible." . . . Indeed, everything is permissible if God does not exist."[5]

Though the atheists of Dostoevsky's day promised to liberate people from religion's backwardness and authoritarianism, Dostoevsky realized that atheism held the keys to unlocking a world of unprecedented evil and brutality, precisely because it removed the divine shackles on human autonomy.[6] Many atheist philosophers share Dostoevsky's concern. Philosopher J. L. Mackie believed that objective morals could not be justified by evolutionary theory, and could not possibly exist without "an all-powerful god to create them."[7] Since God doesn't exist, ethics are illusory and a merely "useful fiction."[8] Philosopher of science Michael Ruse agrees with Mackie, explaining that even though ethics are widely considered "rationally justifiable," they aren't. He writes:

> *I appreciate that when somebody says 'Love thy neighbor as thyself,' they think they are referring above and beyond themselves. Nevertheless, such reference is truly without foundation. Morality is just an aid to survival and reproduction . . . any deeper meaning is illusory.*[9]

But if morality and ethics are nothing but illusions resulting from evolutionary processes, why not ignore them once we've come to realize this?

Premise Driven Morality

Years ago, I had a lengthy conversation with a professor at Yale University who believed that morality is subjectively created and is primarily based upon human values. I pointed out to him that if morality is based on values, then it is essentially the same type of thing as color preference—I value blue, you value red, but neither of us are wrong, since no one could ever prove that one was better than the other. When I suggested that his view ended up in the badlands of moral relativism (the idea that all moral actions are neutral) he didn't agree. His response was strikingly similar to A. C. Grayling's view of subjective morality. Grayling writes:

It will be claimed that it implies relativism to describe morality as a matter for social discussion and negotiation. If morality is the product of temporally and culturally parochial debate, then different societies will come up with different moralities, perhaps radically different, so that what is accepted in one is rejected in another, and there will be no objective standards, and consequently no common standard of adjudication between moral outlooks. [But] relativism is not what follows . . . For there are objective facts about human needs and interests that constrain any possible morality. Very few people like to be cold, hungry, afraid, lonely, threatened, in danger, in physical pain, subjected to psychological suffering, deprived of basic physical and psychological amenities, and the like.[10]

Grayling believes that even though morality is in part a consensus, it is limited by certain facts about humanity. Once these facts are recognized, we can then work together to come up with moral solutions through open dialogue and critical thinking. Similarly, Greg Epstein sees this act of continual exploration as a sort of virtue, saying:

> *if no morality is timeless and eternal, then we will never be able to fool ourselves into thinking that there is one set of easy and obvious answers to questions about euthanasia, abortion, capital punishment, or other such issues. We'll have to argue them out, with neither conservatives nor liberals ever able to say they are right in every case, without thought. What is so wrong with this? Indeed, we Humanists can take pride in our passionate belief in a morality based on unfettered inquiry, on compassionate questioning. Call us "the keepers of the question." We are proud to welcome a future of permanent debate and discussion about moral issues, a world in which we will never stop refining our views, never stop exploring how we can promote human dignity more effectively, never stop trying to better understand and more effectively eliminate human suffering.*[11]

Subjective moralists live in a world of questions with no final answers. It is a worldview that echoes the thoughts of 2 Timothy 3:7, "always learning and never able to arrive at a knowledge of the truth."[12]

One of the problems with this moral position is that it has bypassed the moral conversation entirely, as it assumes a moral foundation that it has not grounded. Out of a desire to escape moral relativism, subjective moralists make a few assumptions about morality, such as harm is bad, humans are valuable, and reason and critical thinking are good things. But what makes them think they can do this? Even if we all agreed that these are morally good things, why are they morally good things and what makes them morally binding? How would we explain to someone else that they were wrong for not agreeing with these basic moral assumptions?

Imagine if someone told you that morality is based upon harming others, only valuing the rich, and believing that reason and critical thinking were a waste of time. As a subjective moralist, you would be at a standstill, since you wouldn't be able to appeal to reason or scientific evidence to argue against this. It is true that if you make a few moral assumptions you can get a moral system up and running; however, who gets to decide which moral truths will be the bedrock of morality?

People today have strong moral convictions, but unlike past generations, they don't have any basis for why they find some things to be evil and other things good. Why is it wrong to arbitrarily harm another human being? The fact that I don't like to be harmed does not logically lead to the conclusion that I ought not harm others. Why do we think that we should filter our ethical decisions through that belief? Tim Keller provides a helpful example of this problem when he writes:

> *Statements that seem to be common sense to the speakers are nonetheless often profoundly religious in nature. Imagine that Ms. A argues that all the safety nets for the poor should be removed, in the name of "survival of the fittest." Ms. B might respond, "The poor have the right to a decent standard of living—they are human beings like the rest of us!" Ms. A could then come back with the fact that many bioethicists today think the concept of "human" is artificial and impossible to define. She might continue that there is no possibility of treating all living organisms as ends rather than means and that some always have to die that others may live. That is simply the way nature works. If Ms. B counters with a*

pragmatic argument, that we should help the poor simply because it makes society work better, Ms. A could come up with many similar pragmatic arguments about why letting some of the poor just die would be even more efficient. Now Ms. B would be getting angry. She would respond heatedly that starving the poor is simply unethical, but Ms. A could retort, "Who says ethics must be the same for everyone?" Ms. B would finally exclaim: "I wouldn't want to live in a society like the one you are describing!"[13]

Keller's example demonstrates how there are no neutral universal objective arguments to convince everyone that starving the poor is wrong. Science and reason are simply incapable of weighing in on foundational moral issues. Ms. B might *believe* that humans are more valuable than rocks or trees, but she cannot prove it.

So far, this take on subjective morality might be called *premise-driven subjective morality*, since it ultimately rests on several unprovable beliefs. Many atheists argue that these premises are universal and are what *ought* to direct all moral dialogue and decisions. Philosopher John Rawls popularized the idea that morality should be based upon universally accessible arguments. However, there aren't any neutral, rational, universally accessible arguments, so these unprovable beliefs can only be accepted on faith. In chapter two, we learned that we all hold unprovable beliefs, so this view is not inherently incorrect. However, we must ask if this view explains morality as well as other moral views. I don't think it does.

Premise-driven subjective morality attempts to have the benefits of both objective and subjective morality without having to defend an objective foundation. It is moral subjectivism restrained by a few "nearly objective" premises that serve to prevent moral relativism. Though we all have unprovable beliefs, we cannot justify any belief we want by simply claiming it is a self-evident truth—otherwise we would be unable to distinguish between truth claims at all and would live in a world without knowledge. Though self-evident truths are the starting point by which all other facts are known, these truths must fit with the other facts that make up our worldview. If we don't ensure compatibility, then every truth claim is allowed to hang freely in mid-air, which would make any claim as valid as the next. Therefore, we must ask whether these beliefs actually fit with the Humanist worldview—a worldview, mind you, that believes in unguided evolution.

If Humanists are going to hold these moral premises, they must show how humanity has rights, dignity, and value in a naturalistic universe.[14] This is extremely difficult. How can a purposeless, non-moral process, produce a moral basis for life?[15] Many non-theists recognize this difficulty, so they knowingly embrace subjective moral relativism. Still, many are not ready to give into that just yet, and so they look to science to provide a solution. In chapter six, we will see if science offers the support needed for premise-driven morality, and then in chapter seven we will look at unguided evolution to see if it is compatible with this moral view.

Truth Is in the Eye of the Beholder

Modern Western culture largely rejects the dogmatism that religions preach on right and wrong. It is a popular belief that everyone should determine for themselves what is morally right. No one person has the right to impose their moral view onto others; instead, individuals within a culture will have their own ideals and values, and when taken collectively, will make up a culture's moral system.[16] However, this means what some cultures believe is morally right, other cultures will believe is morally wrong, and both can be right in their own way—this is moral relativism.

Moral relativism has come under heavy scrutiny in recent years, and there have been some devastating arguments against it. Sam Harris, a proponent of naturalistic objective morality, holds a deep contempt for moral relativism. He argues that moral relativism is a self-defeating argument, since it contradicts its own thesis in the very act of stating it. He explains:

moral relativists generally believe that all cultural practices should be respected on their own terms, that the practitioners of the various barbarisms that persist around the globe cannot be judged by the standards of the West, nor can the people of the past be judged by the standards of the present. And yet, implicit in this approach to morality lurks a claim that is not relative but absolute. Most moral relativists believe that tolerance of cultural diversity is better, in some important sense, than outright bigotry. This may be perfectly reasonable, of course, but it amounts to an overarching claim about how all human beings should live. Moral relativism, when used as a rationale for tolerance of diversity, is self-contradictory.[17]

If all truth is relative, to make that claim is to admit that at least one truth is not relative—the truth that all truth is relative, which is a self-defeating argument.

Moral relativism also suffers from being an unlivable worldview, as it can only be embraced from the comfort of one's living room chair. The reality is, for most of us, when we spot injustice, we can't sit idly by and chalk it up to cultural differences; we know better. If we believe that there are people in the world doing things right now that they should stop doing, no matter their personal beliefs, we have exposed ourselves as objective moralists.[18] The moment we say that one moral idea is better than another, we are admitting to an objective moral standard that we measure both moral ideas to. By doing this, we are admitting to a real morality that is independent of personal opinion. However, if we refuse to admit that such a thing as objective moral truth exists, how can we rationally justify fighting against oppression and tyranny?[19] Theologian G. K. Chesterton wrote about this problem in the early 1900s, saying:

But the new rebel is a Sceptic, and will not entirely trust anything. He has no loyalty; therefore he can never be really a revolutionist. And the fact that he doubts everything really gets in his way when he wants to denounce anything. For all denunciation implies a moral doctrine of some kind; and the modern revolutionist doubts not only the institution he denounces, but the doctrine by which he denounces it . . . As a politician, he will cry out that war is a waste of life, and then, as a philosopher, that all life is waste of time . . . The man of this school goes first to a political meeting, where he complains that savages are treated as if they were beasts; then he takes his hat and umbrella and goes on to a scientific meeting, where he proves that they practically are beasts . . . In his book on politics he attacks men for trampling on morality; in his book on ethics he attacks morality for trampling on men. Therefore the modern man in revolt has become practically useless for all purposes of revolt. By rebelling against everything he has lost his right to rebel against anything.[20]

To say that all moral actions are relative is philosophically unlivable. Even if we are unaware of it, we all measure people's actions by some absolute standard that transcends personal opinion. If right and wrong are relative to the individual, we have no right to do this, yet we do it anyway.[21] When we judge other's actions while claiming that morality is subjective, we reduce ourselves to cultural imperialists who impose our choices onto others. When we step outside of our living rooms and look out at the real world as it truly is, with its terrible injustice, we cannot look the other way. The truth is, we all have moral intuitions that we can't seem to get rid of, even when they clash with our worldview. So, why are they there and where did they come from?

Morality on Loan

It is no secret that nature is largely based upon violence and predation—the strong eat the weak, and suffering is the lot of every creature. But if humans are simply bigger brained animals, why is it wrong for stronger humans to prey on the weaker ones? Violence is a natural part of our world. When one animal devours another animal, we don't believe it is morally wrong, so why is it only wrong for humans to take advantage of the weak?[22]

In the 1940s the Nazis shocked the world with their unimaginable cruelty. We must not forget that Hitler's *Final Solution* did not occur in some barbaric uneducated land, but in Germany, one of the most educated countries in Europe.[23] Yet reason did not persuade them that their fierce tactics towards the Jews were wrong. The Nazis believed they were right based upon their scientific understanding of eugenics. In a time when the liberal intellectuals had largely thrown off their belief in God, on what basis could another German argue for human rights?

Historically in the West, it has been understood that human rights are discovered and not created. The United States' Declaration of Independence states: "We hold these truths to be self-evident, that all men are created equal, that they are endowed by their Creator with certain unalienable Rights, that among these are Life, Liberty and the pursuit of Happiness."[24] But if rights do not come from the Creator, how can we justify their existence? Some argue that since God does not exist, human rights come from nature—some behaviors are better fitting with the way things are, so morality is about encouraging those behaviors. However, as we have already mentioned and will visit in greater depth in later chapters, nature thrives on violence and predation as the strong eat the weak; it is the survival of the fittest. Because of this, philosopher J. L. Mackie argued that human rights could not be derived from any self-evident truths; instead, they had to be created by humans and were developed over time.[25] But if human rights are created by the majority, then there is nothing to appeal to when they are legislated out of existence.[26] American law professor Michael Perry acknowledges that the religious grounds for human rights are clear, but for secular thinkers it is not so clear. He writes:

It is far from clear, however, that there is a non-religious ground — a secular ground — for the morality of human rights . . . Indeed the claim that every born human being has inherent dignity and is inviolable is deeply problematic for many secular thinkers . . . perhaps to the point of being impossible.[27]

German philosopher Friedrich Nietzsche criticized the English intellectuals of his day for throwing off Christianity without also throwing off Christian morality. He saw this as a fundamental inconsistency.[28] Nietzsche argued:

They are rid of the Christian God and now believe all the more firmly that they must cling to Christian morality . . . When one gives up the Christian faith, one pulls the right to Christian morality out from under one's feet. This morality is by no means self-evident: this point has to be exhibited again and again, despite the English flatheads. Christianity is a system, a whole view of things thought out together. By breaking one main concept out of it, the faith in God, one breaks the whole: nothing necessary remains in one's hands . . . Christian morality is a command; its origin is transcendent; it is beyond all criticism, all right to criticism; it has truth only if God is the truth—it stands and falls with faith in God.[29]

Though Nietzsche believed that God was dead (that He did not exist), like Dostoevsky, he was not sure if it was a good thing. Nietzsche contended that if people stopped being loyal to the Christian God, they would transfer their old faith in God to something else. He predicted that people would put their trust in cruel "brotherhoods with the aim of the robbery and exploitation of the non-brothers." Almost prophetically, this is precisely what occurred half a century later with two world wars that led to the deaths of millions.[30]

Nietzsche believed that those who dropped their belief in the Christian God and still held to Christian morality were inconsistent. Similarly, today, many who advocate subjective morality have grown up in a culture that has been deeply shaped by Christian values. Like the English intellectuals, they have thrown off their belief in God, but they can't help but cling to His morality, at least in part. But as Nietzsche pointed out, it is disingenuous to cling to the morality of the Christian God while denying His existence.

While the idea of human rights is commonplace in the West, it is not as much so in the East. For instance, China claims that the idea of human rights is a Western notion that we are attempting to force upon the rest of the world, which amounts to cultural imperialism. If human rights are not universal, then different cultures are entitled to their own moral standards, and we cannot say that any one action is moral while another is immoral.[31] But if morality is similar to color preference, who gets to put their subjective, arbitrary moral preferences into law? The majority? What if the majority decides to exterminate the minority? If you say that's wrong, how do you justify your moral preferences being obligatory for others? If there is no God, then all moral statements are nothing but expressions of our arbitrary, subjective feelings, which means there is no external moral standard to judge them by.[32] Consequently, if God does not exist, it is impossible to justify human rights. Nevertheless, we cannot seem to shake the obvious truth that human rights do exist. Recognizing the full weight of this dilemma, agnostic law professor Arthur Leff bleakly wrote:

> *As things stand now, everything is up for grabs. Nevertheless: napalming babies is bad. Starving the poor is wicked. Buying and selling each other is depraved . . . There is such a thing as evil. All together now: Sez Who? God help us.*[33]

CHAPTER FIVE
The Moral Lawgiver

> *"For the Lord is our judge, the Lord is our lawgiver,*
> *the Lord is our king; it is he who will save us."*
> — Isaiah 33:22

> *"Glory to Man in the highest! For Man is the master of things."*
> — Algernon Charles Swinburne

The moral argument is considered by many to be one of the most powerful arguments for God's existence. The argument goes like this: objective moral values can only exist if God exists; objective moral values do exist, therefore God exists.[1] Christian philosopher and apologist William Lane Craig goes so far as to say that the moral argument for God surmounts to a knock-down argument against atheism, which is quite the bold philosophical claim.[2] Scottish philosopher W. R. Sorley argued that objective moral values could only exist in either matter or minds, and since they can't exist in matter, they must exist in minds. However, since human minds are finite, and therefore limited, objective moral values could only exist in an infinite mind, and so we have God.[3]

While nearly all philosophers agree that morality appears to be objective in nature (discovered truth), many argue that its apparent objectivity is simply an illusion that exists because it is socially advantageous. However, Philosopher William Wainwright believes that one of the strengths of theistic morality is that it offers a simpler explanation for the apparent objectivity of moral values. Since moral values appear to be objective, we have good reason to think they truly are. In this respect, theistic morality has Occam's razor on its side (the simplest explanation is the most plausible one). As we discussed in chapter one, though this can't prove the theory outright, it does add support for it.[4] Theists argue that morality being objective better explains why actions like rape, torture, child abuse, and brutality are generally condemned by all human cultures—they are not merely disadvantageous social behaviors, but are moral abominations that we know are objectively wrong.[5]

Atheists are often offended by the idea that we need God in order to be good; however, this isn't actually what theistic moralists claim. Philosopher Robert Adams, developer of one of the more modern accounts of theistic morality, explains that in the same way people in the past could recognize water before knowing its chemical makeup (H2O), people today can recognize goodness without knowing its divine makeup.[6] While goodness is not God, it does flow from Him as it is part of His essence. It is out of God's goodness that He created human beings as moral agents with an intuition for right and wrong. From the theist's perspective, this explains why atheists can recognize goodness without knowing that it comes from God.[7]

Euthyphro's Dilemma

In Plato's dialogue *Euthyphro*, Socrates asks a question that has forever changed the conversation on morality. He asks whether moral acts are desired by God because they are good, or if they are good because God desires them. At first glance it might not seem like much of a difference, however, either horn of the dilemma has devastating results for theistic morality.[8] The first horn of Euthyphro's dilemma addresses moral rightness being based on a standard outside of God. The problem here is that if God's commands are based on an objective moral standard that is independent of God, then we don't actually need God for morality. When God pronounced His creation "good," He was merely comparing it to values that exist independently from Himself and His creation.[9] But if God is appealing to a moral standard that He did not make, then God is merely a middleman to the real source of morality. This means God is just a messenger or law enforcer at best, and is Himself under the authority of this moral standard.[10] If this is the case, why not just cut out the middleman and work to discover the ultimate source of morality ourselves?

The second horn of the dilemma addresses moral rightness being solely based upon God's commands. God simply decides that He likes certain actions and they become what is morally right, and the ones He doesn't like are morally wrong. However, seventeenth-century German mathematician and philosopher Gottfried Leibniz rightly criticized this position for making morality essentially meaningless when he wrote:

> *in saying that things are not good by virtue of any rule of goodness but solely by virtue of the will of God, it seems to me that we unknowingly destroy all of God's love and all of his glory. For why praise him for what he has done if he would be equally praiseworthy in doing the exact contrary?*[11]

If moral goodness and badness are simply due to God's mood, then it is no longer a significant statement to say that God is good, and there is nothing to prevent Him from changing His mind tomorrow and issuing a new set of moral laws that encourage rape, murder, hating your neighbor, and worshiping false gods.[12] Harvard's Humanist Chaplain Greg Epstein writes, "it would be beneath our dignity to worship such a God. It would not deserve our time or our energy."[13] British philosopher John Stuart Mill proclaimed, "I will call no being good, who is not what I mean when I apply that epithet to my fellow-creatures; and if such a being can sentence me to hell for not so calling him, to hell I will go."[14] C. S. Lewis agreed in part with Mill's criticism when he wrote, "if God's moral judgment differs from ours so that our 'black' may be His 'white', we can mean nothing by calling Him good."[15]

Many atheists believe that Euthyphro's Dilemma is a knockout punch for any theory that relies on God as the source of morality.[16] The first horn of Euthyphro's dilemma shows that if morality is independent of God, then we don't need Him to ground morality since God Himself would also be under the authority of this moral standard. The second horn shows that right and wrong cannot be the mere product of God's choosing, since this would make His moral decrees arbitrary and therefore meaningless. Philosopher Massimo Pigliucci claims that Euthyphro's conclusion has devastated the entire Judeo-Christian-Muslim concept of morality and God, which is why most philosophers conclude that Plato's argument is undisputable.[17] Greg Epstein believes Euthyphro's Dilemma shows that gods don't and can't create values—only humans can, and must do so wisely.[18] However, what non-theists often fail to realize is that naturalistic moral positions also suffer from Euthyphro's dilemma. When it comes to the first horn, how can an objective moral standard exist in a naturalistic universe, and even if it somehow did, what makes us obligated to obey it? For the second horn, if morality is based upon our choices, then it too is arbitrary, since saying, "genocide is morally wrong," merely amounts to saying it is unfavorable right now, though tomorrow this may change. Either way, Euthyphro's Dilemma is a problem for both naturalistic and theistic morality.

Euthyphro's Dilemma is only a true dilemma *if* there are *only* two possible options. However, University of Wisconsin philosopher Keith Yandell has come up with at least seven theistic moral options, showing that Euthyphro's Dilemma commits the logical fallacy known as a *false dichotomy* (which states there are only two choices, when there are, in fact, more).[19] While Euthyphro's Dilemma might offer a powerful critique for some of the world's religions, neither horn of the dilemma accurately fits with the God of Christianity. The Bible teaches that God's commands are the source of moral obligation, while His unchanging nature is the source of moral goodness and value. Because morality's foundation originates from God's nature, then it is not based upon an external standard outside of God, but from within Him (the first horn). While God is free to act in a wide range of possibilities, His freedom is limited by His good and perfect nature. Since God doesn't change, neither can morality since it is derived from His perfect and unchanging nature, which is why He can't suddenly decide that rape is a morally good thing (the second horn).[20] Consequently, this version of theistic morality is immune to both horns of Euthyphro's Dilemma.

One objection to this explanation is that it places limits on God, who is supposedly all powerful.[21] While the Bible is full of passages that clearly teach God is omnipotent, it also teaches He is limited in some ways. For example, He cannot sin, let the wicked go unpunished, stop loving His people, annul His commands, or get tired.[22] But if God is unable to do something, then how is He all powerful? We've all heard the common schoolyard question: "Can God make a rock so big He can't lift it?" or, "Could God eat Himself for breakfast?" Behind these questions lies the suggestion that God lacks power if He is unable to carry out any and all actions. So, is it a contradiction to say that God is all powerful if He is limited in any way? No—not if we correctly understand what omnipotence really is.

Even though God is all powerful, He cannot do contradictory, nonsensical things. For example, since God is perfect love and goodness, He cannot also be evil since, as we discussed in chapter one, this is a logical impossibility. To say that God's inability to do logical impossibilities is a lack of omnipotence is an irrational misunderstanding. If God's nature is perfect, then for Him to sin would be the result of imperfection. Therefore, questioning a perfect God's inability to do imperfect things, is like asking, "Is God powerful enough to not be all powerful?" As C. S. Lewis tells us, this is nonsense. He wrote:

> *Can a mortal ask questions which God finds unanswerable? Quite easily, I should think all nonsense questions are unanswerable. How many hours are in a mile? Is yellow square or round? Probably half the questions we ask—half our great theological and metaphysical problems—are like that.*[23]

If God never changes, then what about in the Old Testament when God orders killing, which breaks the sixth commandment?[24] Isn't this a clear example of Euthyphro's second horn? This argument is based upon a misunderstanding of the sixth commandment, which is often incorrectly translated, "thou shalt not kill," when it should be translated, "thou shalt not murder."[25] In the Bible, God delegates His judicial authority to governments and certain people to judge criminals or kill enemies during war, but individuals are never authorized to take justice into their own hands.[26] Private or personal killing is murder and is strictly forbidden, usually bearing the penalty of death.[27] No matter how much we may dislike it, God, who is the author and giver of life, is the only righteous judge who has authority over life and death. Therefore, when God ordered the conquest of Canaan, He commanded killing, not murder. While this causes an emotional conflict for us, there is no logical conflict here with the sixth commandment.

Perhaps you are thinking that even though this solution works logically, it still doesn't get God off the hook. You might think, "It's just evil, no matter the rationalization!" As a Christian, I resonate with this frustration, as I have deeply struggled with this issue over the years, and if I'm honest, it still troubles me. However, when dealing with difficult issues like this, we must not confuse an emotional problem with an intellectual one. Intellectually, I know there is no logical conflict here, but emotionally it still troubles me regardless of the intellectual justifications. But my goal here has only been to show one of the intellectual responses for this alleged problem, while saving the larger response for later when we deal with the broader topic under which this issue falls: the problem of evil and suffering.

As we have seen, the Christian response to Euthyphro's Dilemma is that morality is neither based on a standard external to God, nor from His ever changing arbitrary will. Instead, it is based upon God's unchanging and perfect nature. However, some skeptics still maintain that we need an independent standard to compare with before we can determine whether God's nature is actually good. But remember our discussion in chapter one—any standard we put forth will be subject to this same difficulty. Unless the regress has a stopping point, knowledge is not possible. Theists believe the regress stops with God, and frame their worldview around His existence.

We Can't Trust Religion

There are several commonly-used counter-arguments against theistic morality. One of them states that even if morality comes from God, we would have no way to know what His laws were unless He told us. Clearly, He hasn't, since all of the world's religions disagree with one another over what God has said. As Christopher Hitchens once put it, "Since it is obviously inconceivable that all religions can be right, the most reasonable conclusion is that they are all wrong."[28] Not only is this an enormous logical leap, but, by Hitchens's own line of reasoning, we shouldn't trust his view either, since it's also just one among many.

This argument also commits the *appeal to the masses* fallacy, which holds that consensus is necessary for truth, which is clearly wrong.[29] As the French poet Anatole France said, "If 50 million people say a foolish thing, it is still a foolish thing."[30] While consensus is helpful, sometimes it only shows that people harbor the same biases.[31] As George Orwell stylishly wrote in his novel

1984, "Being in a minority, even in a minority of one, did not make you mad. There was truth and there was untruth, and if you clung to the truth even against the whole world, you were not mad."[32]

Mystery Is A Cop-out

Another common argument against theistic morality views religion's appeal to mystery (ineffability) as a cop-out that stifles conversation and honest inquiry. A. C. Grayling explains:

> *The last resort of the religious apologist is, familiarly, to invoke ineffability. The apologist challenged to explain what is meant by the word 'god' is apt to say that god is a mystery, too great for our finite minds to comprehend. Again familiarly, this closes down conversation, which of course is a useful result for the apologist.*[33]

There are several problems with this argument, but one of the bigger ones is that we all appeal to mystery at some point, and to not do so would be arrogance of a high order. Strangely enough, Grayling seems to understand this when he writes:

> *In contrast to the certainties of faith, a humanist has a humbler conception of the nature and current extent of knowledge . . . Having the intellectual courage to live with open-endedness and uncertainty, trusting to reason and experiment to gain us increments of understanding, having the integrity to base one's views on rigorous and testable foundations, and being committed to changing one's mind when shown to be wrong, are the marks of honest minds.*[34]

Humanists have no problem with open-endedness and uncertainty when difficult questions are asked of their worldview, and even see it as a virtue of the rational mind—but when theists do, it's a cop-out. So why the double standard?

While writing this book, my two-year-old daughter would frequently come visit me and ask, "What doing Dadda?" I would tell her that I was working on my book, and sometimes I'd pick her up and show her, though she often seemed a bit confused by the lack of pictures. One day, she did this while I was thinking over the skeptic's ineffability (appeal to mystery) argument, and it got me thinking about what it would be like to try to explain to her the concepts we are discussing in this book. Obviously, this would be impossible, as the gap between a toddler's mind and an adult's is too vast. On the same note, if there is such a being as God, why shouldn't we expect the gap between us to be even greater? Just as a dog with all of its canine intelligence cannot comprehend trigonometry, neither can we fully comprehend the Divine.

Religion Is Subjective

Some atheists argue that even though religion claims to have an objective moral foundation, it ends up being subjective anyway. Even if God revealed His moral orders, we would still be in the awkward position of needing human agents to interpret them: priests, preachers, rabbis, imams, gurus, and the like, and this all seems hopelessly subjective and open to far more confusion and doubts.³⁵ However, this wouldn't mean that religious morality is subjective, rather that it isn't always easy to figure out. Theistic morality doesn't pretend to make things uncomplicated or simple—ethics are still a very necessary and complex undertaking. Alvin Plantinga explains this point clearly when he writes: "Although we are divine image-bearers, our knowledge and understanding is of course partial and fragmentary and often shot through with error; nevertheless, it is real."³⁶

Even though theists have a foundation for moral knowledge, they still must strive to figure out how God's moral decrees are to be applied, and mistakes along the way should be expected. As humans, we are fallible and prone to error, and there is no escaping this; however, this does not negate the fact that there is such a thing as truth and we must work to discover it. In the same way that mathematics is almost infinitely complex, so is ethics. No matter your worldview, determining the "ins and outs" of morality is difficult. But just because something is difficult doesn't mean it is subjective or wrong, and to argue otherwise is to commit the logical fallacy known as *personal incredulity*.³⁷

God Is Immoral

Another common argument against theistic morality is made by evolutionary psychologist Steven Pinker, who argues that religious followers don't actually get their morality from their religious texts. For example, he claims the Old Testament is full of brutal commands that encourage genocide, rape, slavery, and stoning people to death for frivolous infractions, yet modern-day Christians don't follow these horrifying commands. Pinker goes as far as saying that the Christian's "reverence for the Bible is purely talismanic... they pay it lip service as a symbol of morality, while getting their actual morality from more modern principles."[38] In *The God Delusion*, Richard Dawkins writes:

> *The God of the Old Testament is arguably the most unpleasant character in all fiction: jealous and proud of it; a petty, unjust, unforgiving control-freak; a vindictive, bloodthirsty ethnic cleanser; a misogynistic, homophobic, racist, infanticidal, genocidal, filicidal, pestilential, megalomaniacal, sadomasochistic, capriciously malevolent bully.*[39]

The point is, since the God of the Bible is so morally malicious, few modern Christians actually take the Bible's commands literally. Instead, they pick and choose what commands to follow, and seem to be guided by the same inner light that guides nonbelievers.[40] No one actually takes the Bible literally, and to do so would be to embrace horrific brutality.[41]

This has led some atheists to call religion a "moving target," claiming that it evolves over time as its followers subjectively interpret their religious texts and decide which parts to follow or ignore. For instance, many Christians used to accept and employ slavery and believe that interracial marriage was wrong, but today we know better, no thanks to the Bible. A. C. Grayling compares challenging religion to engaging in a boxing match with jelly; it is an ever-shifting, unclear, amorphous target, which takes a new shape after every blow.[42] Since religious texts are full of flawed moral instructions, once its followers recognize these flaws, the religion shifts to embrace a more enlightened and modernized moral view. The truth is, they argue, the God of the Bible is evil, which is why even His followers refuse to follow His moral code. This argument has two parts.

The first part claims that Christian belief has progressed morally because of modern, enlightened moral principles. However, this is false, as the change is actually due to theological and historical differences. For instance, the differences between the laws in the Old Testament and the New Testament are almost entirely due to Jesus' coming and fulfilling the rigorous requirements of the Law that we could not.[43] The blood sacrifices in the Old Testament pointed to Christ, and were fulfilled in Him when He died as the perfect and final sacrifice.[44] The priesthood ended because Christ is our high priest who intercedes for us before the Father.[45] The physical temple is no longer needed because Christ's followers are indwelt with the Spirit of God, and function as a living temple.[46] The dietary restrictions that set Israel apart from the other nations have been fulfilled and ended in Christ.[47] The civil laws were given to an ethnically rooted people group (the Israelites) who were being directly ruled by God Himself, but they have ended since the people of God (Christians) are no longer a unified nation state, but are exiles serving as ambassadors in a foreign land.

When it comes to the moral failings of Christians, such as slavery, segregation, and opposing interracial marriage, this was not due to Christian doctrine, but the rejection of Christian doctrine. In Martin Luther King Jr's *Letters from Birmingham Jail*, he encouraged the church to "recapture the sacrificial spirit of the early church" which was "God-intoxicated."[48] He didn't call them to embrace "modern moral principles," but ancient ones derived from the scriptures and natural law, as it was their embrace of modern moral principles that caused their racist views in the first place. Still, skeptics of religion are often some of religion's loudest moral critics, and their critiques shouldn't be disregarded in haste. In theologian Alister McGrath's book *The Twilight of Atheism*, he explains the critical role that atheism has had on Christianity's past moral mistakes:

> *The rise of atheism in the West was undoubtedly a protest against a corrupted and complacent church; yet paradoxically, it has energized Christianity to reform itself, in ways that seriously erode the credibility of those earlier criticisms. Where atheism criticizes, wise Christians move to reform their ways. The atheist dilemma is that Christianity is a moving target whose trajectory is capable of being redirected without losing its anchor point in the New Testament.*[49]

While atheism is right to criticize Christians for their moral failings, the truth is, they are calling them to be more Christian, not less.

The second part of the argument states that God's character is seriously morally deficient. However, this criticism is philosophically bankrupt as it hangs on the problem of evil. Atheists, such as Dawkins, believe that by raising the question of evil they have laid the groundwork for deconstructing theism, but this isn't the case. If there is no God, and no objective moral standard by which to judge actions right or wrong, then neither good nor bad is a meaningful term. For Dawkins's criticism to have any strength, he must first explain how a purposeless, non-moral process can produce a moral basis for life. If we give up the foundation for objective morality (God) and embrace subjectivism, morality is nothing more than applauding whichever particular values we like.[50] In C. S. Lewis's famous book *Mere Christianity*, he explains how it was this idea that directed his shift from atheism to belief in God:

> *My argument against God was that the universe seemed so cruel and unjust. But how had I got this idea of just and unjust? A man does not call a line crooked unless he has some idea of a straight line. What was I comparing this universe with when I called it unjust? If the whole show was bad and senseless from A to Z, so to speak, why did I, who was supposed to be part of the show, find myself in such violent reaction against it? . . . Of course I could have given up my idea of justice by saying it was nothing but a private idea of my own. But if I did that, then my argument against God collapsed too—for the argument depended on saying that the world was really unjust, not simply that it did not happen to please my fancies. Thus in the very act of trying to prove that*

> *God did not exist—in other words, that the whole of reality was senseless—I found I was forced to assume that one part of reality—namely my idea of justice—was full of sense. Consequently atheism turns out to be too simple. If the whole universe has no meaning, we should never have found out that it has no meaning: just as, if there were no light in the universe and therefore no creatures with eyes, we should never know it was dark. Dark would be a word without meaning.*[51]

If we say that the God of the Bible is evil and reject His moral standard, on what basis are we saying that He is evil? By what standard are we judging Him, other than His own?

Religion Is the Product of Primitive Man

Some have said that religion cannot be trusted as an objective source for morality, since it is the product of primitive man's attempt to understand the world. A. C. Grayling writes:

> *religion stems from the period when stories, myths and supernaturalistic beliefs served as, in effect, mankind's earliest science and technology. To the inhabitants of such a culture, natural phenomena are most intuitively explained by seeing them as the work of purposive agents who variously cause the wind to blow and the rain to fall, whose footsteps on the clouds are thunderous, and who are responsible for the cycling of the stars and the growth of vegetation in springtime.*[52]

Grayling believes that religion was humanity's earliest attempt at controlling the world around them.[53] Prayer, sacrifice, and ritual were the major instruments used to influence the gods, and their supernatural experiences are best explained by natural causes, such as: hallucinations, drunkenness, poisoning, and health-related issues.[54]

Atheists like Grayling believe that religion is a hangover from humanity's infancy, from "the superstitions of illiterate herdsmen living several thousands of years ago."[55] Though I am a theist, I think Grayling is partly right. There are compelling arguments that back up his explanation for people's supernatural experiences. However, I disagree that these explanations account for *all* religious experience. Atheists sometimes make the mistake of clumping all religious claims and experiences together, and then proceed to critique them as one. Though religions share similarities, most religions make drastically different truth claims from one another. Not all religions are created equally, nor are all claims of supernatural experience. While hallucinations or wishful thinking might account for *some* religious experience, to say that it accounts for all of them paints with a massively broad brush. For instance, to claim the early Christians merely hallucinated Jesus' resurrection is a serious misunderstanding of the vast amount of historical data we have, which is why modern historical scholarship does not accept this as a viable explanation. The point is, when evaluating religion, we need to respect each group's differences, lest we commit a *straw man* fallacy by misrepresenting what each group actually believes and treating them all the same.

Chronological Snobbery

Skeptics argue that the Bible is outdated and untrustworthy, so it cannot be relied on as a source of objective morality. However, this argument relies on an assumption that British philosopher Owen Barfield and C. S. Lewis termed "chronological snobbery," which is the assumption that whatever has gone out of date has been discredited.[56] Theologian J. I. Packer describes this attitude when he writes: "The newer is the truer, only what is recent is decent."[57] The idea is that humanity suffered in hopeless ignorance for countless generations, until modern science came along and shed light into the darkness of that ignorance.[58] In Barfield's fictional dialogue, *Worlds Apart,* one of the characters, who is a rocket scientist, perfectly demonstrates chronological snobbery when he says:

three or four hundred years ago for some reason or other the human mind suddenly woke up . . . for some reason people began to look at the world around them instead of accepting traditional theories, to explore the universe instead of just sitting around and thinking about it. First of all they discovered that the earth wasn't flat . . . and that it was not the centre of the universe, as they had been dreaming, but a rapidly revolving and whirling speck of dust in empty space. Almost overnight about half the ideas men had had about the universe and their own place in it, turned out to be mere illusions. And the other half went the same way, when scientists began applying the new method—practical exploration—to other fields of inquiry—mechanics, chemistry, physiology, biology, and, later on, animal and human psychology and so forth. Everything that had been thought before, from the beginnings of civilization down to that moment, became hopelessly out of date and discredited.[59]

Chronological snobbery is heavily woven into the fabric of our current cultural mood, despite scholarship having discredited it, and can be clearly seen in the flat earth myth.

Flat Earthers

When I was in elementary school, I remember being taught that for most of human history people believed that the Earth was flat, and it wasn't until the scientific revolution that people began to abandon superstition and ignorance. This is why Christopher Columbus had such a difficult time assembling a crew to sail west to find a new trade route to India, as no one wanted to risk falling off the face of the Earth. Columbus lived in a time of ignorance and superstition, when a belief in antipodes, an upside-down people who lived on the other side of the Earth, was common. Against all odds the hero prevailed, and so here we sit in the New World remembering Columbus's courage to fight against the superstition and religious dogma of his day. While this account of history is undoubtedly fascinating, unfortunately it isn't even remotely factual.

Humanity has known from at least the sixth century BC that the Earth is a sphere.[60] Greek philosophers Pythagoras and Aristotle assumed a spherical planet in their cosmology.[61] In the third century BC, Eratosthenes even measured the Earth's circumference.[62] The flat-earth myth claims that this knowledge was lost and forgotten for over a thousand years, mostly because of Christian theology that suppressed it. Skeptics refer to passages such as Revelation 7:1 and 20:8 that speak of the "four corners" of the Earth, and Daniel 4 that speaks of a tree that could be seen to all ends of the Earth, or Psalm 75:3 which talks about God holding the pillars of the Earth firm, as proof that the biblical authors believed in a flat Earth. These texts are offered as proof that the biblical authors are not reliable sources and shouldn't be trusted.

Though it is understandable why someone might think the Bible teaches a flat Earth, this is only possible from a cursory glance at a few select passages, while completely ignoring their context and genre. For example, when Revelation speaks of the "four corners" it's not actually referring to a flat Earth, but the four cardinal directions: north, south, east, and west. In the book of Daniel, the tree that could be seen "to the ends of all the earth" comes from a dream, and the Bible records many extraordinary dreams that are never meant to be literal depictions of reality. The book of Psalms is written as poetry and is not referring to literal pillars, but is a poetic means of emphasizing God's power and sovereignty over His creation. Also, the Bible is full of passages that indicate a round Earth. Job 26:7-10 describes the Earth as suspended over empty space, hanging on nothing and having a spherical nature. Isaiah 40:22 and Proverbs 8:27 also imply the Earth being a sphere, and Luke 17 implies a round Earth, given people are experiencing day and night simultaneously.

Many atheists argue that even if the Bible doesn't teach a flat Earth, many Christians did for most of Western history, which is why people living in the middle ages believed the Earth was flat.[63] However, this claim has almost no historical evidence to support it. While Columbus did receive some sharp intellectual objections to his plan, no one questioned the Earth being round. Instead, Columbus was told that his plan to reach the Indies would fail, not because of a flat Earth, but because the circumference of the Earth was too great (a point they were right about). Columbus had to fudge his figures to favor a much smaller Earth in order to sell his plan, and if he hadn't run into an unexpected land mass (North America), he and his crew would have perished at sea.[64]

After researching the flat-earth theory, Stephen Jay Gould concluded that it was entirely fictitious and that there was never a period of flat-earth darkness.[65] The Greek knowledge of the Earth's spherical nature never faded and virtually all major Christian scholars have always affirmed the Earth's roundness as an established fact.[66] So how did this myth become so widespread? Gould traced the myth back to two people. The first was French antireligious writer Antoine-Jean Letronne (1787-1848) who intentionally misrepresented the church fathers and their medieval successors as flat-earthers in order to make Christianity look bad. The second was American storyteller Washington Irving (1783-1859) who often wrote historical fiction and is responsible for inventing the fabulous tail of Christopher Columbus standing up for truth against the crowd of flat-earthers. Though the myth began with these two men, it was historian John Draper (1811-1882) who made sure the false account of history was perpetrated in texts, encyclopedias, and major scholarship.[67] Gould concluded that the myth was deliberately fabricated in order to accentuate the warfare model between science and religion, and specifically to promote Darwinian Theory over Creationism. It was a story concocted to promote the army of naturalism under the banner of "science."[68]

We Don't Need Religion Anyway

Several years ago, an agnostic friend suggested that if I stopped believing in God, aside from being able to sleep in on Sundays, not much about my life would change. His point was that we don't need God to be good, and there is no significant difference between atheists and religious believers when it comes to moral goodness. While I agreed that many atheists live comparable, if not superior, moral lifestyles to their religious counterparts, I disagreed that my life wouldn't be lived any differently. There are countless conversion stories that demonstrate the dynamic change that can occur when a person comes to faith in God. One of the most remarkable examples of this is eighteenth-century English slave trader John Newton. Before his conversion, his life was a moral train wreck; he was arrogant, rebellious, and lived immorally. Describing his pre-conversion lifestyle, he wrote, "I not only sinned with a high hand myself, but made it my study to tempt and seduce others upon every occasion."[69] After reading Thomas à Kempis's *The Imitation of Christ*, he came to put his faith in the Gospel. After becoming an Anglican clergyman, Newton became a leading influence in the abolition movement, and even had a profound impact on the great abolitionist William Wilberforce. Newton's newfound faith eventually led him to pen the words of the famous Christian hymn *Amazing Grace*.

If faith can positively change a slave trader like John Newton to become an abolitionist, wouldn't the loss of that faith have some sort of reverse effect? The only way that radical abandonment of a person's worldview wouldn't lead to a noticeable change in their actions would be if they adopted a worldview of similar values, or if they never actually lived by their alleged worldview to begin with.

Religion Is Apple Polishing

In *The God Delusion*, Richard Dawkins argues that if you only try to be good in order to gain God's approval and reward, or to avoid His disapproval and punishment, then you aren't being moral, you are just "sucking up."[70] He writes:

> *If you agree that, in the absence of God, you would 'commit robbery, rape, and murder', you reveal yourself as an immoral person, 'and we would be well advised to steer a wide course*

*around you'. If, on the other hand, you admit that you would
continue to be a good person even when not under divine
surveillance, you have fatally undermined your claim that God is
necessary for us to be good. I suspect that quite a lot of religious
people do think religion is what motivates them to be good,
especially if they belong to one of those faiths that systematically
exploits personal guilt. It seems to me to require quite a low self-
regard to think that, should belief in God suddenly vanish from the
world, we would all become callous and selfish hedonists, with no
kindness, no charity, no generosity, nothing that would deserve
the name of goodness.*[71]

In agreement, atheist philosopher Daniel Dennett believes the idea that heavenly reward is what motivates us to be good is "demeaning and unnecessary."[72] We simply don't need God in order to be good when we can be prompted to the ethical life by our natural human feelings of concern and interest in our fellow man.[73]

Atheists have a valid point; if we *only* obey God because of the promise of punishment or reward, then the entire moral argument for God rests on the logical fallacy of *might makes right*. Explaining how this is problematic, Walter Sinnott-Armstrong writes:

*Consider a small boy who thinks that what makes it morally
wrong for him to hit his little sister is only that his parents told
him not to hit her and they will punish him if he hits her. As a
result, this little boy thinks that if his parents die, then there is
nothing wrong with hitting his little sister. Maybe some little boys
think this way, but surely we adults do not think that morality is
like this. To see morality this way is, in a word, childish.*[74]

It is true that if we are to be morally good, we must strive to live morally for reasons above our self-interest; however, just because a person believes in consequences for immorality doesn't make them a might-makes-right consequentialist.[75] Within Christianity, consequences are not the reason an act is wrong, instead they reinforce its wrongness by providing further motive to avoid the act.[76] This concept can be easily understood by looking at our own laws. We do not believe that drunk driving is wrong simply because we might be arrested, face fines, or serve jail time; instead, these punishments exist to further motivate us to do the right thing.[77]

Even though many atheists are upstanding citizens who care for their neighbors and the good of society, historically, when humanity has no faith in the reward of good or the punishment of evil, we see our true colors. For instance, look at what often occurs in populated areas when natural disasters happen, or when there are citywide blackouts—there is almost always an influx of looting, vandalism, and violence.[78] It is not only the psychopathic minority that act in this way. In Nazi Germany, normal citizens were responsible for many of the horrific crimes committed against the Jews and other minorities.[79] When the threat of punishment is taken away, many "good people" engage in evil to an unimaginable degree. Richard Wurmbrand was a Christian minister who lived through years of horrific persecution and anti-Semitic hatred. In regards to the depths of human evil, he wrote:

> *The cruelty of atheism is hard to believe when man has no faith in the reward of good or the punishment of evil. There is no reason to be human. There is no restraint from the depths of evil which is in man. The Communist torturers often said, 'There is no God, no hereafter, no punishment for evil. We can do what we wish.' I have heard one torturer even say, 'I thank God, in whom I don't believe, that I have lived to this hour when I can express all the evil in my heart.' He expressed it in unbelievable brutality and torture inflicted on prisoners.*[80]

Evidently, humanity is not good enough to live morally without the threat of punishment or the promise of reward, whether that be from a governing police force or fear of God.

Another key factor that atheists often overlook is that morality isn't just about appeasing God's arbitrary desires, which would be nothing more than might makes right. Instead, Christians believe that God's perfect and unchanging nature is the ultimate reality that has always existed and to which our created reality points. This means that goodness in our reality is but a reflection of the goodness in Him. Following God's moral law is to follow goodness for goodness' sake, while simultaneously engaging in behavior that best leads to our flourishing. Therefore, God's nature grounds not only morality's existence, but also moral obligation in a way that avoids both horns of Euthyphro's dilemma.

Maybe you still find theistic morality problematic and believe that there must be a God-independent standard for right and wrong.[81] However, remember that any standard we put forth for grounding right and wrong, whether secular or theistic, will be subject to the same difficulty. For the Humanist who fails to recognize this, it is likely because of a deeply biased skepticism that refuses to acknowledge that all truths have stopping points where rational justification ends and belief takes over, less the regress be infinite. This is why we can't say, "Your worldview is belief based and mine isn't." When it comes to self-evident truths, there are good and bad stopping points, so we need to ask ourselves which ones offer a better explanation and justification for morality in our world.

CHAPTER SIX
The Science of Good and Evil

> *"The pendulum of the mind oscillates between sense and nonsense, not between right and wrong."*
> — C. G. Jung

In chapter two, we discussed Stephen J. Gould's belief that science and religion address different kinds of truth —science tells us how the heavens go, while religion tells us how to get to Heaven.[1] While this view has captured the minds of many, the New Atheists have declared Gould's idea to be wrong, arguing instead that religion has nothing to offer us whatsoever, believing that science can provide definitive, objective answers to moral questions. Though religion used to hold the key to moral truth, science has taken over with a firm declaration: we can discover moral goodness without God.

Many atheists believe that morality is not created, but rather discovered, and exists in the same sort of way as the laws of logic and arithmetic. Since morality is woven into the very fabric of the universe, it is not dependent on God's existence, nor is it founded on personal opinion.

Sam Harris, an advocate for this view, argues that the purpose of morality is to increase the well-being of conscious creatures, and science (specifically neuroscience) holds the key to unlocking the answers to our moral questions.[2] While most Humanists believe human flourishing is the general purpose of morality, there is disagreement over whether morality is discovered or created. If morality is discovered, then it abides by fixed laws that are not up to us; whereas if it is created, then we must work together to build a moral system that best serves our purposes and values.

Sam Harris believes that reason can lead us to see that morality is discovered, and is based on a concern for the well-being of conscious creatures.[3] Once this is recognized, it is a small step to accept that human happiness is a key factor in determining what does and does not classify as well-being. Harris explains:

> *I am arguing that, in the moral sphere, it is safe to begin with the premise that it is good to avoid behaving in such a way as to produce the worst possible misery for everyone. I am not claiming that most of us personally care about the experience of all conscious beings; I am saying that a universe in which all conscious beings suffer the worst possible misery is worse than a universe in which they experience well-being. This is all we need to speak about "moral truth" in the context of science. Once we admit that the extremes of absolute misery and absolute flourishing—whatever these states amount to for each particular being in the end—are different and dependent on facts about the*

universe, then we have admitted that there are right and wrong answers to questions of morality.[4]

Harris believes the purpose of morality is to increase humanity's "well-being"; but should we readily accept this as the foundation for all moral thinking?

Facts and Values

In Harris's book, *The Moral Landscape: How Science Can Determine Human Values,* he argues that Hume's Law is mistaken, since the divide between facts (objective or discovered truth) and values (subjective or created truth) is an illusion.[5] Consequently, science can not only *describe* how reality *is*, but can also *prescribe* how reality *ought* to be. Since neuroscience reveals that our beliefs about facts and values originate from similar processes in the brain, we can rely on it to find out which moral values best contribute to human flourishing. Just as there are right and wrong answers to questions of physics, there are right and wrong answers to moral questions, and as science progresses it will provide further answers to our moral questions.[6]

Historically, this view has been strongly rejected by philosophers and scientists alike. Agnostic philosopher Thomas Nagel has written a powerful critique of Harris's moral view, dismissing his experimental data about the brain as being mostly irrelevant to determining moral truth.[7] Similarly, Massimo Pigliucci adamantly disagrees with Harris's rejection of Hume's Law, saying, "Neurobiology can tell us how people think, but not how they should think."[8] Pigliucci finds Harris's position "comical" and even equates it to "nonsense on stilts," arguing that Harris fundamentally fails to understand the difference between facts and values.[9] Pigliucci writes:

> *To begin with, nobody has ever claimed that scientific and ethical judgments have nothing in common, from the point of view of the brain. More importantly, it most certainly does not follow from this that facts and values are the same sort of thing, only that the brain deals with both in the same areas. (By similar reasoning, since the same areas of the brain respond to having sex and thinking about having sex, it would follow that the two experiences are one and the same.)*[10]

Harris is attempting to remove the divide between facts and values because he desperately wants to defeat both religious fanaticism and subjective moral relativism.[11] However, historically, philosophers have understood that facts are objective (discovered) and values are subjective (created). If Harris can remove this divide, he can safely transfer moral decision making over to science and reason, and then build a foundation from which to say that horrendous acts like female circumcision, child sacrifice, and genocide are objectively wrong, and therefore are not a matter of different cultural tastes.

Reason or Emotion

Humanists who seek to ground morality in human reason have an enormous difficulty to overcome; namely, refuting the objection that moral judgments do not come from reason at all, but are purely emotional responses. This would mean the reasons people provide for their moral beliefs are merely after-the-fact rationalizations to justify their emotional commitments.[12] David Hume believed that human behavior is primarily motivated by passions and emotions, not reason.[13] For example, consider slavery—most Westerners today feel that slavery is morally wrong and should be banished from society. However, in the grand scheme of human history, only the minority would agree that slavery is wrong. So, how could we convince someone that slavery is immoral?

Philosopher John Rawls believed that morality is the product of rational discussion and choice. He argued that laws should not be based upon any particular group's beliefs, but instead upon neutral, belief-free arguments. He invites us to imagine we are sitting around a table discussing the basic structure of a new society, except we don't know what our place in that society will be. In other words, you wouldn't know what your race, gender, religion, sexual preference, health, or wealth would be. Realizing that resources are limited, and considering the basic desires of human beings, we should strive to create a society that works best for everyone.[14]

Rawlsian morality has gained much popularity in the West, as many now believe that laws should be based on neutral, secular, nonreligious, rational arguments. Atheists argue that they can only engage with religious believers on highly controversial issues, such as abortion and euthanasia, so long as the arguments are based on neutral concepts that are available to everyone.[15] Once we've agreed to only use rationally neutral arguments, we can then begin to build a consensus in order to find solutions that work for all people. This is why many are calling for the exclusion of religious views from the public square, since religion is a divisive conversation-stopper for anyone who doesn't share those same beliefs.[16] However, an increasing number of both secular and religious thinkers are admitting that this call itself is religious in nature.[17] University of Texas professor J. Budziszewski points out that this argument seems to say, "Because we don't agree with each other, you must do as I say."[18] He goes on to explain:

> *like John Rawls, they respond that their opinion should have special privileges because it is "political, not metaphysical". Here the argument seems to be, "The ultimate truth of things is unknowable, and that's why you must do as I say." Of course, any view of what is knowable or unknowable presupposes something about ultimate truth, so that too is sleight of hand.[19]*

As we discussed earlier, there are no neutral, universal arguments that bring us to objective morality, so to argue that reason can lead us there not only breaks Hume's Law, but greatly underestimates how much our biases and presuppositions determine our views. It is simply impossible for us to check our worldview's beliefs at the door when we engage in controversial issues.

Pigliucci explains the problem of relying on rationality to build an objective moral argument. When discussing the possibility of using reason to argue that slavery is wrong, he writes:

> *Such an argument would have to rely on certain premises that are not, in themselves, easy to defend on rational grounds. For instance, one could say that it is wrong to limit the freedom of other human beings, or that we should not force on others what we would not want others to force upon us. Yet a hypothetical defender of slavery could counter such arguments with a logic of his own: that it is rational to limit some people's freedoms so that a stronger and more prosperous society can be built, or that it is acceptable to force others to do our bidding if we have the might to impose it on them, and so on. You may not find such proslavery arguments convincing (I certainly hope you don't!), but the point is that one can rationally argue both sides of the debate and that ultimately our moral sense derives from how we feel about slavery, with our arguments elaborating on that feeling, not determining it.*[20]

Pigliucci's point is that you cannot use rationality to get an "ought" from an "is," and rational arguments serve only to reinforce our emotional commitments. Nevertheless, nearly every Humanist agrees that harming others for no good reason is morally wrong. For example, atheist author Walter Sinnott-Armstrong argues that we know rape is morally wrong because it causes harm to others for no good reason. He writes:

> *even if we cannot say why it is immoral to cause unjustified harm to others, that should not make us doubt that it is immoral for moral agents to cause unjustified harm to others. Atheists can, thus, legitimately hold on to objective morality, even if nobody has a fully satisfying account of its ultimate basis.*[21]

However, this moral approach is ultimately circular, since he is essentially saying that rape (harming another person) is wrong because it harms another person, which amounts to saying that rape is wrong because rape is wrong. Arguments like this fail to take morality seriously.

When Humanists assert that science can ground morality, they have erred into scientism, not science. Pigliucci explains this problem, saying:

> Harris's entire project is predicated on the idea that science is the best way to judge the consequences of our actions and to channel them in the direction of increasing human well-being, by which he means an increase in happiness and a decrease in pain. But this project is incredibly philosophically loaded, as Harris is taking for granted a particular consequentialist approach to ethics (utilitarianism), which is far from the only contender in the field ... Needless to say, he does this with neither a scientific (because it is not possible) nor a philosophical (because it is boring) defense of his assumptions.[22]

At this point, it seems appropriate to reflect on what Christopher Hitchens said about unfounded assertions; "That which can be asserted without evidence, can be dismissed without evidence."[23]

Those who believe reason can lead us to morality fail to realize that they are merely cultural warriors imposing their culture's beliefs onto others. Reason plays no part in the foundation of their moral view. This is often demonstrated when people appeal to common sense to justify their moral beliefs. I have heard people say, "It's just common sense that it's wrong to harm another person for selfish gain!" But common sense for whom? Historically, most cultures, including many today, have rejected what we Westerners call "common sense" when it comes to right and wrong. Sam Harris responds to this notion, saying, "Everything about human experience suggests that love is more conducive to human happiness than hate is."[24] Yet, as author David Berlinski retorts, "It is astonishing with what eagerness men have traditionally fled happiness."[25] The truth is, we simply cannot say that reason leads us to morality, as our culture is by far in the minority when it comes to belief in universal human rights. To assert otherwise, on the grounds of reason, is to commit cultural imperialism.

Moral Dissenters

One of the difficulties for naturalistic objective morality is how it handles those who reject the "harm is bad" principle. Sam Harris believes these moral dissenters are irrelevant when determining moral truth because, like in other fields, consensus is not the determiner of truth. Just as people disagree over the nature of scientific truth, there will be those who disagree over the nature of moral truth, so their dissent from moral norms is not important. He argues that there simply aren't any good reasons to think that "demonizing homosexuals, stoning adulterers, veiling women, soliciting the murder of artists and intellectuals, and celebrating the exploits of suicide bombers" are morally good actions.[26] Harris doesn't believe he needs to be able to address every moral problem or moral dissenter for his moral principle of maximizing human well-being to be reasonably true.[27]

In one sense, Harris is right. No moral theory is capable of providing definitive answers for every ethical problem. However, if a moral theory is incapable of dealing with even the most basic moral issues, we should seriously reconsider its worth.[28] Though Harris believes that well-being is an obvious starting point for building an objective moral view, even the basic definition of well-being is highly controversial, since it depends on what you believe the meaning and purpose of life is. For example, Christians believe, as theologian Millard Erickson puts it, "Good is not defined in terms of what brings personal pleasure to humans in a direct fashion. Good is to be defined in relationship to the will and being of God. Good is what glorifies him, fulfills his will, conforms to his nature."[29] Still, Harris is not concerned with those who disagree with his definition of well-being. He explains:

> *Of course, anyone who has an alternative set of moral axioms is free to put them forward, just as they are free to define "science" any way they want. But some definitions will be useless, or worse—and many current definitions of "morality" are so bad that we can know, far in advance of any breakthrough in the sciences of mind, that they have no place in a serious conversation about how we should live in this world. The Knights of the Ku Klux Klan have nothing meaningful to say about particle physics, cell physiology, epidemiology, linguistics, economic policy, etc. How is their ignorance any less obvious on the subject of human well-being?*[30]

Harris explains this idea further with an analogy of human health. Even though someone might disagree that the goal of health is to avoid death, disease, pain, and debilitating illness, there is no reason to take what they say seriously.[31] However, the problem with comparing morality to human health is that what is considered healthy is dependent upon the objective purpose of an organ, whereas moral rightness is dependent on the purpose of human life. For instance, the purpose of the heart is to pump blood through the body, and the lungs are for the intake of oxygen and removal of carbon dioxide. Anything that supports these functions is considered *healthy*, while whatever hinders them is *unhealthy*. However, from a naturalistic perspective, it isn't objectively clear what the purpose of humanity is, or if there even is one. Therefore, determining what does and does not lead to human flourishing is completely dependent upon our worldview beliefs. While Harris is free to *believe* that his worldview beliefs are the foundation for moral thinking, he is not free to declare them to be science.

Some philosophers believe moral goodness and badness are really questions about what is *good* and *bad* for living things.[32] For instance, sunlight and water are necessary for an oak tree to flourish and produce acorns, therefore they are morally *good* things in relation to the oak tree.[33] Likewise, it is a *good* thing to further human flourishing and a *bad* thing to hinder it, so we have an obligation to help, and not hinder the flourishing of our fellow humans.

At a basic level, we can determine what contributes to the health or harm of a living thing; however, beyond this the terms *good* and *bad* quickly become philosophically loaded. For instance, where does moral obligation fit in with this idea in a naturalistic universe? Under strict naturalism, everything is the product of purposeless, blind chance, so people have no unique objective value. A star is no more valuable than a moon, and a person is no more valuable than a rainbow. Take, for instance, the mosquito, who's *good* relies on its ability to extract some of our blood in order to flourish. Under naturalism, why should we think that it is morally acceptable to have lethal intentions towards this creature but not women and children? How can we say that one is more valuable than the other? Just because we can identify that something contributes to a species' survival, does not logically suggest that we have a moral obligation to make that contribution. As J. L. Mackie once wrote, this moral view confuses "what sorts of things are good with the question of what goodness itself is."[34]

In an atheistic universe, why think there would be any moral dimension at all? In a debate with atheist philosopher Walter Sinnott-Armstrong, Christian philosopher William Lane Craig argued:

If there is no God, then what's so special about human beings? They're just accidental by-products of nature that have evolved relatively recently on an infinitesimal speck of dust lost somewhere in a hostile and mindless universe and that are doomed to perish individually and collectively in a relatively short time. On the atheistic view, some action, say, rape, may not be socially advantageous, and so in the course of human development has become taboo; but that does absolutely nothing to prove that rape is really wrong.[35]

If atheism is true, then in a naturalistic universe, human beings are merely bigger-brained animals. Since we don't hold the lower animals morally responsible for their actions, why do we for humans?

Walter Sinnott-Armstrong finds this argument uncompelling. He explains that it is the non-moral differences between human beings and other animals that ground their moral differences. For example, humans can suffer, reason, empathize, fall in love, and set goals in unique ways. The lower animals are not moral agents, nor do they make free choices, therefore their actions are not determined by moral understanding. This explains why moral rules and principles do not apply to lower animals any more than they apply to avalanches or tornadoes.[36] Humans are uniquely capable of recognizing the wrongness in inflicting pointless suffering, abuse, and loss of freedom onto others.[37] While Sinnott-Armstrong is right that our ability to empathize makes us unique, logically, how does the fact that humans have the ability to empathize lead to moral obligation? How does he justify the leap from *describing* reality to *prescribing* moral actions? Hume's question remains unanswered—how do we get an *ought* from an *is*?

So far, naturalistic objective morality has many problems to overcome before it can be thought of as a serious moral system.[38] If the universe is nothing more than the product of a purposeless, non-moral process, it seems an impossible stretch to conclude that there is any objective moral basis for life. However, there is another approach to naturalistic objective morality that we need to look at.

Self-Evident Moral Truths

One possible way to justify objective morality without God is to ground it in self-evident truth.[39] Some atheists, who adhere to objective morality, believe that there are at least some moral facts that are self-evident and serve as the foundation for all other moral truths. For example, when reflecting on the moral claim that, "It is wrong to torture the innocent purely for fun," it requires no further justification or explanation; its truth is obvious.[40] Therefore, when theists like Craig ask, "where do these moral facts come from?" or "on what foundation do they rest?" it is as misguided as when atheists ask, "where does God come from?" or "on what foundation does He rest?" The answer is the same in both cases: they come from nowhere, and there is no external foundation that grounds their existence.[41] They are the ground floor of the building upon which all further knowledge is built.

If you start with the premise that unjustified harm is morally wrong, you will have no trouble condemning harmful actions like rape. However, Craig argues this is circular logic, since it presupposes the very thing it is trying to prove.[42] He explains:

> *[Atheistic moral theories] inevitably just assume gratuitously that on a naturalistic view of man, some feature of human existence, say, pleasure, is an intrinsic good, and then proceed from there.*

> *But the advocates of such theories are typically at a loss to justify their starting point. If their approach to meta-ethical theory is to be . . . 'serious metaphysics' rather than just 'a shopping list' approach, whereby one simply helps oneself to the supervenient moral properties needed to do the job, then some sort of explanation is required.*[43]

Many dispute Craig's argument, claiming it assumes, without proof, that objective morality requires an external foundation—that it can't be self-evident or self-existing.[44] Also, as Humanist philosopher Erik Wielenberg points out, theists also make moral claims that have no external foundation; such as, "God is worthy of worship," and, "we are morally obligated to follow God's commands."[45] Wielenberg writes:

> *not only does Craig fail to provide any good reason to think that there cannot be any basic [self-evident] ethical facts, his own theistic approach to morality depends on such facts. Therefore, both parties to the debate are stuck with a "shopping list" approach; the only difference between them is the contents of their respective lists . . . Once we get past all the talk of unintelligible floating values, circularity, gratuitousness, and shopping lists, it turns out that Craig's position is simply that the brute [self-evident] ethical facts posited by theistic approaches like his own are less arbitrary than the brute ethical facts posited by non-theistic approaches to ethics. Let us, therefore, put to rest once and for all the demand that non-theists ground all of their ethical claims . . . On both types of views, the bottom floor of objective morality rests ultimately on nothing.*[46]

Wielenberg's claim that theists also have their own set of self-evident ethical facts is a bit off, since theistic morality really only boils down to one foundational ethical fact: God's omnipotent and unchanging nature is the standard of moral obligation and goodness. However, Wielenberg is right that this is an unprovable belief, and that both views ground objective morality in self-evident truth.[47] You could say that theists ground morality in the "I Am," while atheists ground morality in "it is." But does this mean that Craig's criticisms are unjustified? Not entirely. While Wielenberg's view is intellectually sensible, I believe it faces some challenging obstacles that theism does not.

Moral Obligation

While both atheists and theists are capable of recognizing the existence of basic, self-evident moral truths, when it comes to justifying moral obligation, an atheist has a problem that a theist does not. In a universe created by God, we are responsible to recognize and live in accordance with these truths; but under atheism, what makes moral truth obligatory? Some have proposed that society can obligate its citizens to obey moral truth, but what obligates a society to obligate moral obedience?[48]

Christian theism avoids this struggle because morality is grounded in God's unchanging nature, and out of His moral nature He issues commands that ground moral obligation. Unlike society, God cannot decide to eliminate moral obligation for His creatures, since this would violate His nature. Because our reality originates from God's reality, His imposing of moral obedience upon us isn't a *might makes right* situation, it's a *reality makes right* situation. Unlike society, God not only has the authority to make morality obligatory, but the power necessary to enforce justice when it is not followed.

Recognizing the problems of grounding moral obligation in ourselves, Wielenberg concludes that moral obligation, along with morality itself, is a self-evident truth. He writes:

> *any being that can reason, suffer, experience happiness, tell the difference between right and wrong, choose between right and wrong, and set goals for itself has certain rights, including the rights to life, liberty, and the pursuit of happiness, and certain obligations, including the duty to refrain from rape . . . Evolutionary processes have produced human beings that can reason, suffer, experience happiness, tell the difference between right and wrong, choose between right and wrong, and set goals for themselves. In this way, evolutionary processes have endowed us with certain unalienable rights and duties.*[49]

Under atheism, the number of self-evident truths are starting to add up in order to ground objective morality outside of God. While self-evident truth being the bedrock of morality is certainly not philosophically indefensible, as I have been arguing for a theistic form of this position myself, I believe that one of the biggest problems with this approach is reconciling it with a naturalistic worldview. Under naturalism, the universe is made up of matter, energy, time, and chance. So if morality exists, independent of human thought or opinion, then how does it exist? Where does it fit in a universe of matter, energy, time and chance?

In a debate on morality, Wielenberg argued that morality exists abstractly.[50] However, if moral truth exists objectively, "at the very bedrock of reality, created by no one, under no one's control, passing judgment on the actions and character of God and man alike," how could it exist abstractly in a naturalistic universe?[51] How could the moral value of justice just exist? We can easily comprehend this when we say that a person is just, but how could justice exist in the absence of any persons? Moral values appear to exist as the properties of conscious persons, not as mere abstractions.[52] Not only that, but abstract ideas only exist conceptually in the minds of persons. For instance, the term *Saturday* represents a period of time; the number *two* represents two entities. So, if morality is an abstraction, what physical object does it point to in a naturalistic universe? Christian theism doesn't have this problem, since morality connects to something beyond nature in the supernatural (God). The atheist has a serious problem once they have recognized morality's existence—where do they place it in a naturalistic universe? You can't turn over a rock and find the moral property of goodness, nor can you find it within a molecule.

While both atheism and theism can technically ground objective morality in self-evident truth, I believe that Christian theism has a distinct advantage in doing so, since it can ground it in something beyond the abstract. Also, while our moral intuitions play an important role in discovering moral truth, our intuitions must fit with our worldview. If they don't, we risk labeling any belief as self-evident truth to avoid all rationale and justification. All claims of self-evident truth must be consistent with our worldview or they cannot be considered self-evident truth. Under theism, there is a symmetry between its moral beliefs and its worldview, but under naturalism, there are enormous difficulties and tensions, which explains why most naturalists tend to share the reaction of theists, who believe that the two are at odds. While consensus doesn't determine truth, it should make us pause and wonder why so many naturalists reject objective morality, even though their intuition cries out that it exists.[53] In the next chapter, we will look at unguided evolution in an attempt to understand why so many atheists reject objective morality.

CHAPTER SEVEN
The Evolution of Morality

"Man is the only creature who refuses to be what he is."
— Albert Camus

The vast majority of naturalist philosophers believe that morality is created, not discovered, since objective morality does not mesh well with a Darwinian worldview. Most naturalists believe that morality is a social construct created by humanity for our evolutionary benefit. As societies evolve, they create ethical rules based upon their cultural beliefs that encourage cooperation, which benefits everyone. According to this thinking, human evolution is the driving force for determining our moral beliefs. Therefore, if we are going to understand this moral position, we must understand evolutionary theory.

Contrary to popular belief, evolutionary theory did not originate with Charles Darwin. However, he did popularize the essential mechanism by which it is believed to operate: natural selection.[1] Richard Dawkins describes natural selection as the blind, unconscious, automatic process that is responsible for the existence of every form of life.[2] Natural selection occurs via random genetic mutation. As genes mutate, they will occasionally produce a new trait that gives a creature a survival advantage.[3] Over time, as the creature reproduces and passes this advantageous gene onto its descendants, its offspring will come to overtake the species, since they have a reproductive advantage over those who do not carry the advantageous gene.[4] The result is the evolution of the species.

In Robert Wright's best-selling book on evolutionary psychology, *The Moral Animal,* he explains that a species' behavior is driven by the instinct to successfully pass along it's genes to the next generation.[5] Consequently, evolutionary psychology interprets our behavior through the lens of reproductive success.[6] From an evolutionary perspective, it is difficult to justify wasting valuable resources on caring for those who cannot contribute to our reproductive success. Biologist J. B. S. Haldane was once asked whether he would lay down his life for his brother. After a quick calculation, reflecting on the fact that we share half of our genes with our siblings and about one-eighth of them with our cousins, he responded that he would lay his life down for two siblings, four nephews or nieces, or eight first cousins.[7] Haldane's point is that from an evolutionary perspective, self-sacrifice for others makes little sense unless it contributes to the passing on of our genes.[8]

Nature Is Red in Tooth and Claw

In his article *On Nature*, philosopher John Stuart Mill explained how life is so harsh that most animals spend their existence either tormenting other animals or being devoured themselves.[9] Similarly, Sigmund Freud argued that men have a powerful instinct and natural desire for aggression, saying:

The result is that their neighbor is to them not only a possible helper or sexual object, but also a temptation to them to gratify their aggressiveness on him, to exploit his capacity for work without recompense, to use him sexually without his consent, to seize his possessions, to humiliate him, to cause him pain, to torture and kill him. Homo homini lupus. [Man is a wolf to his fellow man.][10]

Though naturalists frequently speak of the value of empathy and charity, to expect humanity to act selflessly makes little sense from an evolutionary perspective.[11] Robert Wright explains that the basic evolutionary mechanism by which our genes control us is the deep conviction that our happiness is more important that everyone else's. He writes:

We are designed not to worry about anyone else's happiness, except in the sort of cases where such worrying has, during evolution, benefited our genes. And it isn't just us. Self-absorption is the hallmark of life on this planet. Organisms are things that act as if their welfare were more important than the welfare of all other organisms (except, again, when other organisms can help spread their genes). [It may sound harmless] to say that your happiness is a legitimate goal only so long as it doesn't interfere with the

> *happiness of others, but this is an evolutionary heresy. Your happiness is designed to interfere with the happiness of others; the very reason it exists is to inspire selfish preoccupation with it.*[12]

But if natural selection favors selfishness, why do humans engage in empathetic behavior?

Why We Care for Others

Harvard University's Martin Nowak, professor of biology and mathematics, has come up with five rules that explain why humans cooperate with one another, despite our genes' selfish drive to reproduce. He explains that the reason we cooperate with family members is to pass on our shared genes (kin selection), while we cooperate with non-family members so that they will hopefully return the favor and help us when we are in need (direct reciprocity, or tit for tat). We help strangers, because if we don't help them (or even worse, we exploit them), we will develop a bad reputation in our society, which will hurt us in the long run (indirect reciprocity or paying it forward). The reason larger groups of people band together (like churches, synagogues, mosques, and temples) is that everyone can benefit by agreeing to help one another (network reciprocity). Lastly, the reason that individuals will sacrifice their own success (or even their very lives) in order to help members of their group who aren't carrying their genes, is so their group can succeed against rival groups, which will ensure their genes are passed on through relatives in their group (group selection).[13]

Nowak's five rules tell us the primary motive for humans caring for others is selfishness. Philosopher of science Michael Ruse explains that the reason we are moral is because humans who behave morally tend to do better than those who do not, and therefore are likely to leave more offspring.[14] In agreement, A. C. Grayling explains that the reason people help their neighbors is "because such problems might and probably will eventually become a problem for him too."[15] From an evolutionary perspective, the reason we should worry about the happiness of others is that we can all be happier together than we would be on our own.[16] This is why Greg Epstein believes that when it comes to the reasons for helping others, "we must begin with our individual needs, and then move to others' needs; not vice versa."[17] Consequently, because of its belief in unguided Darwinian evolution, Humanism's ultimate motive for empathetic behavior is selfishness.

The Free-Rider Problem

Societies function best when individuals band together and contribute toward the common good. For instance, cleaning up the environment, offering public schools, maintaining a military defense, and building highways and roads are all examples of individuals contributing small amounts to the benefit of the whole. By everyone giving a little, we can all enjoy much. But under naturalism, what motivation is there for a person to not cheat the system and reap the benefits? In a community of just ten members, attempts to cheat the system are unlikely to go unnoticed, so not being caught is the incentive to play fair. However, in a larger society, it is much easier to avoid detection. So, from an evolutionary perspective, if the primary reason we cooperate with others is due to selfish motives, why not exploit others for our own gain when it is certain we can get away with it?

In Plato's *Republic, Book II*, we find the story of Gyges, who finds a magical ring that gives him the power to become invisible at will. Gyges uses this power to seduce the queen of Lydia into helping him murder the king. He then marries the queen and becomes ruler over the entire kingdom, getting everything he ever wanted. After the story concludes, the character Glaucon questions Socrates on Gyges's actions, asking whether any person would have behaved differently from Gyges if given a ring of power. He argues that morality is nothing more than a social construct, and if it were removed, all moral character would vanish. Glaucon explains:

> *No man would keep his hands off what was not his own when he could safely take what he liked out of the market, or go into houses and lie with any one at his pleasure, or kill or release from prison whom he would, and in all respects be like a god among men . . . a man is just, not willingly or because he thinks that justice is any good to him individually, but of necessity, for wherever any one thinks that he can safely be unjust, there he is unjust. For all men believe in their hearts that injustice is far more profitable to the individual than justice . . . If you could imagine any one obtaining this power of becoming invisible, and never doing any wrong or touching what was another's, he would be thought by the lookers-*

on to be a most wretched idiot, although they would praise him to one another's faces, and keep up appearances with one another from a fear that they too might suffer injustice.[18]

David Hume disagreed with this egoistic approach, arguing that cheaters never win in the end because it is too difficult of a strategy to maintain. The person who is dishonest and unjust for personal gain only when they know they can get away with it will eventually make a mistake and get caught. Since we can never know for sure whether we will get away with cheating, it's best to be moral all the time, so honesty is the best policy. Not only that, Hume argues that exploiting others for the "acquisition of worthless toys" would end up making you unhappy. Therefore, whether you get caught or not, you'll suffer psychologically, so you shouldn't cheat.[19] His point is, cheaters never win, and even if they do, they will feel like scumbags and won't be happy anyway—so don't cheat.[20]

Even though we tell ourselves that cheaters never prosper, deep down, we know better. The fact is, it often does pay to cheat, and sometimes the payday can be significant. University of Miami philosopher Mark Rowlands agrees when he writes:

Cheaters never prosper, we tell ourselves. But the ape in us knows it's not true. Clumsy, untutored, cheats never prosper. They are discovered and suffer the consequences. They are ostracized, excluded, despised. But what we apes despise is the clumsiness of their effort, the ineptness, the gaucherie. The ape in us does not despise the cheating itself; on the contrary, it admires it.[21]

If our charitable behavior is primarily driven by selfish motives, then aren't those who behave better simply more enlightened egoists?[22] If moral laws are merely social guidelines to help selfish creatures work together for mutual benefit, then the motive for being compassionate towards others is for our good, not theirs. Sam Harris recognizes this, though he argues that it shouldn't concern us, since the feeling of love happens to be one of our greatest sources of happiness, so it is perfectly rational to seek our own happiness by caring for others.[23] Recognizing the paradox of being loving for selfish motives, Harris concludes, "We discover that we can be selfish together."[24]

Harris realizes that natural selection works by creating species that believe their happiness is more important than everyone else's. He argues that this doesn't have to result in the strong constantly oppressing the weak, since we have evolved to the point where we have realized we can get more by working together. However, most evolutionary psychologists reject this, since evolution has designed us to not worry about anyone else's happiness unless it benefits us personally.[25] It seems then that from a Darwinian perspective, selfishness is the quintessential virtue.

Truth Is in the Eye of the Beholder

In *Why People Believe Weird Things*, Michael Shermer argues that morality is created, so it cannot be held to any absolute standard or criteria, and to argue otherwise is scientifically indefensible. Since morals do not exist in nature, they cannot be discovered, and so they are up to us to decide. Morality, being nothing but a human creation, is subject to cultural beliefs and social constructs, which means that actions become moral or immoral only when someone judges them to be. After all, every culture has different moral views, so they can't all be objectively true. Shermer argues that each culture's moral beliefs are similar to musical preferences, saying, "Just as there is no absolute right type of human music there is no absolute right type of human action."[26] Therefore, just as we must decide what kind of music we like, we must also decide what kind of morality we like.

If morality is up to society to decide, then what prevents a society from embracing oppression, rape, and violence as perfectly natural moral behavior given our evolutionary heritage? While reading Robert Wright's book *The Moral Animal*, it struck me how this view of reality is deeply sexist and oppressive towards the weak and powerless—but given its beliefs about the world, why shouldn't it be? Wright paints a picture in which nearly everything about human nature is built for the purpose of survival through sexual reproduction. However, if reality is really like this, then how can we escape the conclusion that morality is entirely relative to the individual? Though people have their personal feelings about right and wrong, that's all they are. This leaves us without a foundation to challenge moral evil, since evil is subjective to the individual. Therefore, the logical result of subjective morality is no real morality at all (moral relativism). Still, Shermer disagrees, saying:

> *I'm not an ethical relativist—that is a dangerous road to go down. I think that there really are moral principles that are nearly absolute—what I call provisional moral truths, where something is provisionally right or provisionally wrong. By this I mean that for most people in most places most of the time behavior X is right or wrong. I think this is as good as it can get without an outside source like God.*[27]

The dangers of moral relativism are clear, which is why Shermer advocates for "nearly absolute" moral principles. However, how can he say it is wrong to prey on the weak given his naturalistic Darwinian worldview? Calling them "nearly absolute" moral principles is merely word play, since they are still subjective to the individual. Though he tries to avoid it, he cannot escape the inevitable conclusion that moral truth is relative. Even so, he denounces it anyway, saying:

> *Does this mean that all human actions are morally equal? Of course not, any more than all human music is equal. We create hierarchies of what we like or dislike, desire or reject, and make judgments based on those standards. But the standards are themselves human creations and cannot be discovered in nature.*[28]

If morality is a human construct based upon what we "like or dislike, desire or reject," then moral belief is the same sort of thing as color preference—I value blue, you value red, and at the end of the day the majority, or those with the most power, will "create hierarchies" of what they "like or dislike," and force them upon everyone else.

This is the *might makes right* principle, which is often characterized as two wolves and a sheep deciding what's for dinner. While Shermer wishes to denounce moral evil, his worldview prevents him from doing so in any way that holds up. This is why Robert Wright believes that Darwinism shows us that morality simply comes down to choice. He writes:

> *Whether, for example, we want to live in an egalitarian society is a choice for us to make; natural selection's indifference to the suffering of the weak is not something we need emulate. Nor should we care whether murder, robbery, and rape are in some sense "natural." It is for us to decide how abhorrent we find such things and how hard we want to fight them. But once we've made such choices, once we have moral ideals, Darwinism can help us figure out which social institutions best serve them.*[29]

For the most part, atheist philosophers recognize the dangerously close proximity that moral relativism has to their naturalistic worldview. Though many resist this connection, under a naturalistic, subjective worldview there is simply no way to avoid the conclusion that human rights only exist if we choose to create and enforce them. But as we saw in chapter four, if human rights are created, then there is nothing to appeal to when they are legislated out of existence.

The Moral Zeitgeist

In his book, *The God Delusion*, Richard Dawkins argues that despite our evolutionary heritage, morality evolves and progresses over time, in what he calls "the moral zeitgeist." In agreement, Peter Singer explains that throughout history there has always been a "right side" on moral issues. For example, there was a "right side" on the issue of slavery. There was a "right side" on the workers' battles for unionization, limiting working hours, and better working conditions. There was a "right side" on women's right to vote, be admitted to universities, and own property. And there was a "right side" in the war against the Nazis. Similarly, there is also a "right side" on the great moral struggles of our time, and so we must strive to be on the "right side" of history.[30]

The moral zeitgeist works by moral shifts occurring over time in an upward direction, which results in moral improvement. While there will always be those who lag behind the moral curve, moral progress inevitably marches on.[31] Dawkins explains:

> *Some of us lag behind the advancing wave of the changing moral Zeitgeist and some of us are slightly ahead. But most of us in the twenty-first century are bunched together and way ahead of our counterparts in the Middle Ages, or in the time of Abraham, or even as recently as the 1920s. The whole wave keeps moving, and even the vanguard of an earlier century . . . would find itself way behind the laggers of a later century.*[32]

But if morality improves over time, then how can the moral zeitgeist account for the horrific moral reversals such as Nazi Germany? Dawkins believes this isn't a problem since moral advancement does not come at a consistently progressive pace, but overall moves in a progressive direction.[33] He explains that as wicked as Hitler was, his ideas and intentions were not self-evidently more evil than men of prior times, such as Caligula or some of the Ottoman sultans. The major difference is that Hitler and Stalin had twentieth-century weapons at their disposal, while wicked men of the past did not. Setbacks and all, morality continues in a steadily-upward trajectory that results in moral improvement that is independent of religious belief.[34]

Though it might be true that Hitler and Stalin were not anymore evil than men of prior times, this only shows that morality moves in a horizontal direction, not an upward one. If Dawkins's moral theory is right, and morality truly progresses in an upward direction, then why is evolution still producing the same kind of moral monsters that it has in the past? If we are evolving morally over time, then shouldn't humanity be leaving such moral evils behind? While Dawkins might argue that evolution produces fewer moral monsters over time, how does he determine what is and is not moral improvement?

The belief that morality evolves progressively over time has at least two major problems. The first is what C. S. Lewis called, "The worship of the future." In *God in the Dock: Essays on Theology and Ethics,* Lewis explained that if things can improve, then there must be some standard of good to measure it by. But if morality is subjective, then how can we legitimately say that it is becoming better? Lewis explained:

> *There is no sense in talking about 'becoming better' if better means simply 'what we are becoming' — it is like congratulating yourself on reaching your destination and defining destination as 'the place*

you have reached' . . . *[For this reason,] the worship of the future, is a fuddled religion.*[35]

Lewis's point is that when we refer to moral progress, we mean changing for the better, not simply changing. If no set of moral beliefs were truer or better than any others, then there would be no sense in preferring civilized morality to savage morality, or Christian morality to Nazi morality.[36] So, when Dawkins says that morality progresses over time, whether he is aware of it or not, he is measuring human action by some sort of transcendent moral standard. But what gives him the right to do this given his naturalistic worldview, and especially his subjective view of morality? Ultimately, this approach to morality leaves us blind from knowing whether or not we are on the right side of history.

In 1908, G. K. Chesterton argued against the moral zeitgeist in his classic Christian apologetic work, *Orthodoxy*, where he questioned the basis by which a naturalist could fight against apparent injustice. He wrote:

But how can we rush [to fight injustice] if we are, perhaps, in advance of our time? How can we rush to catch a train which may not arrive for a few centuries? How can I denounce a man for skinning cats, if he is only now what I may possibly become in drinking a glass of milk? . . . What on earth is the current morality, except in its literal sense— the morality that is always running away?[37]

Chesterton's point is that the moral zeitgeist leaves us incapable of knowing whether our evolutionary watch is running fast or slow, since there is no objective standard to measure it by. Without a moral standard, we are left morally blind and without a measuring tool for determining which moral position is the right one. Therefore, according to this theory, moral knowledge is impossible.

The second problem with the moral zeitgeist is that it is nearly universally agreed upon that evolution is non-progressive in nature, which simply means that evolution has no end goal in mind.[38] While the general public may find the moral zeitgeist to be a reasonable moral theory, this is largely due to the evolutionary metaphors they are familiar with that make evolution easier to understand (Mother Nature, evolutionary intentions, progress to a higher stage of civilization, etc.).[39] But the problem with metaphors is they are always inaccurate depictions of the real thing. The truth is, unguided evolution is a purposeless and sightless process whose only function is a creature's brute survival. Though we talk about natural selection "designing" creatures with certain traits, this is only a metaphor, as evolution is not a conscious process; it simply preserves the traits that contribute towards a creature's survival. When we properly understand unguided Darwinian natural selection, we can see why biologist George Williams concluded that morality is "an accidental capability produced, in its boundless stupidity, by a biological process that is normally opposed to the expression of such a capability."[40]

In 1871, Charles Darwin published *The Descent of Man*, and wrote of how human morality might have evolved very differently, saying:

> *If, for instance, to take an extreme case, men were reared under precisely the same conditions as hive-bees, there can hardly be a doubt that our unmarried females would, like the worker-bees, think it a sacred duty to kill their brothers, and mothers would strive to kill their fertile daughters; and no one would think of interfering.*[41]

This brutal sort of evolutionary thinking led the people of Darwin's day to be worried about how the theory would affect the moral order. The *Edinburgh Review* wrote that if Darwin's theory was right, "a revolution in thought is imminent, which will shake society to its very foundations by destroying the sanctity of the conscience and the religious sense."[42] The main reason Darwin's theory was largely rejected wasn't for its biological observations, but its dangerous philosophical ramifications. Robert Wright acknowledges that this concern isn't entirely off base, since religious sense has indeed waned since Darwin's day, especially among the intelligentsia. Wright explains:

> *Among ethical philosophers, there is nothing approaching agreement on where we might turn for basic moral values—except, perhaps, nowhere. It is only a slight exaggeration to say that the prevailing moral philosophy within many philosophy departments is nihilism . . . Sympathy, empathy, compassion, conscience, guilt, remorse, even the very sense of justice, the sense*

> *that doers of good deserve reward and doers of bad deserve punishment—all these can now be viewed as vestiges of organic history on a particular planet. What's more, we can't take solace, as Darwin did, in the mistaken belief that these things evolved for the greater good—the "good of the group." Our ethereal intuitions about what's right and what's wrong are weapons designed for daily, hand-to-hand combat among individuals. It isn't only moral feelings that now fall under suspicion, but all of moral discourse.*[43]

Though Wright goes on to advocate a form of utilitarianism, he stops to ponder the ramifications of evolution, saying, "If plain old-fashioned Darwinism has indeed sapped the moral strength of Western civilization, what will happen when the new version [evolutionary psychology] fully sinks in?"[44]

The Great Illusionist

Philosopher Michael Ruse believes that evolution reveals that morality is a matter of psychology, without any actual foundation. Morality is an illusion put in place by our genes to get us to cooperate with others.[45] Though most people believe murder is objectively wrong, it is merely a psychological belief, as there is no absolute, objective basis for morality or human rights. In philosophy this view is called *The Noble Lie*.

While discussing philosopher Jeremy Bentham's dismissal of inalienable human rights as being "nonsense upon stilts," atheist philosopher Daniel Dennett comments on how Bentham may have been right, saying:

> *Perhaps talk of rights is nonsense upon stilts, but good nonsense ... It might seem then that "rule worship" of a certain kind is a good thing, at least for agents designed like us. It is good not because there is a certain rule, or set of rules, which is provably the best, or which always yields the right answer, but because having rules works—somewhat—and not having rules doesn't work at all.*[46]

Dennett is saying that even though morality doesn't exist, at least not in the traditional way most of us think it does, humanity has evolved to believe it does exist, and this false belief is for our benefit. But notice that Dennett is still appealing to an objective standard. Dennett suggests that even if Bentham is right that inalienable human rights are "nonsense on stilts," they are still "*good* nonsense," and "rule worship" is "a certain kind of *good* thing."[47] Dennett is essentially saying that even though moral goodness does not exist, it's morally good that we think it does. If anything amounts to "nonsense on stilts," surely it would be this sort of circular logic.

The truth is, naturalistic subjective moralists cannot live in harmony with their worldview. This is why Michael Ruse admits that even though his worldview informs him that morality does not exist, once he leaves his philosophy chair and goes back out into the real world, his psychology takes over and he doesn't bother with his moral skepticism. Even though objective morality doesn't exist, evolution has led us to believe it does, so we are none-the-worse off behaving as if it really does exist. He writes:

> *If we knew that morality was subjective and that we could ignore it, then very quickly morality would break down and people would start cheating and before long there would be general mayhem. But because we think that morality is objective, we all obey it more or less. In other words, I'm saying it is a Darwinian adaptation that we should be deceived about the justificatory status of morality. Morality may have no foundation, but it is in our biological interests that we should think that it has. Hence we do think that it has.*[48]

But if the noble lie is true and morality is purely psychological, what prevents those of us who discover this from abusing those who haven't? Ruse argues that even though we could do this, we would do so at our psychological expense, and so we shouldn't—which fits with Hume's idea that we shouldn't cheat because it will make us unhappy.[49]

As we have seen, evolutionary psychology tells us that we are naturally inclined towards the false belief of objective moral truth because of natural selection. Humans who act morally tend to do better than those who do not, which produces a survival advantage.[50] In agreement, naturalist philosopher Patricia Churchland explains that natural selection is not interested in truth, but advantageous behavior: feeding, fleeing, fighting and reproducing.[51] Once again, though our intuitions tell us one thing, modern evolutionary theory reveals them to be deceptions put in place for our survival, and so we cannot trust them.

Similarly, many atheists consider our intuition of God's existence to be just another deception caused by the evolution of our minds.[52] Because humans don't like randomness, we look for ways to explain the mysteries we find around us and come up with supernatural causes, since any explanation is better than no explanation.[53] Describing how we evolved to believe in God, Michael Shermer writes:

> *God is a pattern, an explanation for our universe, our world, and ourselves. God is the key actor in the story, "the greatest story ever told" about where we came from, why we are here, and where we are going. God is a myth, one of the most sublime and sacred myths ever constructed by the mythmaking animal. God is the ultimate enforcer of the rules, the final arbiter of moral dilemmas, and the pinnacle object of commitment . . . People believe in God because we are pattern-seeking, storytelling, mythmaking, religious, moral animals.*[54]

But even if naturalists are right that religion is an evolutionary false positive, this still doesn't tell us whether God exists or not.[55] Instead, they proceed on the assumption that no God exists, and explain the belief away as a byproduct of evolution. This is the logical fallacy known as *Bulverism*, which explains how someone came to their wrong belief without having first shown it to be wrong.[56] Nevertheless, naturalists maintain that our intuition that God exists is just another one of the illusions caused by natural selection.

The Illusion of Free Will

Right and wrong, lawmaking, and justice all depend upon the existence of free will. But if the universe is determined and we don't have free will, it makes very little sense to hold people accountable for their actions. Despite this problem, most naturalistic scientists have concluded that free will cannot be reconciled with the current understanding of the natural world.[57] Paraphrasing classical scholar and poet A. E. Housman, Richard Dawkins writes, "DNA neither cares nor knows. DNA just is. And we dance to its music."[58] In agreement, Sam Harris believes that all human behavior can be traced to biological events of which we had no conscious knowledge. He writes:

> *Did I consciously choose coffee over tea? No. The choice was made for me by events in my brain that I, as the conscious witness of my thoughts and actions, could not inspect or influence ... How can we be 'free' as conscious agents if everything that we consciously intend is caused by events in our brain that we do not intend and of which we are entirely unaware? We can't.*[59]

Robert Wright claims that free will is "a fairly useful fiction," though it is "beginning to outlive its usefulness."[60] While we still need to hold people responsible for their actions, he likens this to holding robots responsible for their malfunctions.[61] In agreement, Harris argues that when we hold people responsible for their actions, we need to recognize how much luck is involved, since if we had been born with that person's genetic makeup and life experiences, we would have acted the same way.[62] The point is, everything is determined, and the belief that we have free will is scientifically indefensible.

Atheist philosopher Daniel Dennett has written a strong critique of Harris's work on free will. He explains that if no one is responsible, then the prisons should be emptied, since we can't hold anyone accountable for anything.[63] As a naturalist himself, Dennett realizes that neuroscience is rapidly leading to the conclusion that free will is nothing but another evolutionary illusion. As a potential solution, he looks to quantum mechanics in hope that it might offer the foundation necessary to ground our intuition of free will. Quantum mechanics theorizes that particles can randomly pop into existence at the subatomic level, and so our thoughts could be the result of these random occurrences.[64] However, though Massimo Pigliucci agrees with Dennett that determinism undermines morality, he disagrees that quantum mechanics can be of any help in saving us from determinism, since quantum mechanics could only lead to *random will*, not free will. No one sees free will as random decision making, as if our brains were a roulette table that decided our course of action by the random spin of the wheel.[65]

Atheist philosopher J. L. Mackie pointed out that one of the main reasons most people are committed to believing in free will is that we experience the feeling (or intuition) of freedom. Whenever we choose to do one thing instead of another, we are immediately aware that we could have chosen otherwise.[66] Nevertheless, naturalism cannot support this intuition and so it joins the ever-growing pile of evolutionary illusions.[67]

So far, the cost of philosophical naturalism is heavy, which is why historically there is a close connection between atheism and nihilism. Naturalism presents us with a universe of blind fate, meaninglessness, and chance, which challenges our core intuitions. If it is true, as Richard Dawkins suggests, that the universe has "no design, no purpose, no evil, no good, nothing but blind, pitiless indifference," then what hope is there for the belief that life has any meaning?[68] This is why most atheists conclude that morality cannot exist in any sort of objective way, given the truths of modern evolutionary theory. Ethicist Kai Nielsen puts it sharply:

> *We have not been able to show that reason requires the moral point of view, or that all really rational persons should not be individual egoists or classical amoralists. Reason doesn't decide here. The picture I have painted for you is not a pleasant one. Reflection on it depresses me . . . Pure practical reason, even with a good knowledge of the facts, will not take you to morality.*[69]

CHAPTER EIGHT
The Meaning of Life

"That it will never come again is what makes life so sweet."
— Emily Dickinson

"Regarding life, the wisest men of all ages have judged alike: it is worthless."
— Friedrich Nietzsche

"I am the bread of life. Whoever comes to me will never go hungry, and whoever believes in me will never be thirsty (John 6:35).
— Jesus

Can life have any meaning in a naturalistic universe? Physicist Steven Weinberg doesn't think so. He writes, "The more comprehensible the universe becomes, the more it also seems pointless."[1] But if the universe is pointless, what does that say for the meaning of our lives? French philosopher Albert Camus believed that there was really only one serious philosophical question, "Should, or should I not commit suicide?" The great Russian novelist Leo Tolstoy was haunted by this question, which nearly led to his suicide. Recounting his experience, he wrote:

> *My question—that which at the age of fifty brought me to the verge of suicide—was the simplest of questions, lying in the soul of every man from the foolish child to the wisest elder: it was a question without an answer to which one cannot live, as I had found by experience. It was: . . . "Is there any meaning in my life that the inevitable death awaiting me does not destroy?"*[2]

None of us know how long our lives will be, but we know it has a bad ending, and if the end is truly the end, this harsh truth overshadows whatever joy or meaning we might find. Still, many believe that even though life has no higher meaning, we're able to construct meaning for ourselves. For example, Stephen Jay Gould wrote:

> *We are here because one odd group of fishes had a peculiar fin anatomy that could transform into legs for terrestrial creatures; because comets struck the earth and wiped out dinosaurs, thereby giving mammals a chance not otherwise available . . . We may yearn for a "higher" answer—but none exists. This explanation, though superficially troubling, if not terrifying, is ultimately liberating and exhilarating. We cannot read the meaning of life passively in the facts of nature. We must construct these answers for ourselves.*[3]

Gould's point is that even though life has no meaning, we are free to give it whatever meaning we please. But how can we derive meaning from the meaningless? If nature has no inherent meaning, yet we say our choices have meaning, then we are really saying that one part of nature actually does have inherent meaning: our choices.[4] But if our universe has no meaning, then neither do our choices, since we are just another part of the universe. The truth is, in a naturalistic universe, life can have no meaning that overcomes the deafening finality of the grave.

Still, Humanism holds that life is worth living and that we can find real meaning in our lives without God. Outside of religion, Westerners tend to believe that the meaning of life is to find happiness, whether through career, love, family, money, possessions, or social standing. Christianity rejects this hedonistic thinking, instead believing that the meaning of life can only be found in God. When we reject the Creator, we leave a God-shaped hole in our hearts that we desperately try to fill with created things.[5] Recognizing that we are all gap fillers by nature, Richard Dawkins believes that gap filling isn't a response to a longing for God, but is a natural attempt to give our lives meaning and purpose. Explaining what gives him meaning, Dawkins writes, "My way includes a good dose of science, the honest and systematic endeavour to find out the truth about the real world."[6] While Dawkins recognizes that we are all gap fillers by nature, his solution of trying to fill the gap with *things* instead of God, has at least two major problems.

The first problem is that gap fillers never seem to satisfy—we always want more, and our thirst is never satiated. Stuart Walker, sailboat racer and author, speaks of the hollowness of using winning as a gap filler, saying:

Winning doesn't satisfy us—we need to do it again, and again. The taste of success seems merely to whet the appetite for more. When we lose, the compulsion to seek future success is overpowering; the need to get out on the course the following weekend is irresistible. We cannot quit when we are ahead, after we've won, and we certainly cannot quit when we're behind, after we've lost. We are addicted.[7]

Walker realizes that winning can't quench his never-ending thirst for meaning and significance, but he can't stop. He knows there is a gap that must be filled, and so he continues trying to fill it the only way he knows how, with winning, even if the satisfaction is short lived.

Religions such as Buddhism have suggested we give up on the gap-filling endeavor entirely by living a detached life. However, not only is this impossible, but even if we could eliminate all desire, why would we want to? This would result in a passionless existence where our loved ones meant nothing to us at all. The problem isn't that we care about things, it's that we try to make these good things into ultimate things in order to give our lives meaning.[8]

The second problem with gap filling is that even if we could find something to fill the gap, we will eventually lose it—whether it be love, career, money, or health.[9] Deep down, we are all painfully aware that whatever gap fillers we look to for meaning will die the same death that awaits us. Beauty fades, loved ones die, health never lasts, and success is short lived. In this life, suffering is guaranteed and whatever happiness we have is temporary. If we center our life's meaning on things to give us happiness, we will face disappointment and loss until it eventually crushes us.

If life's meaning is about finding personal happiness, then can't we justify any despicable act so long as it makes us happy?[10] Many Humanists argue against this, believing that meaning is better found in devoting our lives to the betterment of our world, through the reduction of unnecessary human suffering. Attempting to ground this way of thinking, Philosopher J. L. Mackie argued that once we claim our happiness or pleasure is a good thing, we should be able to recognize that our happiness is no more desirable or good than anyone else's, so we should work towards everyone's happiness.[11] However, this can only be grounded in belief since, as we've seen, reason cannot take us to morality. Also, arguing for charitable behavior assumes individual choice, which, as we saw in the last chapter, is deeply problematic for naturalistic morality given our apparent lack of free will. Not only that, but if life's meaning is best found in the reduction of human suffering, then wouldn't the painless annihilation of all life in the universe be a drastically effective way of accomplishing this? Certainly, Humanists would not endorse this as a worthy goal, but why not? Clearly, some other moral principle is necessary to ground life's meaning.[12]

Inherent Value

If the reduction of human suffering cannot lead to a meaningful life, what about filling our lives with things that have intrinsic value? It seems plausible that our lives can have meaning without God so long as there are things that exist in our world that have value in and of themselves. But how can anything have intrinsic value in a naturalistic universe? How can we get meaning from the meaningless? Erik Wielenberg believes intrinsic things do exist outside of God, such as falling in love, engaging in intellectually stimulating activity, being creative, teaching, and experiencing different kinds of pleasure.[13] But how does this fit with naturalism? As we saw in the last chapter, so many things that naturalists believe to be intrinsically valuable are nothing but the result of natural selection instilling false beliefs in us to contribute toward our survival.

If humanity is, as Bertrand Russell famously stated, nothing but "the product of causes which had no prevision of the end they were achieving, that his origin, his growth, his hopes and fears, his loves and his beliefs, are but the outcome of accidental collocations of atoms," then how can there be any intrinsic meaning or purpose for our lives?[14] Under naturalism, we are the children of accidental natural forces that did not have us in mind. What is love but a biochemical evolutionary illusion to help us raise our children and protect the survival of our genes? What is helping a friend but a tit-for-tat effort to ensure a future return? What is beauty but a neurological hardwired response to particular data? We find lush environments beautiful because there is food there, and since this helped our ancestors survive, it was passed down.[15] Intellectual activity goes too, if, as neuroscience suggests, we don't have free will, since our thoughts are nothing more than the result of the unconscious chain of events that occurred beforehand. In a naturalistic world, what good activity is not stripped of all intrinsic meaning by unguided Darwinian natural selection? Still, grounding intrinsic goodness is not even naturalism's greatest difficulty. The greater problem is that even *if* things actually do exist that have intrinsic value, which of them can survive death's cold embrace?

The Death of Everything

For some time now, scientists have known that all life will eventually cease to exist as the universe expands into a vast, frozen wasteland. In the end, all stars will burn out and the corpses of planets, stars, and galaxies will separate and expand into an empty nothingness. The entire universe is steadily marching toward its grave.[16] But if the goal of life is the grave, how can anything we do have meaning? Humanists, such as Walter Sinnott-Armstrong, argue that even though the people we help will eventually die, much good can still be accomplished since our good acts permanently and forever reduce the amount of suffering in the universe.[17] Greg Epstein agrees when he writes:

so long as we continue to grow in some way, we are living, not dying. None of us will ever fully recover or be healed from the human condition. No amount of repairing the world will ever actually fix it. But we can grow tremendously in our abilities to understand and to feel and give love and affection and empathy. We can build up those around us, and we can build a better world.[18]

Sinnott-Armstrong and Epstein are certainly right that we have the ability to reduce the amount of suffering in our world, however, is this really enough to give meaning to our lives?

Imagine you are spending time with some close friends, maybe watching a sports match or playing board games. Suddenly, you receive news that there is a nuclear missile headed for your city that will arrive within the half hour. Realizing that your death is assured and running is futile, how do you spend the last thirty minutes of your existence? Your Humanist friend suggests that you quickly gather up whatever food you can find and go feed the homeless in your neighborhood. Another friend chimes in, "What's the point? We will all be dead in less than thirty minutes and the bomb will wipe out whatever accomplishments we've made!" Your Humanist friend, unmoved by this argument, begins explaining how whatever good that is accomplished in the next thirty minutes will have forever reduced the amount of suffering in the world, and so this is the only way to give true meaning to these last moments of your lives. So, do you begin bagging up food to go and hand out?

I hope the point of the story is obvious: the finality of death swallows up everything. Maybe you still disagree, but why? If you can see the absurdity within the story, but still think that life can have meaning without God, how do you justify it? Does replacing thirty minutes with hours, days, or decades change things? I don't see how.

In Cormac McCarthy's *The Sunset Limited*, an atheist professor named Black (played by Tommy Lee Jones) attempts to kill himself by stepping in front of a subway train, but is stopped by a Christian ex-con named White (played by Samuel Jackson). Afterwards, White takes Black back to his run-down, overcrowded apartment, and tries to convince him that suicide is not the answer to his problems. Black's nihilistic response is breathtakingly disheartening as he explains what led to his suicide attempt:

> *the world is basically a forced labor camp from which the workers, perfectly innocent, are led forth by lottery, a few each day, to be executed. I don't think that's just the way I see it. I think that's the way it is. Are there alternative views? Yes. Will any of them stand close scrutiny? No . . . The shadow of the axe hangs over every joy. Every road ends in death, every friendship, every love. Torment, loss, betrayal, pain, suffering, age, indignity, hideous lingering illness . . . and all of it with a single conclusion for you and everyone and everything you have ever chosen to care for.*[19]

Black believes that suffering and human destiny are one and the same, and if people could see their lives for what they truly are, without their dreams and illusions to blind them from cold, harsh reality, they would be unable to offer any sound reason why they should not elect to die as soon as possible.[20] Like the great atheist philosophers of old, such as Voltaire, Sartre, and Nietzsche, Black is well aware of what his atheistic worldview entails; namely, the ridiculousness of life and the pointlessness of everything.

In a universe that has, as Richard Dawkins describes, "no design, no purpose, no evil, no good, nothing but pitiless indifference," Black's cynicism makes all too much sense.[21] Before his conversion, Christian apologist Ravi Zacharias came to understand the full depths of such cynicism, which resulted in his own suicide attempt. Explaining what brought him to such lows, he writes:

> *But eventually, belief in a world birthed by accident, a life that has no purpose, morality without a point of reference except for those absolutes that have been smuggled in—well hidden behind the mask of relativism—and death that ends in oblivion made me prefer the possibility of this oblivion to the sheer weight of the emptiness of a God-less world. Contrary to what atheists imply, the dead weight of their beliefs leads to a heartless, pointless, and hollow existence.*[22]

The Myth of Sisyphus

In Greek mythology, the fate of Sisyphus demonstrates the futility of human existence. In the story, Sisyphus is punished by the gods and condemned to roll a boulder up a hill for all eternity. Right before the bolder reaches the top, it rolls back down, and he is forced to begin the futile task all over again. The philosophical dilemma is whether his life can have intrinsic meaning despite the meaninglessness of his eternal activity. Like Sisyphus, we too are condemned to struggle against an adversary that inevitably conquers us all—death. The question remains, can life have meaning in the face of futility?

Philosophers have come up with two possible ways to give Sisyphus's life meaning. The first option imagines the gods being merciful and instilling a passionate desire within Sisyphus to roll the stone up the hill. Though his situation is the same, Sisyphus is infatuated with rolling the stone and so he cannot get enough of it. The second option sees his situation slightly altered. Instead of rolling the same stone, he now rolls many different stones to the top of the hill and uses them to construct a great temple that adds beauty to the world. However, both of these options have problems.

The first option makes the mistake of assuming that happiness can provide meaning to our lives. It is the idea that a meaningful life is dependent on doing what we enjoy. Atheist philosopher Erik Wielenberg brilliantly points out the absurdity of this idea. He invites us to imagine a Sisyphus who is not condemned to rolling a stone up a hill, but is instead condemned to eating feces for all of eternity. Obviously, this is a horrible existence, but the gods are merciful and so they have instilled within him a true passion for eating excrement. And so, Sisyphus gobbles it down all day long; he simply cannot get enough. According to the "happiness can give our lives meaning" view, the grinning excrement eater's life has just as much meaning as a Sisyphus who is condemned to be a concert pianist and create beautiful music for the gods for all of eternity. Both lives are equally meaningful so long as Sisyphus enjoys what he is doing. Wielenberg rightly criticizes this, saying:

A grinning excrement-eater who passes up a pianist's life for the sake of eating excrement is a fool, and if the gods get him to make such a choice by instilling in him a passion for eating excrement, then their's [sic] is a cruel joke rather than an act of mercy. No matter how great his passion, no matter how big his grin as he spoons it down, he should be an object of pity rather than of envy. If we want to find an adequate way of dealing with internal meaning we must look elsewhere.[23]

What about the second option? Can Sisyphus's life have meaning if he rolls many stones to build a great temple? This option assumes that meaning is based on objective values, while the first option assumes meaning is based on subjective values (what matters to us personally). But even if Sisyphus creates a beautiful temple, in a naturalistic universe, the stones still end up rolling back down, since the temple, like everything else, will eventually wither, decay, and turn to dust. Whatever we make will eventually be undone by that great destroyer named death, and as the atheists of old concluded, death is the great eradicator of all our achievements and efforts. Therefore, both options have insurmountable difficulties.

Some philosophers have concluded that perhaps it doesn't matter that life is meaningless. For example, Albert Camus believed that life is absurd and meaningless, and any philosophy that says otherwise is deluded. Without God to give our lives meaning, we face a lifelong struggle that we can only lose. In light of this, the only way to exist in our meaningless and absurd reality is to accept the ridiculousness of our situation.

Camus understood that death is the great destroyer of all our accomplishments and efforts; nevertheless, he concluded that once we've accepted the absurdity of our situation, we could rebel against death by throwing ourselves into life and choosing activities that we feel give our lives meaning.[24]

While Camus's approach may appear similar to the claim that happiness determines meaning, its difference is that it recognizes that life is ultimately meaningless. "Life has no meaning," it says, "but so what? Rebel against death and live your life as if it is meaningful!" This idea, called the Noble Lie (or error theory), holds that if we lie to ourselves and say that there are things worth living for, we'll be better off, since we'll be able to live as if life has meaning.[25] Philosopher Thomas Nagel explains this idea, saying:

> *Even if life as a whole is meaningless, perhaps that's nothing to worry about. Perhaps we can recognize it and just go on as before. The trick is to keep your eyes on what's in front of you, and allow justifications to come to an end inside your life, and inside the lives of others to whom you are connected. If you ever ask yourself that question, "But what's the point of being alive at all?"—leading the particular life of a student or bartender or whatever you happen to be—you'll answer "There's no point. It wouldn't matter if I didn't exist at all, or if I didn't care about anything. But I do. That's all there is to it.*[26]

Nagel explains how some people find this approach completely satisfying, while others find it deeply depressing. He believes that we all naturally try to give our lives intrinsic meaning even though no such thing exists. This is partially because we take ourselves too seriously, since we desperately want to feel that what we are doing is not just important to ourselves, but important, period. Realizing that this harsh reality may "take the wind out of our sails," Nagel goes on to conclude:

> *If life is not real, life is not earnest, and the grave is its goal, perhaps it's ridiculous to take ourselves so seriously. On the other hand, if we can't help taking ourselves so seriously, perhaps we just have to put up with being ridiculous. Life may not be only meaningless but absurd.*[27]

One of the greatest obstacles to living our lives with meaning is the fear of death. But in a naturalistic universe, how can we avoid this fear? Some atheists believe that the act of striving to overcome our fear of death is a part of living a life of dignity. Others recommend accepting that death can strike anyone at any time, and by keeping this in mind, death can never surprise us.[28] For instance, Erik Wielenberg finds comfort in understanding that we are all in this life together, and death takes us all in the end. He writes:

> *The life of man is a long march through the night, surrounded by invisible foes, tortured by weariness and pain, toward a goal that few can hope to reach, and where none may tarry long. One by one, as they march, our comrades vanish from our sight, seized by the silent orders of omnipotent death. Very brief is the time in which we can help them, in which their happiness or misery is decided . . . [Therefore] let us remember that they are fellow*

sufferers in the same darkness, actors in the same tragedy with ourselves.[29]

In a naturalistic world, our lives almost certainly have no meaning. Still, we are told to press on and live as if life has meaning anyway, since it will make us happier in the end. Death is the great destroyer and there is no avoiding it. But we should try to live a life of dignity and learn to live valiantly underneath death's shadow. While this approach certainly has a sense of stoic bravery, we should seriously question whether it is even possible to live this way.

An Unlivable Worldview

In the past few chapters, I have attempted to show that the values of Humanism are in irreconcilable conflict with unguided Darwinian evolution. In a naturalistic world, if we try to ground Humanism's values into an objective moral framework (discovered morality), we find that it is impossible unless we accept it as a self-evident truth. While this is logically tenable, reconciling this with an evolutionary account of human nature is an enormous difficulty, which is why most atheists do not attempt it. On the other hand, if we try to ground Humanism's values in a subjective moral framework (created morality), then we find that it has dangerously close ties to moral relativism. If morality is based upon human values, then it is difficult to avoid the conclusion that human rights only exist if the majority, or those with the most power, say that they do. This means that there is nothing to appeal to when they are legislated out of existence.[30] Nevertheless, many atheists outrightly reject these conclusions and are strong supporters of justice and human rights, even though they are deeply irreconcilable with their naturalistic worldview.

We must ask ourselves: if moral behavior is at such great odds with natural selection, why can't we live without it? Robert Wright recognizes the remarkableness of this when he writes, "Indeed, if you ponder the utter ruthlessness of evolutionary logic long enough, you may start to find our morality, such as it is, nearly miraculous."[31] C. S. Lewis had a different take on the matter. He believed that the reason atheists cling to morality, despite naturalism's ruthless logic, is that deep down they know better. Lewis noticed that the moment after naturalists finished explaining that good and evil and meaning and purpose were evolutionary illusions, he'd find them urging everyone to work towards the betterment of the future, education, revolution, and living and dying for the good of the human race. Lewis wrote: "Holding a philosophy which excludes humanity, they yet remain human. At the sight of injustice they throw all their Naturalism to the winds and speak like men and like men of genius. They know far better than they think they know."[32]

If naturalism is true, then there are many human behaviors that simply do not make sense from an evolutionary perspective. Massimo Pigliucci provides a few examples, such as deciding to have two or fewer children, volunteering for a humanitarian organization, sending money to take care of children on the other side of the world who do not carry our genes, or sacrificing our lives for a cause we deem worthy, which amounts to evolutionary suicide. He concludes:

> *None of these decisions make sense from a purely biological standpoint, which would have us focus our efforts on two and only two things: survival and reproduction . . . The widespread existence of human behaviors like the ones just mentioned (and many others, of course) is a real problem for any strong evolutionary theory of morality.*[33]

Steven Pinker agrees, explaining that if we followed the logic of natural selection "men would line up outside sperm banks and women would pay to have their eggs harvested and given away to infertile couples."[34] Yet most of us don't do these sorts of things.

Some Humanists have suggested that the reason we behave ethically is that we have partially overcome our evolutionary heritage. Sam Harris argues that evolution couldn't have foreseen all the things necessary for our ultimate fulfillment, such as the need for stable democracies, alleviating climate change, saving animals from extinction, containing the spread of nuclear arms, or any other issue that is crucial to our happiness in this century. He goes on to say, "As with mathematics, science, art, and almost everything else that interests us, our modern concerns about meaning and morality have flown the perch built by evolution."[35] Though evolution may have selected "territorial violence, rape, and other patently unethical behaviors as strategies to propagate one's genes," our collective well-being depends on opposing these natural tendencies.[36] The point is that we can leave our "red in tooth and claw" heritage behind, and choose a different path that will lead humanity to a better tomorrow. However, Thomas Nagel rightly asks, "what mental wings have allowed us to fly this perch, and how do they enable us to reach truth?"[37] The problem is, if we are going to rise above naturalism and our evolutionary heritage, what is it that enables us to do so?

In *The Selfish Gene*, Richard Dawkins explains that if you want to build a better society where people contribute generously and unselfishly toward the common good, you can expect little help from biological nature. He writes, "Let us try to teach generosity and altruism, because we are born selfish."[38] Some Humanists believe we can build a charitable world without God in spite of our evolutionary history. However, Ethicist Richard Taylor strongly disagrees, saying:

The modern age, more or less repudiating the idea of a divine lawgiver, has nevertheless tried to retain the ideas of moral right and wrong, not noticing that, in casting God aside, they have also abolished the conditions of meaningfulness for moral right and wrong as well. Thus, even educated persons sometimes declare that such things as war, or abortion, or the violation of certain human rights, are 'morally wrong,' and they imagine that they have said something true and significant. Educated people do not need to be told, however, that questions such as these have never been answered outside of religion . . . Contemporary writers in ethics, who blithely discourse upon moral right and wrong and moral obligation without any reference to religion, are really just

> *weaving intellectual webs from thin air; which amounts to saying that they discourse without meaning.*[39]

Despite the harsh reality of naturalism, Humanists remain committed to their moral position, regardless of how irreconcilable it is with their worldview. While many naturalists are perfectly comfortable with this incongruity, others find it irresponsible. In response to Harris's presentation at the Salk Institute, atheist and professor of psychology Scott Atran had this to say:

> *I find it fascinating that among the brilliant scientists and philosophers at the conference, there was no convincing evidence presented that they know how to deal with the basic irrationality of human life other than to insist against all reason and evidence that things ought to be rational and evidence based. It makes me embarrassed to be a scientist and atheist.*[40]

In a naturalistic world, either evolution is the end-all be-all explanation for human nature, or it isn't—you can't have it both ways. So, while atheists can be good without God, this stands not as a testament to their worldview, but as a denial of it. For our lives to have meaning and for morality to exist, purpose is necessary. But in a naturalistic universe, meaning, morality, and purpose have no place and are best left to the fiction aisle.

CHAPTER NINE
A New Hope

> *"I hate mankind, for I think myself
> one of the best of them, and I know how bad I am."*
> — Samuel Johnson

> *"And he who was seated on the throne said,
> "Behold, I am making all things new."*
> — Revelation 21:5

The story of the Bible has been called the greatest story ever told, a great drama consisting of four acts: creation, fall, redemption, and restoration.[1] The book of Genesis says that in the beginning, God created the heavens and the Earth: energy, time, and matter—and His creation was good, very good.[2] From the very first words in the book of Genesis, humanity's purpose is established by God. We were created for a reason, and this reason gives our lives purpose and meaning.

The Bible tells us that God created humanity for the purpose of living in a perfect, loving community with Himself and others. Unlike naturalism, which believes that love is the product of blind physical forces and biochemical reactions of the brain, and other religions that do not believe in a God of love, Christianity believes that love lies at the very center of the universe, as "God is love."[3] This teaching is demonstrated in the doctrine of the trinity, which holds that God has forever existed in a trinity of three persons: Father, Son, and Spirit. Though the doctrine of the trinity is profoundly mysterious to us, without it, God's nature would be radically different. Unless God is a triune being, He can't be a God of love. He could still be a God of wisdom, power, holiness, justice, goodness, and truth, but not love, since love only exists between persons. If God is unipersonal then love didn't exist until He created other beings, which means that love is not an essential part of God's nature. Only if God is triune by nature can love be a part of His essence.[4]

When God created humanity, He wasn't creating us to fill a relational void, but instead to take part in what C. S. Lewis called, "the dance of God." Lewis explained that the God of Christianity is "not a static thing—not even a person—but a dynamic, pulsating activity, a life, almost a kind of drama. Almost, if you will not think me irreverent, a kind of dance."[5] Lewis believed that each part of the trinity circles around the other, just like in a dance. The Father, Son, and Spirit love, adore, and glorify each other, as they have centered their happiness on the happiness of one another. This is the kind of loving relationship we were created to be a part of, the dance we were created for.

Because humanity was made for the purpose of living in relationship with God, there are at least three truths that naturally follow. The first is that our value lies not in what we can do, but in what we are. Unlike Humanism, Christianity holds that humanity is made in the very image of God (the Imago Dei), and so we have inherent value. J. L. Mackie demonstrated the vast difference between these two worldviews when he claimed that humans are not intrinsically valuable for what they *are* but for what they *can do*. He wrote: "It would be more reasonable to think of the right or claim to life as growing gradually in strength, but as still being very slight immediately after conception."[6] Mackie, like many today, understood human rights in terms of capacities. If humans are merely complex organisms and not divine image bearers, then our understanding of human rights is drastically altered. If you believe that human rights and values are based on people's capabilities—like their ability to reason, make choices, live independently, or hold personal preferences—then you end up with varying levels of human rights. The more you are able to do these sorts of things, the more valuable you are, and the less you are able to, the less valuable you are.[7] It is from this kind of subjective Hitlerian logic that our society justifies horrific acts such as abortion and euthanasia. Christianity strongly disagrees with this type of thinking, instead holding that all humans are intrinsically valuable for what they are, not for what they can do. Since each and every person is created in the image of God, they all bear the mark of the divine, and nothing can take that away: not handicap, age, nor desirability.[8]

The second truth that follows from the creation account has to do with the idea of gap filling that we discussed in the last chapter. Because we were created to live in a perfect, loving community with God and others, we have been instilled with certain desires that can only be satisfied by living in harmony with our created purpose. This is why any attempt to fill the God-shaped hole with *things* can never work. C. S. Lewis offered a significant insight into this problem when he wrote:

Creatures are not born with desires unless satisfaction for those desires exists. A baby feels hunger well, there is such a thing as food. A duckling wants to swim: well, there is such a thing as water. Men feel sexual desire: well, there is such a thing as sex. If I find in myself a desire which no experience in this world can satisfy, the most probable explanation is that I was made for another world. If none of my earthly pleasures satisfy it, that does not prove that the universe is a fraud. Probably earthly pleasures were never meant to satisfy it, but only to arouse it, to suggest the real thing.[9]

An essential part of our created purpose includes worshiping God, and though this concept is offensive for many, it shouldn't be. Greg Epstein, like many atheists, finds this doctrine deeply repulsive. Criticizing the Bible's Ten Commandments, he writes:

it simply makes no sense that the first words in this purportedly most important of all ethical statements, the one that people fight to have posted at courthouses and on public lawns, would not be about, well, peace or justice, or love, or compassion, or neighborliness, or anything like that. No, they are about "Worship Me. Properly. Or Else."[10]

Religious skeptics often think that a God who demands worship is an egotistical, petty being, with serious character flaws—He's simply not a good person. While this criticism is stronger against a unipersonal God, it doesn't work if God is triune in nature. The God of the Bible already receives perfect adoration, love, and praise within the trinity, so He doesn't need it from us. Why then are we commanded to worship Him?

There are two main reasons we are told it is proper to worship God. First, if God is the greatest conceivable being that exists or could ever exist, then He is the standard of beauty and goodness. For any rational moral being to withhold worship isn't just rebellion, it is irrational and perverse. Secondly, it is for our good. If we refuse to take our proper place in the dance, we are left with an unquenchable, unfillable void in our lives.[11] Bart Ehrman, an agnostic author who left Christianity after attending seminary, explains how he sensed a void after dropping belief in God, saying:

> *I have such a fantastic life that I feel an overwhelming sense of gratitude for it; I am fortunate beyond words. But I don't have anyone to express my gratitude to. This is a void deep inside me, a void of wanting someone to thank, and I don't see any plausible way of filling it.*[12]

If you don't live for God, you will live for something else, and that something else will never satisfy you. Author H. P. Lovecraft recognized this when he wrote,

"Take away his Christian god and saints, and he will worship something else."[13] Similarly, at a commencement address at Kenyon College in 2005, American novelist David Foster Wallace gave an astonishing speech explaining how we all worship something. He said:

In the day-to-day trenches of adult life, there is actually no such thing as atheism. There is no such thing as not worshipping. Everybody worships. The only choice we get is what to worship. And an outstanding reason for choosing some sort of God or spiritual-type thing to worship . . . is that pretty much anything else you worship will eat you alive. If you worship money and things—if they are where you tap real meaning in life—then you will never have enough. Never feel you have enough. It's the truth. Worship your own body and beauty and sexual allure and you will always feel ugly, and when time and age start showing, you will die a million deaths before they finally plant you. On one level, we all know this stuff already . . . Worship power—you will feel weak and afraid, and you will need ever more power over others to keep the fear at bay. Worship your intellect, being seen as smart—you will end up feeling stupid, a fraud, always on the verge of being found out. Look, the insidious thing about these forms of worship is not that they're evil or sinful; it is that they are unconscious. They are default-settings.[14]

Although Wallace was not a religious person, he still recognized that we are all worshippers at heart. As Augustine of Hippo's renowned prayer states: "You have made us for yourself, and our heart is restless until it finds its rest in you." If you don't worship and live for

God, you will live for something else and it will never satisfy you—it will "eat you alive." Sadly, Wallace understood this all too well, as he killed himself only a couple of years later.[15]

The third truth that follows from the creation account has to do with God's laws. Many people view God's laws as oppressive restrictions, but for Christians, they are the instructions for the dance with God that leads to our flourishing, not our enslavement. Following this train of thought, Thomas Aquinas's "natural law theory" understands God's laws as the directions for running the human machine.[16] For instance, a barber's scissors are made for the purpose of cutting hair. If we try to use them for some other purpose, say to cut sheet metal, the blades will be damaged and no longer able to fulfill their created purpose. In a similar way, people who try to live outside of their created purpose and ignore the instructions for running the human machine will not only damage themselves, but others.[17] Christian theologian G. K. Chesterton explained how finding the right limitations actually serves to liberate our nature rather than restrict it.[18] He wrote:

> *You can free things from alien or accidental laws, but not from the laws of their own nature. You may, if you like, free a tiger from his bars; but do not free him from his stripes. Do not free a camel of the burden of his hump: you may be freeing him from being a camel. Do not go about as a demagogue, encouraging triangles to break out of the prison of their three sides. If a triangle breaks out of its three sides, its life comes to a lamentable end.*[19]

Similarly, God's laws are not meant to hinder our nature, but to lead to our flourishing. They exist to help us live and carry out our created purpose, which is the only way to have meaning in life. It is because we refuse to follow in step with God that our lives have so much difficulty and hardship.

Stepping Out of the Dance

It is difficult to avoid the conclusion that there is something deeply and terribly wrong with our world. We live in a world of child sex trafficking, gang violence, continuous warfare, terrorism, racism, hatred, and random public shootings. We cannot escape the unsettling suspicion that there is something fundamentally broken within us. Yet still, many deny this brokenness, instead believing that humanity is essentially good, and that our environment is the cause of our problems. We tell ourselves that if we only had better education, living conditions, and jobs, then people would come to see that violence and oppression are inferior ways of living. British journalist Malcolm Muggeridge once commented on this, saying, "The depravity of man is at once the most empirically verifiable reality but at the same time the most intellectually resisted fact."[20] No matter how obvious this truth is, we search endlessly for ways to explain it away.

The Times magazine once asked prominent authors to write a response to the question, "What's wrong with the world?" in which G. K. Chesterton supposedly responded:

Dear Sirs,
I am.
Sincerely yours,
G. K. Chesterton.[21]

Chesterton understood that humanity's core problem is not our environment, our bad choices, lack of education, but sin, and it has affected us all. If we're honest with ourselves, deep down we all know that there is something wrong with us, and so we try to mask our flaws with *things*, whether it be a lucrative career, hobbies, money, sex, or drugs. We convince ourselves that if we just had *that*, then our lives would have meaning, and we would be happy, but these accomplishments never satisfy us for long, and so we live our lives in an endless cycle of trying to prove ourselves over and over again. But no matter what we do, we always come up empty, just short of contentment.[22]

The biblical concept of sin is deeply offensive to many and is often seen as a burden that causes needless guilt and anxiety. Many people believe that if we could drop the notion of sin, we could move on and happily enjoy our lives. Prominent atheists claim that the notion of sin comes from an earlier, pre-scientific time in humanity's infancy, when we believed in wrathful and angry gods that needed to be appeased through worship and sacrifice.[23] But does removing the concept of sin really make us better off? C. E. M. Joad, a socialist philosopher whose atheistic worldview was shattered after World War II, didn't think so. He wrote: "It was because we rejected the doctrine of original sin that we on the Left were always being so disappointed; disappointed by the refusal of people to be reasonable . . . by the behavior of nations and politicians . . . above all, by the recurrent fact of war."[24] After the Holocaust, British historian Lord David Cecil said, "The jargon of the philosophy of progress taught us to think that the savage and primitive state of man is behind us . . . But barbarism is not behind us, it is [within] us."[25]

We all contribute to the cumulative evil in our world by our individual selfish actions. The Bible tells us the world is not made up of "good guys" and "bad guys," but as Aleksandr Solzhenitsyn said, "The line between good and evil passes not through [states, classes, nor between political parties] but right through every human heart."[26] In a major sense, we are the villain of the story. Perhaps the concepts of sin and total depravity offend you, but I would suggest that this might be because you don't understand them the way Christians do.

In the Bible, sin isn't just a list of the bad things that we do; it is the distortion of good things into ultimate things in an attempt to give our lives meaning and satisfaction.[27] It's saying to the Ruler of the Universe, "I know better, this is how I should live my life." Sin, then, is an attempt to create an all-new dance, trying to get things and people to revolve around us. But this never works. Dallas Cowboys coach Tom Landry was one of the most successful coaches in all of NFL history. However, Landry realized that achievement and success couldn't bring lasting happiness and fulfillment. He explained:

> *Even after you've just won the Super Bowl—especially after you've just won the Super Bowl—there's always next year. If [as the expression goes] 'Winning isn't everything. It's the only thing', then 'the only thing' is nothing—emptiness, the nightmare of a life without ultimate meaning.*[28]

A while back, I came across a section from Marquis de Sade's story *Justine* that captures this idea pointedly. In the story, a lascivious friar comments on his never-ending lust for sexual desire:

> *Spending the night with one woman always makes me want another in the morning. Nothing is quite as insatiable as our urges; the greater the offerings we make to them, the hotter they burn. Of course, the outcome is always pretty much the same, yet we always imagine that there is better just around the corner. The instant our thirst for one woman is slaked is also the moment when the same drives kindle our desire for another.*[29]

When we pursue good things and make them into ultimate things, we corrupt ourselves and God's creation.[30] As theologian Jonathan Edwards put it, "God is the highest good of the reasonable creature. The enjoyment of him is our proper happiness; and is the only happiness with which our souls can be satisfied."[31] Make no mistake, there is such a thing as evil; however, Lewis and Edwards help us see why sin is not just "doing bad things," but is putting good things in the place of God —"badness is only spoiled goodness."[32]

Christianity Is Pessimistic

While the Bible's message is ultimately one of hope and joy, it doesn't start there. It begins with a diagnosis of a deadly condition. However, many skeptics believe this message is overtly negative and contributes to needless guilt and problems. In his book, *Letter to a Christian Nation*, Sam Harris writes, "[Christianity's] principal concern appears to be that the Creator of the universe will take offense at something people do while naked. This prudery of yours contributes daily to the surplus of human misery."[33] Harris and many others believe Christianity restricts human flourishing with its outdated beliefs about human well-being, especially in regard to sexuality. Not only does Harris trivialize the impact that sex has on us, but he ignores the fact that we all believe there are right and wrong approaches to sexuality; we all believe in at least some restrictions. Christianity believes that God created sex to be enjoyed within the confines of a marriage, between one man and one woman. Others disagree, believing that sex is to be enjoyed at will, but *only* between consenting adults, so long as no "harm" occurs. But notice that both sexual narratives put restrictions on sexuality—the first limits it to heterosexual marriage, while the second restricts it to consenting adults. Therefore, the struggle is not over whether to impose restrictions on sexuality, but instead finding the right restrictions that lead to human flourishing. The principle concern of Christian sexuality is not what people do while naked; rather, it is following the guidelines the Creator has given, which brings Him glory and leads to our flourishing. If there is a God who made us, then He is the one who knows the purpose of sex and how it works best, since He's the one who invented it.

I once had a conversation with a woman who told me that she could never accept the God of the Bible because the Bible was so restrictive and pessimistic. She saw the doctrine of sin as a low view of humanity and an attempt to control people through guilt and superstition. Her thoughts were very similar to what many modern Humanists believe. For instance, PZ Myers doesn't want to live a purpose-driven life. He comments, "You'd have to be insane to aspire to a life defined by someone else."[34] Dan Barker, former Christian pastor turned atheist, believes that life's purpose must be personal, and if someone else directs you how to live then you are not free, but are a slave.[35] A. C. Grayling maintains that Christianity offers an ugly view of humanity, saying:

> *[Christianity] tells us that we are created diseased by a certain doctor—"All people are initially damned to hell" it says—that only this doctor has the cure, and that we must completely submit to this doctor, in continual worship, praise and obedience, in order to get the cure. The fact that people simply ignore these kinds of utterances, and pass them by with a shrug, is perverse.*[36]

Richard Dawkins complains that Christianity has "a nasty little preoccupation" with "sin sin sin sin sin sin sin."[37] The atheistic concept of the God of the Bible is that He is a sadistic megalomaniac who is hell-bent on sin, guilt, and punishment. Their point is, it is incredibly offensive for Christians to preach this repulsive message of sin and damnation.

Several years ago, my father went to the doctor after having a hoarse voice for over a month. After several appointments, he was told that he had a very rare type of cancer on his vocal cord that would require chemotherapy, radiation, and surgery to remove that vocal cord. This procedure would result in his voice being forever altered to the sound level of a loud whisper. This obviously came as a shock, especially because he was a pastor of over thirty years who relied on his voice for his vocation. But despite the gravity and sadness of this news, he didn't get upset with the doctor for bringing it, nor did he refuse the "restrictive" treatment plan. Why not? Because it was true! For the doctor to not tell him the deadly seriousness of his condition would have been the most unloving thing that he could have done, and for my father to refuse the treatment because it was restrictive would have been a death sentence. This illustrates why the question is not "Does Christianity's message depress us or offend us?" but "Is it true?" For if Christianity is true, then it doesn't matter if its message depresses or offends us.

The unpopular doctrine of sin leads us to the even more unpopular doctrine of Hell. For the most part, our Western culture believes that there is simply no rational way to believe that a God of love could also be a God of divine punishment—the two are at odds. It is the doctrine of Hell that sent many of the great atheists of old, such as Bertrand Russell, running from Christianity.[38] Even as a Christian, the doctrine of Hell has deeply troubled me over the years. I've never had a problem believing in a God of love, but a God of judgment who created Hell seems unfathomable to me. In my college years, I really struggled with this issue, and it wasn't until I began reading Tim Keller and C. S. Lewis's written works that this doctrine started to make sense to me. Although it still troubles me at an emotional level, it no longer troubles me at a philosophical level: here is why.

As Westerners, our revulsion of Hell is largely based on our cultural location and time. If Christianity is not simply the product of any one culture, but is the transcultural truth of God, then it would make sense that it would offend every human culture at some point, since all human cultures are different, ever-changing, and imperfect. It was Keller who helped me see that though our culture is offended by a God of justice and punishment, traditional cultures are deeply offended by a forgiving God who commands us to turn the other cheek. Traditional societies are repulsed by aspects of Christianity that Western people cherish and are attracted to the aspects that Westerners despise. So unless we are ready to say that our culture is superior to all other cultures that have been, are, and will be (which amounts to cultural imperialism), then we must not say that our culture's objections to Christianity necessarily trump others. If Christianity is the transcultural truth of God, then it would have to offend each culture in different places. For us Westerners, Keller concludes, "maybe this is the place, the Christian doctrine of divine judgment."[39]

But isn't the God of the Bible supposed to be a God of love? Condemning someone to an eternity in Hell is the opposite of love. While this criticism is understandable, it largely comes from a misunderstanding of God's nature.

In the Bible, love is just one of the many attributes of God's nature. To name a few, He is also just, holy, righteous, unchangeable, gracious, jealous, all powerful, all knowing, all present, sovereign, transcendent, triune, and wrathful toward sin. But aren't love and wrath polar opposites? In Rebecca Pippert's book, *Hope Has Reasons*, she explains that when you see someone or something you love being destroyed, it makes you angry. You are wrathful towards whatever it is that is ruining the person or object, not despite your love, but because of it. The opposite of love isn't wrath, but hate, and the final form of hate is indifference.[40] As theologian E. H. Gifford wrote, "Human love here offers a true analogy; the more a father loves his son, the more he hates in him the drunkard, the liar, the traitor."[41] Because God is loving, He hates seeing His creation being ruined by sin and death, so He opposes and condemns the evil that is ruining it.[42]

If you don't believe in a God who will eventually judge the Earth and put all things right, then you will be tempted to take justice into your own hands. However, because there is a righteous judge who will not allow injustice to go unanswered, we have the power to refrain from settling the score ourselves. However, if there is no God to judge our actions, then all that's left is power—you take out my eye, so I'll retaliate and take out both of yours. Without a wrathful God who judges sin, it is nonsense to tell people to turn the other cheek. It's incredibly naïve to insist that violence won't solve anything to someone who's seen their home burned, their family raped and murdered, and their possessions taken from them. Keller points out that unless there is a God of justice who is wrathful towards injustice, we will be unable to turn the other cheek and will be "pulled inexorably into an endless cycle of vengeance, of strikes and counterstrikes nurtured and justified by the memory of terrible wrongs."[43] If we don't believe that God is the righteous judge, we inevitably become the judge, jury, and executioner ourselves.

When I was younger, I thought of Hell as the place God sent us for refusing to "get saved." When a person died, God would cast them into the burning fires of Hell kicking and screaming as they pleaded for God to save them. However, this kind of thinking results from a serious misunderstanding of the nature of sin, and if we don't understand sin, we can't understand Hell. Sin isn't just making a mistake, or a failure to obey God's "dos and don'ts." Sin is, as Psalm chapter two explains, deliberate, high-handed rebellion against the sovereign Lord of the universe. Lewis put it pointedly:

Someone or something whispered that they could become as gods —that they could cease directing their lives to their Creator . . . [Humanity] wanted to 'call their souls their own'. But that means to live a lie, for our souls are not, in fact, our own. They wanted some corner in the universe of which they could say to God, 'This is our business, not yours.'[44]

Sin is the creation's foolish attempt to overthrow the Creator and be free from His rule and reign, which is a sad joke. Sin is treason. And what do all good and just

Kings do when treasonous rebels are at their gates? They crush them.

Sin is high-handed rebellion that eventually leads to our complete devolution as we become more entrenched in our rebellion against God. Explaining this idea, C. S. Lewis wrote:

> *People often think of Christian morality as a kind of bargain in which God says, "If you keep a lot of rules I'll reward you, and if you don't I'll do the other thing." I do not think that is the best way of looking at it. I would much rather say that every time you make a choice you are turning the central part of you, the part of you that chooses, into something a little different from what it was before. And taking your life as a whole, with all your innumerable choices, all your life long you are slowly turning this central thing either into a heavenly creature or into a hellish creature: either into a creature that is in harmony with God, and with other creatures, and with itself, or else into one that is in a state of war and hatred with God, and with its fellow-creatures, and with itself.*[45]

According to Lewis, sin is the radical warping and perversion of our nature to the point where we eventually become a hellish creature who only has one desire left—hateful rebellion towards God.

Discussions on divine wrath and punishment nearly always bring up questions about the problem of evil. If you feel like this brief discussion hasn't dealt with all of your objections, hopefully they'll be better addressed in the next chapter when we look more closely at the problem of evil and suffering. However, for the remainder of this chapter I'd like to look at what the Bible says God did about our sin and rebellion.

The Resurrection

The Christian story isn't just about sin and Hell; it is a love story about the great lengths that God was willing to go to save us. Nothing captures the Gospel message more clearly than John 3:16: "For God so loved the world, that He gave His only Son, that whoever believes in Him should not perish but have eternal life."[46] This is the Gospel, the good news, and it tells us what God did for us so that we can rejoin the dance of God. However, many modern listeners struggle to accept the Gospel's message of hope and joy because they doubt the trustworthiness of those who recorded its supernatural claims.

Several years ago, an agnostic friend of mine introduced me to Bart Ehrman's book *Misquoting Jesus*. In the book, Ehrman introduces his readers to textual criticism, which is a method used for attempting to understand what the Bible's original manuscripts said. This is a necessary task because the original manuscripts of the Bible are either missing or have been destroyed. What we do have are thousands of copies of New Testament manuscripts dating from the first to the fifteenth centuries AD. When examining these copies, we discover that there are scribal errors, alterations, and, in a few cases, additions to the text. Because of this, skeptics like Ehrman argue that textual criticism reveals that we can't trust the Bible, as it is nothing more than a collection of writings that have been copied and recopied by fallible scribes who had their own religious agendas. In Ehrman's view, the classic children's game *telephone* illustrates how the original message was distorted again and again, which resulted in the error-filled Bible we have today.[47] In Christopher Hitchens's book, *God is Not Great: How Religion Poisons Everything*, he reasoned that the Bible is obviously man-made, saying:

> *The contradictions and illiteracies of the New Testament have filled up many books by eminent scholars, and have never been explained by any Christian authority except in the feeblest terms of "metaphor" and "a Christ of faith." . . . The Gospels are useful, however, in re-demonstrating the same point as their predecessor volumes, which is that religion is man-made.*[48]

In agreement with Hitchens, Richard Dawkins claims that scholars have demonstrated since the nineteenth century that the Gospels are not reliable, and in fact, they were all written long after the death of Jesus, which explains why the authors cannot agree on anything of importance.[49]

The *Jesus as Legend* view claims that the stories of Jesus developed and evolved over time. The historical Jesus was simply a religious teacher who got into trouble with Rome and ended up being executed for it. After His death, His followers began to feel Jesus' presence in their lives and began to believe He was resurrected. Though Jesus Himself didn't physically walk out of the grave, the Jesus idea did. Eventually the Jesus idea grew into the Gospel message we hear today. Though this might seem plausible at first glance, there is a problem—this narrative doesn't fit at all with the actual evidence. Scholars have shown that the Christian church's core beliefs were established very early on. Nearly all scholars agree that Paul's letter to the Corinthians was written in a city near Turkey around AD 55, a little over twenty years after Jesus' death. In the letter, Paul writes: "For what I received I passed on to you as of first importance: that Christ died for our sins according to the Scriptures, that He was buried, that He was raised on the third day according to the Scriptures, and that He appeared to Cephas [Peter], and then to the Twelve."[50] Such a short amount of time is simply not enough for legend to develop and take hold, since many of the eyewitnesses were still alive. Paul wasn't establishing some new creed; he was repeating what the church already believed.

Dawkins claims that the Gospels can't agree on anything of importance, but this is hardly the case. Interestingly enough, some skeptics, like Dawkins, claim the Gospels are too *dissimilar* to be trusted, while other skeptics argue they are too *similar* to be trusted (referred to as the synoptic problem). It is no secret that the first three Gospels, Matthew, Mark, and Luke, are very similar in content, and because of their similarities they are called the Synoptic Gospels. Since the Gospels have so many similarities, many scholars have suggested that they had a common source from which they obtained their content —referred to as the *Q source*. However, there is no direct historical evidence that a *Q source* ever existed; the early church fathers never mentioned it, nor have any portions or fragments been discovered. It is simply a naturalistic hypothesis to help explain how the Gospels are so similar without invoking the supernatural.

What about the claim that historians have discovered numerous other Gospels that were not added to the Bible because they were too embarrassing and conflicted with the original gospels? Dawkins mentions the Gospel of Thomas, which tells of Jesus as a child abusing His magical powers like a mischievous fairy would, doing things such as transforming his playmates into goats, turning mud into sparrows, and giving His father a hand with the carpentry by miraculously lengthening a piece of wood.[51] Dawkins claims that Mathew, Mark, Luke, and John were chosen, more or less, arbitrarily out of at least a dozen other Gospels, including the Gospels of Thomas, Peter, Nicodemus, Philip, Bartholomew, and Mary Magdalen.[52] He concludes the four canonical Gospels are simply legend, written by people who almost certainly never met Jesus personally and had a pre-scientific understanding of the world. They are as factually dubious as the stories of *King Arthur and his Knights of the Round Table*.[53]

Though some of the ideas found within the non-biblical Gospels have become popularized through novels and movies (Dan Brown's *The Da Vinci Code* for example), virtually no professional scholar takes these Gospels seriously. One of the main reasons for this is that they came much too late. For instance, the earliest date for the Gospel of Thomas is AD 175, more than one-hundred years after the canonical Gospels were in widespread use.[54] The *Jesus as Legend* view relies on the assumption that the biblical Gospels were written late—so late that they are not reliable sources for the events of Jesus' life. But once again, it is the assumption of naturalism that drives scholars towards a later date rather than an earlier one. For example, when a naturalist reads the Gospels' account of Jesus' prophesying of the coming destruction of Jerusalem (which occurred in AD 70 by the Roman Emperor Tiberius), they conclude, in the face of contrary evidence, that it must have been written later, since supernatural prophecy is impossible. They are once again interpreting the data through the lens of naturalism.[55]

The skeptic's assumption of naturalism is clearly demonstrated in a debate that took place between Christian apologist William Lane Craig and Bart Ehrman. In the debate, Ehrman argues that it is impossible to conclude a miracle happened in history, because historians cannot make judgments about God or the supernatural. He argues that any naturalistic theory, no matter how improbable, is infinitely more probable than a miracle, because miracles are, by their very nature, the most improbable thing there is.[56] He explains: "Since historians can establish only what probably happened in the past, they cannot show that miracles happened, since this would involve a contradiction—that the most improbable event is the most probable."[57] But there are two problems with Ehrman's argument. First, it is contradictory. If historians truly cannot make judgments about God or the supernatural, then he cannot historically say that the resurrection is improbable, because that conclusion makes a supernatural determination. The question is not whether Jesus rose *naturally* from the dead, but whether *God* raised Jesus *supernaturally* from the dead. No one doubts that Jesus rising naturally from the dead is preposterously improbable; the question is, if Jesus is God, how probable is it that He could rise from the dead?[58]

Secondly, Ehrman assumes it is improbable that Jesus rose from the dead. Why? Because throughout all of human history, dead bodies don't come back to life. Therefore, he asserts, "you can't ever verify the miracle on the basis of eyewitnesses." But this is just an old, defeated argument; in fact, David Hume made it hundreds of years ago. One of the embarrassments of Hume's reasoning was he readily admitted that, based upon it, no person living in the tropics should ever accept the testimonies from travelers that water could exist in the form of a solid. No matter how many eyewitnesses validated water turning into ice, based upon this Humean logic, the islander would have to reject the truth because it contradicted what he knew. Similarly, when it comes to the resurrection of Jesus, for naturalists like Ehrman, even if the bulk of the evidence is better explained by a miracle, this conclusion is ruled out from the start since it is incompatible with their worldview.[59]

Atheists frequently assert that the burden lies entirely on Christians to prove that Jesus rose from the dead. However, this isn't entirely true. If the Bible is based on legend and not eyewitness accounts, then skeptics have a great difficulty in explaining the rise of the early Christian church. For example, the first eyewitness accounts are said to be women, who had such a low status in the first century that their testimony wasn't even admissible in a court of law. If the story is based on legend, then it makes no sense that the early Christians wouldn't have removed these women from the accounts.[60] Also, the canonical Gospels portray the disciples of Jesus as fools who just never seem to understand what Jesus is saying. In the Gospel of Mark, the apostle Peter even denies Jesus three times. In Matthew 28, the disciples met the resurrected Jesus and they worshipped Him, though "some doubted." If the Gospels are based upon legend, then it makes no sense that the early church would claim its first eyewitnesses were women, nor to portray their founding leaders as fools. You don't do things like this if you are trying to start a religious movement to gain power.

If Jesus rose from the dead, then we have a plausible explanation for how the Christian church rose up nearly overnight and forever changed history. But if Jesus didn't rise from the dead, then skeptics must also provide an alternate account for how the church got started. In attempting to provide alternate explanations, many skeptics fail to realize the extreme religious culture in which Christianity arose. The Jewish people believed in a unipersonal God, and to worship anything but Him was blasphemy punishable by death. The fact that Jesus' ministry lasted three years, or even three hours for that matter, is miraculous enough. When looking for plausible explanations for the rise of the Christian church, we must seriously consider the cultural context in which Jesus lived. Whatever it was that caused the followers of Jesus to not only worship Him as God, but also give their lives for this belief, must have been significant.

Nearly all of the disciples of Jesus, as well as many of the early Christian leaders, died for their faith. It was not a faith of power and aggression, but a faith that taught its followers to selflessly serve and love their enemies. Without a doubt, the blood of the martyrs is one of the strongest evidences that the early church really believed that Jesus rose again. They were so convinced of the miracles they saw and the message they heard that they were willing to give up everything: religion, possessions, family, and their very lives.

One of the main objections to this that I've encountered goes something like this: "Just because the early Christians died for their faith doesn't prove anything. Many religions have people who die for their faith, so you can't say that Christianity is any different for it." On one hand, it is true that many religions have followers who die for their faith, suicide bombers being a rather current example. So, skeptics are partly right—dying for your faith only proves that you really believe what you believe is true. However, there is a fundamental difference between a modern-day suicide bomber and the early Christian believers. The early Christian believers were in a position to actually know if their beliefs were true. The disciples were there—they saw Jesus' life and ministry. Unlike suicide bombers or modern Christians who die for their faith, the disciples of Jesus weren't relying on the testimony of others for the validity of their beliefs, they were relying on the testimony of themselves and the others who witnessed Jesus' life. This is an important difference. Regardless of whether you find these arguments convincing, the followers of Jesus, in the face of their doubts and conflicting beliefs, must have really believed they saw the risen Jesus.

For Christians, everything depends on the resurrection of Jesus. The apostle Paul wrote that if Christ didn't rise from the dead, then Christians have no hope and they should be pitied above all men.[61] The resurrection of Jesus is the vital center of Christianity. If Christ didn't rise from the dead, then Christianity doesn't matter and we should ignore it. But if Christ did rise from the dead, it changes everything.[62]

But what about all the Bible's inconsistencies, its incompatibility with science, and the Old Testament's barbarism? While these are good questions, and I believe there are good answers for them, if you are a skeptic looking at the Bible, perhaps for the first time, you shouldn't begin with those questions. The first and most important question you need to answer is, "Who was Jesus?" At first, your primary concern shouldn't be whether the Bible has errors; instead, it should be whether its basic portrayal of Jesus is accurate. Tim Keller explains how it was this question that led him to trust in Jesus and the Bible:

> *I am not here trying to argue for the complete trustworthiness of the Bible, only that its portrayal of the life and teaching of Jesus is historically accurate. If it is, then we can draw conclusions about who Jesus is from the information we read there. If eventually we*

> *put our faith in Jesus, then his view of the Bible will become ours. Speaking personally, I take the whole Bible to be reliable not because I can somehow "prove" it all to be factual. I accept it because I believe in Jesus and that was his view of the Bible.*[63]

Keller isn't saying, "You just have to take it on blind faith." He's appealing to our reason and urging us to ask ourselves who Jesus was. Did He really rise from the dead? Why have so many people died for their belief that He rose from the dead? This is an important question. It is the resurrection of Jesus on which Christianity rises and falls.[64]

The Restoration of All Things

The resurrection of Jesus is important because it tells us that the natural order has been forever changed through one Man's defeat of sin and death. It is a love story in which God Himself rescues His bride from certain death and complete destruction. When explaining the differences between Christianity and other religions, I often tell people that Christianity is the only religion that isn't a religion. What I mean is that most religions tell us what we have to do in order to please God and earn His approval. If you obey the list of "dos and don'ts," then God will owe you His blessings and you'll live a happy life. However, Christianity is fundamentally different. It tells us what God has done for us so that we can reenter the dance of God. Where religion is about our performance, Christianity is about Christ's performance. Salvation is not a record of our moral achievements that we hand over to God; instead, Christ's perfect record is given to us by grace through faith so that we might live anew.

Every person who has come to faith in Jesus has come to realize their total inability to obey God's laws, and for me personally, this is one of the most compelling reasons I believe Christianity is true. No other religion or worldview gives such a clear diagnosis of the human heart. Building our life's meaning on either religious moral achievements or secular ones are both ultimately ways of trying to save ourselves.[65] Before I came to understand grace, I approached Christianity as a moralistic religion and tried to follow the rules so that I would be a good person, so God would accept me. For years I had tremendous guilt because I knew I wasn't good enough to fully live up to His standard. Though I believed that salvation was by grace through faith in Jesus, I still approached it as something I did instead of a gift. My level of faith was the determiner of my salvation. Because of this wrong approach to grace, I started to panic as I grew older and began to wrestle with doubt. I eventually came to realize that it's not the strength of my faith but the strength of the object of my faith that matters.[66]

To believe that we must remove all of our doubts and fears before turning to Christ is another way of trying to earn our salvation and put God in our debt.[67] This is moralism, not Christianity. The Gospel is entirely different; it is about what God has done for us in order to save us, not what we must do to save ourselves. When you finally see the beauty of the Gospel, it changes you forever. It not only cripples feelings of pride and superiority over others, but also self-loathing and guilt, while giving us a new identity: Christ's identity. Instead of seeing moral obedience as a currency to gain God's approval, we come to see it as an act of love to please God. In the same way that a bride adorns herself before the wedding ceremony to meet her groom, so do Christians adorn themselves with good works in preparation to meet our savior, Jesus Christ.

In the book of Revelation, we read of the future restoration of all things, a new Heaven and a new Earth, and the grand finale of God's great redemption story. Unlike other religions, the people of God are not carried away to some mystical spiritual realm, but rather to Earth, reborn as God meant her to be.[68] Because of one man's sin, humanity was cut off from God, but because of another Man's obedience, we can live forever with Him.[69] The creation that once groaned for its restoration is made whole with the removal of death, crying, mourning, and pain, for they have passed away.[70] While the Bible is heavily focused on the restoration of humanity's fallen nature, it stands alone from other world religions in promising the restoration of the physical world. This offers tremendous hope, since Jesus didn't come to free humanity from creation, but to restore it, even above and beyond its former glory. For the people of God, though this is the end of their redemption story, it is only the beginning of the great story that will continue on forever.

As C. S. Lewis described in his final book of The Chronicles of Narnia:

> *But the things that began to happen after that were so great and beautiful that I cannot write them. And for us this is the end of all the stories, and we can most truly say that they all lived happily ever after. But for them it was only the beginning of the real story. All their life in this world and all their adventures in Narnia had only been the cover and the title page: now at last they were beginning Chapter One of the Great Story, which no one on earth has read: which goes on for ever: in which every chapter is better than the one before.*[71]

CHAPTER TEN
Evil and Suffering

> *"People speak sometimes about the 'bestial' cruelty of man, but that is terribly unjust and offensive to beasts, no animal could ever be so cruel as a man, so artfully, so artistically cruel."*
> — Fyodor Dostoyevsky

> *"Our God is in the heavens; he does all that he pleases."*
> — Psalm 115:3

We live in a world of unimaginable cruelty and suffering that includes both moral and natural evil. When it comes to moral evil, every hour, more than five children die from violence, which amounts to more than one hundred per day. While child mortality rates have declined in the past couple of decades, in the year 1960, one in ten children never reached the age of five.[1] Child pornography is now a global, multibillion-dollar industry that thrives on the dark web (the part of the internet not available to search engines) and its evil includes toddlers and even infants. In the United States, someone is sexually assaulted every two minutes. When it comes to natural evil, 150,000 people die every single day, which is comparable to a small city being wiped out.² Family members are suddenly torn away from their loved ones, resulting in all their dreams and aspirations coming to an abrupt end. The mortality rate for humanity is one hundred percent and it's not getting any better. If you have not yet experienced evil and suffering, just wait a little while, you will.

During my time in seminary, one of my professors told us that there was only one truly unsolvable problem in all of Christian theology. While other theological problems exist, we ultimately have plausible and rational ways for making sense of them. Not so with the problem of evil. The problem of evil and suffering (also called theodicy) was first advanced by Greek philosopher Epicurus and was further developed by Scottish philosopher David Hume. The problem goes like this: Why would a good, all-powerful God allow evil and suffering? If God allows evil and suffering to exist because He can't stop it, then He might be good, but He's not all powerful. But if God allows evil and suffering to exist when He could stop it, then He might be all powerful, but He's definitely not good. Either way, the existence of evil proves that the good and all-powerful God of the Bible couldn't exist.³

If there is a God, how could He allow such horrifying evil like the Holocaust, where men, women, and children were thrown alive into fiery ovens and their blood-chilling cries could be heard throughout the camp? Couldn't God hear their cries? Surely if a good and all-powerful God exists, He would have stopped this, right? The problem of evil and suffering is a serious one that has led many to abandon their belief in God. For Bart Ehrman, this is precisely what happened. In his book on evil and suffering, he writes:

> *If there is an all-powerful and loving God in this world, why is there so much excruciating pain and unspeakable suffering? The problem of suffering has haunted me for a very long time. It was what made me begin to think about religion when I was young, and it was what led me to question my faith when I was older. Ultimately, it was the reason I lost my faith.*[4]

One might assume that a textual critic like Ehrman would have lost his faith over the reliability of the Gospel record, but no, it was ultimately over the problem of evil. Likewise, it wasn't Charles Darwin's theory of evolution that led him to reject the Christian concept of God; it was the problem of evil and suffering in regards to Hell and the death of his daughter.[5] Many atheists have concluded that the problem of evil and suffering is insurmountable, and proves one thing—the God of the Bible couldn't exist.[6] Humanist author Greg Epstein says that if the only way to get to Heaven is by worshiping a God who had the power to prevent the Holocaust but chose not to, then He doesn't deserve our worship.[7] While many see the problem of evil and suffering as a knock-down argument against belief in God, the Bible does offer several explanations for its existence.

Free Will

Early Christian theologian Augustine believed that evil was largely the result of man's free will. Instead of seeing evil as a property or an object, Augustine saw it as the absence of goodness, similar to darkness being the absence of light. When God created humanity with free will and intelligence, evil was made possible.[8] In *Mere Christianity*, C. S. Lewis explained this idea further when he wrote:

> *God created things which had free will. That means creatures which can go either wrong or right. Some people think they can imagine a creature which was free but had no possibility of going wrong; I cannot. If a thing is free to be good it is also free to be bad. And free will is what has made evil possible. Why, then, did God give them free will? Because free will, though it makes evil possible, is also the only thing that makes possible any love or goodness or joy worth having. A world of automata—of creatures that worked like machines—would hardly be worth creating. The happiness which God designs for His higher creatures is the happiness of being freely, voluntarily united to Him . . . Of course God knew what would happen if they used their freedom the wrong way: apparently He thought it worth the risk . . . If God thinks this state of war in the universe a price worth paying for free will—that is, for making a live world in which creatures can do real good or harm and something of real importance can happen, instead of a toy world which only moves when He pulls the strings—then we may take it it is worth paying.*[9]

As Westerners, we are naturally drawn to the free will theodicy, as choice and individualism are nearly sacred to us. While the free will theodicy can certainly help us better understand moral evil, how can it account for natural disasters, such as earthquakes, hurricanes, and tsunamis?[10] Augustine's solution was that natural evil is the result of moral evil. When Adam and Eve sinned in the garden, Satan and his fallen angels were given the power to carry out natural evil upon the Earth. Human actions are also able to cause natural evil through famines, droughts, and floods. Therefore, according to this idea, both moral and natural evil can be explained as the result of free will.

Free will certainly contributes to evil and suffering, however, it cannot work as a complete explanation since it relies on an unbiblical view of free will. In philosophy, there are three major views on free will: we have it, we don't have it, and both. The first view is the libertarian view of free will, which holds that God could not have created us to always do good without violating our free will. Since He created us with free will, evil was always and necessarily possible.[11] However, free will explanations, like Lewis and Augustine's, have several major problems. First, the Bible teaches that God Himself is unable to sin and yet is completely free. So why couldn't God, in His omnipotent power, have created us free, yet unable to sin just as He is unable to?[12] Second, in the Bible, sin is never portrayed as freedom, but as slavery, which prevents us from being able to exercise true freedom. Sin diminishes our nature; it doesn't enhance it. The Bible tells us that true freedom will only be experienced in eternity when the people of God are fully glorified and beyond the possibility of sin. Until then, we are, at least in part, slaves to our sinful passions that prevent us from being our true selves and loving God fully. While the libertarian view of free will offers some insight into the problem of evil, it is ultimately an unbiblical concept if we try to make it a total explanation for the problem of evil and suffering.

The second view on free will is often called determinism (or fatalism), which is the idea that our choices are predestined to happen. Though Adam and Eve chose to sin, their choice was predestined and so they could not have chosen otherwise. Bart Ehrman points out some of the problems with this view when he writes:

> *If people do bad things because God ordains them to do them, why are they held responsible? If Adam and Eve were foreordained to eat the fruit, why were they punished for it? If Judas betrayed Jesus and Pilate crucified him because that was God's will, how can they be held accountable? In the Bible God is typically portrayed as the all-powerful Sovereign of this world who foreknows all things, yet human beings are portrayed as responsible for their actions.*[13]

Contrary to both the libertarian and determinist views, the Bible teaches a third view called compatibilism. Instead of being *either/or*, it is *both/and*. History is one hundred percent determined by God's will, yet humanity is one hundred percent responsible for our behavior.[14] As Westerners, this concept seems like a contradiction to us, as we tend to think of things in terms of either/or. However, the Bible clearly teaches that divine sovereignty and human responsibility are not a contradiction, but a paradox. God sovereignly determines the course of the future, not in spite of our choices, but through them. This is clearly seen in the Old Testament when God uses the pagan nations to judge Israel. Even though they were His instrument of judgment, He still held them responsible for their decision to wage war against God's people. This paradoxical language is seen throughout the Bible. For example, Proverbs 16:9 says, "The heart of man plans his way, but the Lord establishes his steps." In Genesis 50:20, Joseph tells his brothers that though they intended evil when they sold him into slavery, God intended it for good.[15] The Bible clearly teaches that God is in complete control of history, yet humanity's choices are not determined.[16]

If you hold to one side of the paradox at the expense of the other, you will lean towards unbiblical beliefs and behavior. For instance, if you embrace a libertarian view of free will, then you will not only have a weak and powerless God, but you'll be paralyzed and unable to make wise decisions because the anxiety of making those decisions will overwhelm you. If history is completely determined by our choices, then every single choice we make causes a butterfly effect that we cannot possibly comprehend. On the flip side, if you embrace determinism, you'll believe that everything is fixed despite our choices, so you'll be passive and won't act responsibly. Standing in opposition to both of these extremes is the compatibilist view of the Bible, which teaches that our choices matter—there are consequences for bad choices. However, we don't need to panic or be anxious because God is the one who is in complete and absolute control. This is why Paul could confidently say in Romans 8:28, "And we know that for those who love God all things work together for good,"—even evil and suffering.[17] While the free will theodicy helps us understand one aspect of evil and suffering, it ultimately fails to explain why God sovereignly orchestrated it from before the foundations of the world.[18] Though it provides a partial answer, it still leaves the problem unsolved.

Suffering as Punishment

In the Bible, suffering is used by God to accomplish His divine purposes. For example, God sometimes uses suffering to punish sin. In the Garden of Eden, suffering and death enter the world as a curse from God for humanity's rebellion against Him. A few chapters later, God wipes out all of humanity for their sin with a worldwide flood, only sparing Noah and his family. Throughout the Old Testament, God uses all kinds of disasters to punish Israel when they sin and turn their back on Him. The Bible's message is clear—God hates sin and He will judge it accordingly and without exception. Both the Old and New Testaments repeatedly speak of God using suffering as punishment to judge wicked people, both in this life and at the end of time on the Day of Judgment.[19] The Bible clearly teaches that those who disobey God can expect hardship, suffering, and eventually physical and spiritual death.[20]

In the prologue to the book of Job, we are introduced to a man who is about to experience intense suffering. Job is described as a man of complete integrity who was blessed by God with great wealth, family, and prosperity. He was a man who had everything.[21] After introducing Job, the scene abruptly shifts from Earth to Heaven, where God asks Satan to consider the great character of His servant Job. Satan isn't impressed and argues that Job only obeys God because God rewards him for it; take away Job's prosperity and he'd curse God to His face. To the shock of modern readers, God accepts Satan's challenge and permits him to take away all of Job's possessions. Job loses everything. His ten children die suddenly by a strong wind that collapses a roof onto their heads, and his livestock are either stolen or destroyed. But in spite of Job's great loss, his response is astonishing: "Naked I came from my mother's womb, and naked shall I return. The Lord gave, and the Lord has taken away; blessed be the name of the Lord."[22] The chapter finishes by saying, "In all of this Job did not sin or charge God with wrong."[23]

But Satan isn't satisfied. He argues that a man's possessions are nothing in value compared to his health, so if God would take away Job's health, then he would surely curse God to His face. Once again, God accepts Satan's challenge and gives him permission to take away Job's good health, but not his life. Job is struck down with horrific sores from head to toe. After the loss of his possessions, family, and health, Job's wife urges him to "curse God and die."[24] But in spite of all of Job's losses, he tells his wife that she is speaking foolishly and refuses to curse God. So, God wins the bet with Satan, while Job is left completely devastated.[25] Though Job never curses God, he has one simple question for Him, "Why?"

Job's view of God was deeply shaken by what happened to him. The people of Job's time believed that

God's justice operated on the basis of the righteous being blessed and the wicked being punished. But Job was a righteous man, so why was he being treated like the wicked? When we look at the response of Job's wife, though it was wrong, it was understandable. She knew firsthand that Job was a righteous man, so she concludes that if this is how God treats His faithful servants, then it is better to die. Though Job understood he was a sinner, he knew that his life did not merit the suffering he was receiving when compared to the wicked. So, Job begins to doubt and question whether God's system of justice was working properly, or if God had forgotten about him.[26]

In the next act, Job's friends arrive. Upon seeing Job's distress, they respond empathetically with weeping, mourning, and sitting with him in silence for seven days. When they break their silence to offer Job advice, they tell him that God is treating him like the wicked because he must be wicked. Job's first friend reasons that Job's suffering is because of his sin, refusal to repent, and a lack of fear for God.[27] Job's second friend goes even further and claims that Job's children were killed by God for their great sin, and if Job would simply repent, he'd be restored.[28] His third friend is even harsher and says that Job actually deserved much worse than he got, and that he was mocking God by refusing to admit his sin.[29] Job rejects the counsel of his friends because he knew his suffering was not punishment for some great evil. Instead, Job wonders if something has gone terribly wrong with God's judicial system.[30]

After Job and his three friends end their conversation in disagreement and frustration, Job's youngest friend Elihu steps forward to offer his opinion. Elihu is irritated with all of them. He's upset with Job for focusing on justifying his character instead of God's, and with the three friends because they hadn't refuted any of Job's arguments, yet they condemned him anyway. Job had challenged his friends to show him his sin and how he merited such punishment. Though they knew that Job's character was astounding, they insisted that he must have brought this punishment upon himself for some great sin. Job's friends had similar theology to that of modern-day prosperity Gospel preachers, who teach that God blesses the righteous and punishes the wicked. For them, the problem of theodicy is simple: it's the carrot or the stick. If we simply obey God's list of *dos* and *don'ts* we'll have a healthy, wealthy, and prosperous life. While other religions might view God this way, Christianity does not.

Christian Smith, professor of sociology at the University of Notre Dame, researched American young adults and concluded that most of them are, what he calls, "moralistic therapeutic deists."[31] Smith found that most American young adults believe that the central goal of life is to be happy and feel good about yourself. Fittingly, they also believe in a God who created the world with order, watches over human life, and wants people to be good, nice, and fair to each other. If you are nice, fair, and generally a good person, then God will bring you to Heaven when you die. Unlike religions that claim God demands our worship, God really doesn't need to be involved in your life, but He can help resolve your problems if you ask Him to.[32] Like Job's friends, American young adults assume that God will give us a good and happy life if we strive to be a good and honest person. But as Job came to discover, often the good do suffer while the wicked flourish. The inevitable result of this spiritually entitled worldview is that when suffering comes, and it surely will, it crushes you. Ultimately, this view of God reduces Him to a genie who exists to grant our wishes and satisfy our idolatry.

In the final chapters of the book, Job gets his wish when God shows up, speaking to him from a whirlwind. But God doesn't start listing off all of the reasons why He allowed Job to suffer; instead, He bombards Job with a series of sarcastic questions that aim to show him his complete inability to comprehend God's ways. "Who is this that questions my wisdom with such ignorant words? Brace yourself like a man, because I have some questions for you, and you must answer them."[33] God never tells Job about the conversation with Satan, nor does He offer any sort of explanation for why the good sometimes suffer while the evil flourish. Instead, God's series of questions serve to demonstrate the vast gap between God's knowledge and man's. Though God rebukes Job, it is not for an immoral life, like his friends suggested—it is for his ignorance. God's point is clear: man does not know enough about God to judge His ways.

Instead of walking away bitter about God's refusal to answer him, Job responds in proper worship. After getting a tiny glimpse of God's glory, you see him whisper back to God, "I am unworthy. How can I reply to you? I put my hand over my mouth. I spoke once, but I have no answer —twice, but I will say no more."[34] Job realized what Paul spoke of in the book of Romans about God's sovereignty: "But who are you, O man, to answer back to God?"[35] In the end, Job's suffering didn't lead him away from God, it brought him closer to Him.

The book of Job essentially puts God on trial for evil and suffering. The book ends with God exonerating Job's character by rebuking Job's friends, with the exception of Elihu. Though God blessed Job with a long life and twice as much as he had before, Job never found out all the reasons for his suffering. While many see Job's story as a simple bet between God and Satan, a closer look shows it is packed full of explanation for why evil and suffering exist. Contrary to what Job's friends believed, suffering isn't always punishment for sin. This means that we can't automatically conclude that those who are suffering are being punished or are less worthy.[36] In Job's case, God used suffering to not only humiliate Satan and bring Himself glory, but to impact countless others throughout the ages through Job's story. God also used it to humble Job and keep him from a greater evil, to test and strengthen Job's faith, and to lead Job to trust and love God regardless of his circumstances.

Suffering Is Redemptive

In the Bible, God sometimes uses suffering to discipline His children, just as a loving parent would, in order to lead them to become more holy.[37] As children, our parents would discipline us in varying ways in order to focus our attention and teach us truths that we couldn't have learned otherwise. So why think that God couldn't do the same thing to an even greater degree with pain and suffering? C. S. Lewis once explained how pain and suffering have a unique way of grabbing our attention. He wrote, "God whispers to us in our pleasures, speaks to us in our conscience, but shouts in our pains: It is His megaphone to rouse a deaf world."[38] For whatever reason, suffering has the ability to focus our attention on what matters in a way unlike any other.

A couple of years after my father's treatment of an extremely rare and deadly throat cancer, I asked him about his experience and how it affected his faith in God. He told me that though he wouldn't want to repeat the experience, since in many ways it was truly horrifying, he wouldn't trade it either. His experience with cancer shaped and strengthened his faith in a unique and radical way that couldn't have happened otherwise. Suffering has a unique way of testing our faith so that it always results in one of two things: it either brings us closer to God or pushes us further away from Him. The one thing it won't do is leave us where we are.

The Bible offers many different explanations for why evil and suffering occur. Sometimes it is used to punish people for sin or to discipline God's children in order to bring them to spiritual maturity. Suffering is used to glorify God by our response to it, while other times it's used to prevent us from future evil. It is also inflicted on us by forces that are opposed to God. Some suffering has no purpose other than to bring a person to love God for who He is, and not what He gives, which is the only way to have lasting peace and joy.[39] But if suffering contributes to so many good things, then is it a good thing that ought to be embraced cheerfully?

In *The God Delusion*, Richard Dawkins explains how approximately 95 percent of the population of the United States believes they will survive their own death. But if this is the case, he asks, why do they mourn and fear death? Shouldn't they respond how the Abbot of Ampleforth did when Cardinal Basil Hume told him that he was dying? "Congratulations! That's brilliant news. I wish I was coming with you."[40] If Christians truly believe in life beyond the grave, why don't they beam with anticipation when a close friend or family member is given months to live? After all, aren't suffering and death God's tools to bring about a greater good?[41]

In the eleventh chapter of the book of John, Jesus receives word from Mary and Martha that their brother Lazarus is sick and dying. Though Jesus cares deeply for Lazarus and his sisters, He intentionally delays two days before going to him. Jesus tells His disciples, "This sickness will not end in death. No, it is for God's glory so that God's Son may be glorified through it."[42] After two days, Jesus tells His disciples that it is time to go see Lazarus because he's dead, but He's glad He wasn't there for their sake so that they might come to belief.[43] By the time Jesus and His disciples arrive, Lazarus has already been in the tomb for four days, so it's too late for Jesus to heal him.

Jesus seems to have carefully planned for Lazarus's death so that He could raise him from the dead, in order to bring glory to God and help the disciples come to belief. However, before He raises him from the dead, Jesus responds in a very unexpected way for someone who deliberately planned for this. The text says that when He saw Mary and the others crying, He was deeply moved in spirit and troubled. We then read the shortest verse in the entire Bible: "Jesus wept."[44] Why would Jesus cry over the death of Lazarus when He had not only planned for it, but was about to raise him from the dead?

In Tim Keller's book *Encounters with Jesus*, he explains his frustration with the way most Bible translations translate John 11, verse 38, which says: "Then Jesus, deeply moved again, came to the tomb."[45] Keller explains that the Greek text uses a word that means "to bellow with anger." He goes on to say:

> *Jesus is absolutely furious. He's bellowing with rage—he is roaring. Who or what is he angry at? . . . Jesus is raging against death. He doesn't say, "Look, just get used to it. Everybody dies. That's the way of the world. Resign yourself." No, he doesn't do that. Jesus is looking squarely at our greatest nightmare—the loss of life, the loss of loved ones and of love—and he's incensed.*[46]

Jesus' response helps us see why Christianity's response to evil and suffering is very different from other worldviews. Fatalism says to heroically endure it, while Christianity is more empathetic, recognizing the devastation it brings. Buddhism says to accept it as a natural part of life, while Christianity recognizes it as an intruder of the natural order. Karma says to pay it since you owe it for past mistakes, while Christianity recognizes that suffering is often unfair. Secularism says to avoid or fix it, while Christianity understands that suffering can be meaningful and ultimately cannot be avoided. Christianity recognizes the partial truths within each of these worldviews, but realizes that they are ultimately too simplistic.[47] While God uses pain and suffering to accomplish a greater purpose, ultimately, He hates evil and suffering and wants to eradicate it.[48]

Does any of this soften the problem of evil and suffering? After all, we still haven't found an ultimate explain-it-all answer for why a good, all-powerful God would allow evil and suffering. Isn't the most probable explanation for their existence, God's non-existence? Bart Ehrman asks:

If God had come into the darkness with the advent of the Christ child, bringing salvation to the world, why is the world in such a state? Why doesn't he enter into the darkness again? Where is the presence of God in this world of pain and misery? Why is the darkness so overwhelming?[49]

This question is a reasonable one; however, the argument for the problem of evil ultimately rests on three unfounded assumptions.

First, the argument of theodicy wrongly assumes that omnipotence means that God can do anything. Atheist author A. C. Grayling demonstrates this incorrect assumption when he writes:

> *Omnipotence strictly implies that anything is possible. But this cannot mean that it [an omnipotent being] could do logically impossible things, like for example both existing and not existing at the same time, or being 'greater' or 'more perfect' than itself. It is not clear whether omnipotence implies that a possessor of it could do things that are not so obviously logically impossible, such as eat itself for breakfast ... These are phrases that appear to have meaning but on examination turn out to make no sense.*[50]

As we discussed in chapter five, it makes no sense to think that omnipotence means being able to do impossible things.[51] As C. S. Lewis once wrote, "Nonsense remains nonsense even when we talk it about God."[52] British philosopher Richard Swinburne shows us why we can't understand omnipotence to mean "able to do anything." He explains:

> *A logically impossible action is not an action. It is what is described by a form of words which purport to describe an action, but do not describe anything which it is coherent to suppose could be done. It is no objection to [God's] omnipotence that he cannot make a square circle. This is because "making a square circle" does not describe anything which it is coherent to suppose could be done.*[53]

Once we understand what omnipotence is, we can begin to understand that God couldn't eradicate evil without eradicating us. It is indisputable that humanity is one of the major causes of evil and suffering in our world. If God showed up today and wiped it out entirely, then there would be no people left, since we all contribute towards the selfishness, evil, and pain of our world.[54] Evil is a parasite, and suddenly wiping it out would wipe out its host. This is why asking, "Why didn't God simply wipe out evil without wiping out us?" equates to a nonsense question.

The second unfounded assumption is the assumption of strong rationalism. Though the Bible has many different examples of how God uses pain and suffering to accomplish a greater good, the answer is ultimately a mystery to us. The problem of theodicy wrongly assumes that because we can't come up with an ultimate explanation for why a good and all-powerful God would allow evil and suffering, means that there isn't one. Romans 8:28 tells us that all things work together for good for those who love God. If we can see small glimpses for how evil and suffering bring about a greater good some of the time, why couldn't it be that God is using all evil and suffering for a greater good that couldn't otherwise have been attained? Why couldn't the existence of evil and suffering be necessary for the greatest possible good?[55] Are we really ready to say that just because our three-pound, sin-fallen, finite, human brain can't think of a good reason for why an infinite God would plan history to include pain and suffering means that there can't be one? Alvin Plantinga asks, "Suppose God does have a good reason for permitting sin and evil, pain and suffering: why think we would be the first to know what it is?"[56]

Founder and Rabbi of Humanistic Judaism, Sherwin Wine, demonstrated the third assumption when he said, "Sometimes, the nicest thing you can say about God is that he doesn't exist."[57] The assumption is that if God exists, He has failed to do the right thing, and so He has violated some moral standard. But as we've been discussing throughout this book, if God doesn't exist, then by what standard are we judging Him to prove His guilt in the first place? To say the God of the Bible is evil and has failed to do the right thing assumes the existence of objective moral values, which are extremely difficult to ground in a naturalistic universe. By making this argument, we are essentially cutting off the branch we are sitting on. The argument relies on God's existence in order to argue against His existence, which obviously doesn't work. This problem is what eventually led C. S. Lewis away from atheism as he became convinced that the logical problem of evil is an even greater problem for atheism than it is for Christianity.

Christianity tells us that even though God uses evil and suffering to accomplish a greater good, we are right to long for its final destruction. However, atheism paints a very different picture, which is why Charles Darwin wrote:

Believing as I do that man in the distant future will be a far more perfect creature than he now is, it is an intolerable thought that he and all other sentient beings are doomed to complete annihilation after such long-continued slow progress. To those who fully admit the immortality of the human soul, the destruction of our world will not appear so dreadful.[58]

Though death is final, unavoidable, and certain, atheists must believe it is neutral since it is a natural part of the universe. Demonstrating this belief, A. C. Grayling writes:

Because, on a naturalistic view, being dead is identical to being unborn, nothing about death in itself makes it good or evil. It is what it takes away from us that makes it one or the other. If it takes away suffering, it is good; when it takes away hopes, possibilities, relationships with those beloved, it is bad.[59]

Humanists advocate courage when facing the reality of death and coming to terms with it being a natural part of life. Fear of death's finality is natural; however, we should fight against its paralyzing power that takes away the current joys of living.[60] Greek Stoic philosopher Epictetus taught that one way of facing death with courage was by coming to grips with its harsh, cold reality. He wrote:

When you kiss your child, or your brother, or your friend, never give way entirely to your affections, nor free rein to your imagination; but curb it, restrain it . . . Remind yourself likewise that what you love is mortal, that what you love is not your own . . . What harm is there while you are kissing your child to murmur softly, 'Tomorrow you will die'?[61]

Those who advocate a neutral view of death are not championing bravery, but indifference. Death is the sudden removal of everyone and everything we love and cherish, and by embracing an attitude of courageous indifference towards death, we are really striving to become indifferent towards our loved one's very existence. Even though it is easy to say that we should not fear death, in reality, we still do. The eternal loss of everyone and everything we love was not what we were created for.

In the end, the argument of the problem of evil (theodicy) doesn't hold up so well, and as philosopher William Alston said, is now acknowledged on (almost) all sides to be completely bankrupt.[62] What at first appeared to be an argument against the existence of God, actually makes God's existence more probable, since objective moral values struggle to find a footing without Him. Christianity tells us that God has good reasons for allowing evil and suffering to exist, and though it is still largely a mystery to us, there is a silver lining that will somehow make it worth it all in the end.

In Romans 8:18, Paul tells of this silver lining: it is the glory that Christ brings at the end of time that is so great it makes our current suffering look like nothing at all. This is not an attitude of indifference towards evil and suffering, rather it is a high view of the glory that awaits all those who love God. As C. S. Lewis famously said: "They say of some temporal suffering, 'No future bliss can make up for it,' not knowing that Heaven, once attained, will work backwards and turn even that agony into a glory."

The Emotional Response

So far, we have been looking at the intellectual response to evil and suffering, but for many of us (if not all of us), intellectual solutions are simply not enough to carry us through our darkest hour. Hearing that suffering is a mystery and that we have good reasons to trust God isn't likely to provide much comfort or relief when we are in the thick of it. We need something else.

In *The Brothers Karamazov*, the skeptical brother Ivan rejects all intellectual responses to evil and suffering. For Ivan, the hurt is too deep and the pain is too real. In the story, he asks his religiously devout brother Alyosha to contemplate the horrible injustice of God's world. He tells Alyosha a story of an eight-year-old boy who accidentally bruised the leg of a general's favorite dog. In his outrage, the general responds by releasing a pack of hounds upon the child who rip him to shreds right before his crying mother's eyes. So, Ivan asks, "Is this God's perfect justice?" Ivan can't imagine how this boy's suffering could ever be made just, so he refuses to accept any intellectual justifications for it. He can't fathom it, so he dismisses its possibility. Ivan declares that even if God has some explain-it-all answer, some justification that makes all suffering worth it in the end, the pain is too real for him, and so he wants nothing to do with a God who is ultimately responsible for it. One tear of a suffering child is not worth the price of admission to learn the intellectual justification for it, and so, Ivan returns God his ticket.[63]

Ivan, like many of us, has an emotional, gag-like reflex to the problem of evil that prevents intellectual responses from resonating. For those of us like Ivan, something else is needed. In Romans 8:31-34, Paul points us to something that has the power to shatter any emotional doubts about evil and suffering. He writes:

> *What, then, shall we say in response to these things? If God is for us, who can be against us? He who did not spare his own Son, but gave him up for us all—how will he not also, along with him, graciously give us all things? Who will bring any charge against those whom God has chosen? It is God who justifies. Who then is the one who condemns? No one. Christ Jesus who died—more than that, who was raised to life—is at the right hand of God and is also interceding for us.*[64]

Although these verses do not tell us the reason why God allows evil and suffering, they do tell us one reason it can't be—it can't be because God doesn't love us; He's neither cold nor indifferent to our pain, and He proved this on the cross.[65]

On the cross, God Himself entered into our suffering to face its full blow so that we wouldn't have to. English writer Dorothy Sayers explained that on the cross, God had the "honesty and the courage to take His own medicine."[66] As sinners, there was a debt to be paid that we could never pay, but out of His immense love, Christ paid it. The Bible tells us that while we were still sinners, living in our rebellion as enemies of God, Christ entered into our suffering and died for us.[67] This is the emotional response our hearts are looking for. Knowing that God Himself entered into our suffering changes everything.

He didn't duck and run. He faced it when He didn't have to, and He did so out of His incredible love. In the book of Ephesians, it tells us that God did this not because of who we are, but because of who He is. It was out of His great love that He died for us.[68]

Perhaps you are like Elizabeth Anderson and find it offensive to be told that you are so sinful that God Himself had to die for you. In *The Portable Atheist*, Anderson writes:

> *If God is merciful and loving, why doesn't He forgive humanity for its sins straightaway, rather than demanding His 150 pounds of flesh, in the form of His own son? How could any loving father do that to his son? I find it hard to resist the conclusion that the God of the Bible is cruel and unjust and commands and permits us to be cruel and unjust to others.*[69]

Anderson assumes that because God is loving and merciful, He should just forgive people outright. It's simply a choice; if God wanted to, Anderson reasons, He could and therefore He certainly should. But do we know that He could simply choose to forgive everyone? While it is true that God is loving and merciful, He is also righteous and just and so He must do the right thing. Therefore, it would be morally wrong for God to forgive people without any recompense.

Imagine someone murdered one of your loved ones in cold blood. After months of litigation in a clear-cut case, the judge announces the verdict, saying: "Though you committed murder in cold blood, and deserve to be punished severely for it, you are forgiven. There will be no punishment. Go and live your life to the fullest!" Is this justice? Of course not, and you'd be right to be furious. Was this merciful and loving? Perhaps in a way, but in another major way, it was absolutely not loving towards the victim's loved ones. Justice was not upheld, and your loss was made into a mockery. In a similar way, to say that God should just "forgive" is a deep-seated failure to understand the notion of justice.

Considering human relationships can help us better understand why forgiveness requires suffering. If somebody wrongs you (perhaps they lie about you in a way that ruins your reputation or they steal money they can't repay), you have two options. You could seek retribution through vengeance or repayment, or you could take the loss, which is a form of suffering. They pay or you pay. Either way, the debt cannot be simply dismissed, and must be absorbed by someone. Similarly, our sin created a debt, and it was a debt that demanded payment.[70] The night before Jesus died, He desperately asked God the Father if there was some other way to pay the debt. There wasn't. Either He paid or we paid. But because God wanted to end evil and suffering without ending us, He paid it.[71] The cross proved once and for all that God is really on our side.[72]

Entering the Relationship

I mentioned before that evil and suffering never leave us where we are, and that they either move us towards God or away from Him.[73] Some respond like Ivan and want to get as far away from God as possible. But for many others, it brings them closer to God in a deep and intimate way. For a woman from my church, this is precisely what happened in the midst of every parent's worst nightmare. On the anniversary of the death of her three-month-old son, Cameron, she wrote:

> *Today marks the day that my heart broke so hard so fast that I couldn't breathe. It was the day that I knew what it was like for my whole body to scream. It shook the foundation of my faith to its very core. I begged God to change His mind every night, and every morning after, I realized He answered "no". It was also the day that began to strengthen my bond with my best friend in a way I never could have imagined. It was the day that made me so incredibly grateful for what I had. A beautiful boy that needed me now more than ever, a husband that stood like a rock when I couldn't, parents that dropped everything and came the moment they heard those unforgettable words "mom I need you". Family that came from everywhere to hold us. An amazing church family that was not only there that day, but has grown with us to support us through this journey. Friends, whether we'd talked that week or not in years, rallied to be there to walk with us. The outpouring of love that comes together in the good times is amazing, but truly life changing when it happens on your darkest day. Most importantly, I realized and am continuing to realize, that I serve a God that loves me. I don't know why [God allowed this to happen] . . . I don't need to. What I do know, is that God is faithful. He put people in my life to pull me through. He turned me to Jeff, when I could have so easily shut him out. He gave me the courage to have Charly, when I was terrified to ever try. He was patient with me, as I worked through my anger. He spared me from turning to anything that could hurt me and my family. He blessed me with Bren, who was [the one who] drove me to open my*

eyes every day. For that I am forever grateful. Mommy misses you bud, today and every day. I love you with all of my heart.

The terrible loss this mother experienced didn't result in her cursing God, but in her drawing closer to Him. Why? What is it that determines the direction we go when the darkness comes?

For those like Ivan, evil and suffering turn them away from God. They are completely disinterested in intellectual justifications for the existence of evil and suffering because it is emotionally gut wrenching. "Any God who allows this isn't good, no matter what!" they think. However, they've missed the thing that changes everything—they've missed the cross. If Ivan had even a glimpse of the true beauty of Jesus and God's love for us displayed on the cross, his emotional frustrations would have melted away by the overwhelming splendor and brilliance of Christ's glory. And when you've seen that, it changes you forever.

Hearing about God's great love and how far He was willing to go to save us can easily move us emotionally, and maybe even bring us to tears; however, unless it draws us into a relationship with Him, it still won't be enough. We must actually grab hold of His love or we will inevitably turn away from Him when evil and suffering come. Famous preacher Charles Spurgeon once spoke of how someone can grab hold of Christ's love by comparing it to entering through a door. On the outside of this door is written Matthew 10:32: "Whoever acknowledges me before others, I will also acknowledge before my Father in heaven."[74] So is that it? If you want

Christ's love, just muster up your best religious effort to walk through the door? No. Spurgeon, a complementarian, explained that once you've walked through the door, you would look back and see written above it John 15:16, "You did not choose me, but I chose you," and John 6:44, "No one can come to me unless the Father who sent me draws them."

When we first approach God, we think in terms of what we have to do to earn His favor. But once we've encountered the cross of Jesus, we see that the Gospel is actually the opposite of this; it's about what God has done for us so that we can be with Him.[75] This is why everyone who's gone through the door of salvation has come to realize that they are accepted by God, not because they are smarter, humbler, more moral, or even more spiritual than other people, but because of God alone who loved them and saved them. As C. S. Lewis once said, all of our moral effort must lead us to the vital moment when we turn to God and say, "You must do this. I can't."[76]

The Biblical view of evil and suffering is unique amongst all of the worldviews. Christianity offers an incomplete answer, while all other worldviews offer an insufficient one. While free will is a partial explanation, ignoring it entirely leads to determinism. The existence of Satan and other spiritual forces is a partial explanation and ignoring this leads to a serious failure to comprehend the true depths of evil in our world. Sometimes evil and suffering are the result of punishment or discipline, but as we saw in the book of Job, this isn't always the case and the good do die young. Sometimes evil and suffering are used to keep us from a greater evil, while other times they are used to bring God glory. However, in the end, all of these are only partial explanations, and evil and suffering are still ultimately a mystery to us, but *not* a blind mystery. Most importantly, the cross of Jesus proves that we can trust God when He says, "No eye has seen, nor ear heard, nor the heart of man imagined, what God has prepared for those who love Him." This is the hope we are offered. It doesn't promise to give us all the answers or even give us a comfortable life. But it will give us a hope that allows us to face anything while still praising and trusting God for who He is, not for what He gives us. It's a hope that will allow us to say as the Psalmist did:

> *Whom have I in heaven but you?*
> *And there is nothing on earth that I desire besides you.*
> *My flesh and my heart may fail,*
> *but God is the strength of my heart and my portion forever.*[77]

CHAPTER ELEVEN
The Evidence for God

"For since the creation of the world God's invisible qualities—his eternal power and divine nature—have been clearly seen, being understood from what has been made, so that people are without excuse."
— Romans 1:20

"In the absence of any other proof, the thumb alone would convince me of God's existence."
— Isaac Newton

So far, we have been comparing the theistic worldview (represented by the Christian narrative) with the atheistic worldview (represented by the Humanist narrative) to see which story offers a better explanation for human knowledge and experience, morality and human rights, evil and suffering, and the meaning of life. One narrative informs us that our intuitions are mostly trustworthy, while the other holds that most of them (if not all) are illusions put in place by evolution's natural selection. One says that evil and suffering are not a part of the created order, and we are right to be repulsed by their existence, while the other says they are as natural as air and water. One tells us that life has intrinsic meaning that comes from God, while the other believes that life has no meaning, though we can give it subjective meaning by living for things we deem meaningful. One says that this world is a broken and dim reflection of the world to come, while the other says this world is all there is. After examining atheism closely, it is difficult to avoid the conclusion that if God doesn't exist, morality and human rights are merely human conventions, evil and suffering are natural, and life has no real meaning. The only escape from this appears to be an appeal to first principles (self-evident truth) to ground our moral intuition, while at the same time awkwardly holding to a worldview that severely undermines our intuitions. Therefore, from a Humanistic perspective, it is difficult to avoid the conclusion that if God is dead, then everything is morally permitted.

Perhaps it doesn't matter, and this is just the cold, harsh truth of it all. After all, atheists have always prided themselves on facing reality boldly and honestly, no matter how dark or unpleasant it may be. Perhaps even if we preferred God's existence, the evidence just isn't there. Surely if an all-powerful, all-knowing God existed who wanted to prove His existence, He could have done it in a way that is plain and obvious to everyone. American scientist Carl Sagan posed this question when he asked why God hasn't settled the issue once and for all by doing something blatantly obvious, like engraving the Ten Commandments on the Moon or placing a hundred-kilometer crucifix in Earth's orbit for all to see. "Why should God be so clear in the Bible and so obscure in the world?" Sagan asked.[1] Humanist author Greg Epstein explains that it's not that atheists have made it their goal to mock religion, it's just that they have high standards when it comes to deciding whether a story is true or not. Those arguing for God's existence should be able to produce serious, credible, testable evidence to support their claim.[2] But since there is no credible evidence for the existence of God, it can only be accepted by blind faith.

At the beginning of this book, I said there were three major reasons for why I believe the Christian narrative: the philosophical, the historical, and the experiential. So far, we have looked at some of the philosophical arguments for God's existence and have briefly touched on the historical when addressing common atheistic arguments and misconceptions when they intersect. Since this is a book primarily arguing for the philosophical evidence for God's existence, it should come as no surprise that I strongly disagree about there being no credible evidence for God's existence. Aside from what we've already looked at so far, I believe there are a handful of powerful arguments that support God's existence. Let's look at a few of them.

Intelligent Design

Imagine that you are walking along a beach and notice a rock and a watch lying in the sand. What conclusions might you draw about these two objects and how would they differ? You begin examining the rock by digging around it and discover that it is actually the tip of a very large boulder that is buried deeply beneath the sand. You conclude that there is a good chance that this boulder has been there for a very long time, and that it wasn't designed, created, or placed by any human intelligence. You then examine the watch, noticing the face, minute and hour hands, and the numbers marked clearly in sequential order. Unlike the rock, you immediately perceive that the watch has been designed by an intellect with an intended purpose. So why did you conclude that the one is designed and the other is not?[3]

The ability to distinguish between the intelligent design of a watch and the lack of such in a rock is the foundation for what philosophers call *the teleological argument* for God. This argument was first developed by Aristotle and further advanced by eighteenth-century philosopher William Paley. Paley argued that evidence of design indicates a designer. When we inspect the watch, we perceive that it consists of several parts that are framed and put together for a purpose, and if just one of these mechanisms were removed, it would no longer function. Paley viewed the universe in this same sort of way, as a system of complex mechanisms designed and constructed to achieve a purpose.[4] For example, the human brain is an immensely technically-ordered mechanism that consists of billions of neurons connected in numerously complex ways, resulting in an astronomical number of different possible brain states and functions. The human brain is immensely more complex than any watch, so the argument follows that if we can recognize the watchmaker behind the watch, shouldn't we also recognize the creator behind the creation?

In *The Blind Watchmaker*, Richard Dawkins argues that our natural intuition of a designed universe is a false one, and we don't need a designer to explain organized complexity. He explains:

> *Biology is the study of complicated things that have the appearance of having been designed with a purpose . . . All appearances to the contrary, the only watchmaker in nature is the blind forces of physics . . . A true watchmaker has foresight: he designs his cogs and springs, and plans their interconnections, with a future purpose in his mind's eye. Natural selection, the blind, unconscious automatic process which Darwin discovered, and which we now know is the explanation for the existence and apparently purposeful form of all life, has no purpose in mind. It has no mind and no mind's eye. It does not plan for the future. It has no vision, no foresight, no sight at all. If it can be said to play the role of watchmaker in nature, it is the blind watchmaker.*[5]

Once again, though our intuitions tell us one thing, we dare not trust them since they've been misled by natural selection. This is why British molecular biologist Francis Crick warned that biologists must constantly keep in mind that what they see was not designed, but evolved.[6] Though the universe looks like a put-up job, it really isn't, since natural selection can fully explain the complex lifeforms we see today. But is the theory of unguided natural selection really capable of explaining the marvelous complexity in our world?

Irreducible Complexity

American biochemist Michael Behe caused a stir when he argued that systems exist at the biochemical level that are irreducibly complex.[7] These biological systems have mechanisms that have at least two interacting parts, which completely depend on one another for proper function. If either one of them is removed, the system will no longer work.[8] According to Behe, there are numerous examples of irreducibly complex systems within the biological world that could not have come about by gradual Darwinian evolution.[9] As we discussed earlier, evolution's natural selection works by random genetic mutation. All genetic changes that provide a survival advantage are passed on through the host's offspring, and over time end up replacing those who do not have the advantageous gene. However, if evolution works by small genetic changes over time, then how could these irreducibly complex systems have developed through small, successful modifications? After all, natural selection has no purpose, "no mind and no mind's eye. It does not plan for the future. It has no vision, no foresight, no sight at all."[10]

In the biological world, one of the clearest examples of an irreducibly complex system is the mammalian eye, which consists of numerous interworking parts and functions like a camera.[11] If life has evolved by purposeless, unguided chance through small beneficial mutations over time, then how could the eye have evolved? For an eye to give vision, there are a multitude of parts that need to be working simultaneously. Vision begins when light rays are reflected off an object and enter our eyes through the cornea (the clear outer covering of the eye). The cornea then refracts the rays through a round hole called the pupil. The colored part of our eye (the iris) opens and closes to make the pupil bigger or smaller, functioning as an adjustable shutter that shrinks and expands in order to let in just the right amount of light, so we can see in bright and dark conditions. The light rays then pass through the lens, which further bends the rays to focus them on the back of the eye. The retina is a thin layer of tissue at the back of the eye that contains millions of tiny, light-sensing nerve cells that detect color, motion, and fine detail. The small cells within the retina then convert the light into electrical impulses that are sent through the optic nerve to the brain where the image is reversed, processed, and produced.[12]

As complex as this might sound, it is only a basic explanation of how the eye actually works. In reality, the eye is much more complex, with numerous mechanisms at work. The point is, if the eye evolved slowly over time for the sole purpose of providing vision, then there appears to be a problem; namely, the numerous evolutionary steps would have had to lead to an advantage of some kind in order to have been preserved and passed down. Remember, natural selection is blind, so we can't think that it preserved these parts for the future purpose of one day constructing the eye. Generally, each mutation must have provided its host some sort of advantage in order to have been preserved.[13] The alternative is to assume that the eye evolved rapidly, which doesn't fit well with unguided natural selection.

Charles Darwin admitted that, at first glance, it seems ludicrous to think that something as complex as the human eye could have been formed through natural selection. Still, he believed that science would one day discover the evolutionary steps needed to get from a simple eye to a complex one.[14] Evolutionary biologist Stephen Jay Gould agreed with Darwin's conclusion, suggesting that the pre-evolved eye was used for something besides sight.[15] Richard Dawkins suggests that the eyes of ancient animals may have been used for 5 percent vision, which of course is better than total blindness.[16] The argument is, there very well may be a plausible scientific explanation for the evolution of the eye that we just haven't discovered yet.

Philosopher Alvin Plantinga has pointed out that Dawkins's explanation for the eye's evolution confuses the question "What good is 5 percent of an eye?" with "What good is 5 percent vision?" There is a monumental difference between the two. What scientific evidence is Dawkins relying on that suggests that 5 percent of an eye is somehow able to produce 5 percent vision? As Plantinga points out, as far as we know, there may not be any 5 percent of an eye that is capable of producing 5 percent vision.[17] While biologists like Gould and Dawkins have offered some theories, based on observing other creatures' eyes for what the various stages of the eye's evolution might look like, their theories boil down to guesswork at best and do not demonstrate that Behe's argument of irreducible complexity is wrong. In Dawkins's book *The Blind Watchmaker,* he admits that the larger the evolutionary change, the less probable it becomes; however, he tells us that his feeling is that scientists will one day discover the evolutionary steps needed for the evolution of the eye.[18] While it is fine for Dawkins to *feel* this way, it hardly proves what he set out to prove, which is a "universe without design."[19]

American philosopher Paul Draper pointed out that Behe's argument of irreducible complexity fails to provide irrefutable evidence that it is impossible for these irreducibly complex systems to have evolved through natural selection. For all we know, there very well might be an explanation for how it happened and we just haven't discovered it yet.[20] In order for Behe to prove that the human eye could not have evolved through unguided natural selection, he would have to show that it is impossible, or at least monumentally unlikely, to have evolved in a Darwinian fashion.[21] Alvin Plantinga agrees with Draper's argument since we have no way of measuring the probability of Behe's argument.[22] However, even though Behe's argument fails to show that it is impossible for natural selection to account for systems that appear to be irreducibly complex (like the mammalian eye), neither has anyone been able to prove that these systems are not irreducibly complex. We will return to this argument later, but for now, the takeaway is that Behe's argument of irreducible complexity is scientifically inconclusive.

A Universe Tuned for Life

Prior to the 1960s, many astrophysicists held to the steady-state theory, which claims that the universe has always existed and will continue to forever. But then scientists discovered background radiation from the big bang, which almost entirely put an end to the steady-state theory. The big bang theory claims that our universe came about billions of years ago when all of the matter in the universe was compressed into an extremely small entity (called a singularity). Then something like an explosion happened and all of the matter shot out and collected into clumps, which eventually resulted in the galaxies, stars, planets, and organic life that we see today. With this new theory discrediting the steady-state theory, many turned to the oscillating universe theory, which claimed that our universe moves in an eternal cycle between the big bang and the big crunch. After a big bang occurs, matter expands for billions of years until gravity eventually pulls it all back into a singularity, which results in another big bang. However, the oscillating universe theory lost its sway when the Hubble Space Telescope launched in 1990 and discovered that the universe was expanding at a steady rate.[23] The result is that the universe will continue to expand forever until it is a vast wasteland of frozen nothingness (also called the big freeze or heat death). Most importantly, this strongly indicates that our universe is not eternal.

If our universe had a beginning and will have an end, then something must exist that is timeless. But what could that be? We know that our universe isn't eternal, because it began to exist. All things that begin to exist have causes, and because nothing is caused by itself, something must have caused our universe. This is the idea behind Kalam's Cosmological Argument, which was developed by both Aristotle and Thomas Aquinas. The idea holds that there must be an uncaused cause or an unmoved mover—someone or something that exists outside of time that created our finely tuned universe.

Building upon *the teleological argument* (evidence of design indicates a designer), the fine-tuning argument observes the universe and sees numerous, highly-improbable cosmic coincidences that give the appearance of having been designed. Francis Collins, scientist and director of the Human Genome Project, explains the incredibly fine-tuned nature of the universe, saying:

> *When you look from the perspective of a scientist at the universe, it looks as if it knew we were coming. There are 15 constants—the gravitational constant, various constants about the strong and weak nuclear force, etc.—that have precise values. If any one of those constants was off by even one part in a million, or in some cases, by one part in a million million, the universe could not have actually come to the point where we see it. Matter would not have been able to coalesce, there would have been no galaxy, stars, planets or people. Some have said that it is as if there were a large number of dials that all had to be tuned to within extremely narrow limits—and they were. It seems extremely unlikely that this would happen by chance.*[24]

According to Paul Davies, physicist, cosmologist, and astrobiologist, "Scientists are slowly waking up to an inconvenient truth; which is, the universe looks suspiciously like a fix."[25] Davies explains that for over forty years, physicists and cosmologists have been quietly assembling examples of all-too-convenient "coincidences" concerning the fundamental laws of the universe that are necessary for life to exist. By changing just one of these, the consequences would be lethal for biological life.[26] In a 1987 BBC documentary, Davies explains:

> *The really amazing thing is not that life on Earth is balanced on a knife-edge, but that the entire universe is balanced on a knife-edge. You see, even if you dismiss mankind as just a mere hiccup in the great scheme of things, the fact remains that the entire universe seems unreasonably suited to the existence of life—almost contrived—you might say a "put-up job".*[27]

Scientist Stephen Hawking pointed out that life is only possible because the universe is expanding at just the right rate to avoid recollapse.[28] Explaining the delicate nature of our universe, Richard Dawkins writes: "We live not only on a friendly planet but also in a friendly universe . . . Physicists have calculated that, if the laws and constants of physics had been even slightly different, the universe would have developed in such a way that life would have been impossible."[29] Without a doubt, the universe gives the appearance of having been fine-tuned for life. This is why distinguished cosmologist and atheist Fred Hoyle, who has been accused of supporting intelligent design, concluded that the fine-tuning argument was so compelling that it was *almost* beyond question. It was, Hoyle said, as if "a super-intellect has monkeyed with physics."[30]

If the universe appears to be fine-tuned, then we should ask ourselves which worldview offers a better explanation for it. If theism is true, then the fine-tuning of the universe is not at all surprising, since a designer who intended for there to be life would have tuned the conditions for it. However, under atheism, the fine-tuning of the universe is highly surprising since it is attributed to blind, highly improbable, unintentional chance.[31] Therefore, isn't theism a better explanation for the fine-tuning of the universe?

Astronomical Improbability

Despite the overwhelming odds naturalism faces, atheists tend to find the fine-tuning argument uncompelling. Realizing the enormous improbabilities, atheist philosophers have come up with potential ways to lessen the odds against them. One way is by completely negating the relevancy of the odds. This argument states, "It doesn't matter if the odds are against us. The fact is, we are here having this conversation, so it obviously must have happened, regardless of how unlikely it was."[32]

Canadian philosopher John Leslie compares the probability of a finely-tuned universe to a man who is sentenced to death by a firing squad of fifty expert marksmen. They all fire at the man from six feet away, and somehow all miss. Like the fine-tuning argument, there are two rational explanations. First, it is possible that even an expert marksman could miss from that close, so it is technically possible that all fifty of them just happened to miss at the same time. The chances are incredibly low, but it obviously happened this way because if it hadn't, the man wouldn't be around to ponder it. However, no one in their right mind would bet on these kinds of odds, nor is this the best explanation. A better explanation is to conclude that the chance of fifty expert marksmen missing from 6 feet away is so astronomically improbable, they must have conspired to miss.[33] Similarly, while it might be *technically* possible that our finely tuned universe came about by random chance, it makes no sense to bet on those odds.

In *The God Delusion*, Richard Dawkins argues that the probability of the universe being fine-tuned for biological life from blind chance alone is not astronomically unlikely, since there may be trillions of universes in existence. While the odds of just one universe being fine-tuned for life by blind chance is extremely low, given that there are a vast multitude of universes, it was bound to happen that at least one of them would be. Considering we are here, pondering the fine-tuned nature of the universe, it is obvious that we happen to be in one that is, or else we wouldn't be here pondering it.[34] While it is technically possible that God could exist, we don't need Him in order to explain the existence of our universe, its fine-tuning, or biological life. Since Darwinian natural selection is capable of producing improbable things on an enormous scale, God is simply out of a job.[35] Not only that, but God's existence is incredibly improbable, even more so than naturalistic theories. Therefore, the multiverse theory successfully solves the fine-tuning problem without the need of an even more improbable designer.

It has been said that the chance of life coming about from unguided Darwinian evolution is about as likely as a tornado going through a junkyard and assembling a fully operational Boeing 747. However, Richard Dawkins argues that God's existence is even more improbable than that, and so God is the ultimate Boeing 747.[36] Any God capable of producing the marvels of the universe (fine-tuned and all) would have to be even more complex than the universe He created. A God who is capable of continuously monitoring and controlling every particle in the universe cannot possibly be simple. Therefore, by intelligent design's own line of reasoning, God's existence cannot serve as an explanation for our universe since it requires a mammoth explanation in its own right.[37] In comparison, any naturalistic theory (including the extravagant multiverse theory) is by default more probable than the God hypothesis and should be preferred.[38]

But is the God hypothesis actually more complex than all naturalistic theories? Better yet, is God complex at all? Alvin Plantinga doesn't think so. Even by Dawkins's own definition of complexity, God isn't complex, since he defines something as complex if it has parts that are "arranged in a way that is unlikely to have arisen by chance alone."[39] The Christian God has no parts at all, being neither material nor a part of the created order. John 4:24 says that God is Spirit, which is why Christians have traditionally held that God is not a material being and is more like a mind than anything else.[40] Nevertheless, Dawkins misunderstands intelligent design's argument; the goal is not to give a complete accounting for the origin of organized complexity, but only one manifestation of it; namely, the material universe, and biology is no different in this regard.[41]

Atheists believe that looking to God as the explanatory source of our universe merely kicks the can down the road. If everything requires a causal explanation, as the intelligent design argument states, then why think that God is immune to this regress?[42] Even children recognize this problem when they ask, "but who made God?"[43] Since theists have no answer to this, they usually just cite a verse about God being mysterious in nature, which completely dodges the issue; it is an anti-science conversation stopper. Offering an explanation by invoking something that is itself unexplained, amounts to no explanation at all.[44] Therefore, God cannot serve as an explanation for the existence of our universe.

Demanding an explanation for God's existence is only reasonable if we reject the existence of self-evident truth and believe that everything must be proven. However, as we discussed in chapter one, this is impossible; there must be some knowledge that is not the result of other knowledge. From the theist's perspective, asking for a causal explanation for God's existence is similar to asking why two plus two equals four. Theism is not alone in this, as all casual explanations are incapable of providing an ultimate explanation for reality. To expect theism to provide an ultimate explanation for everything when naturalism cannot is a double standard. For instance, take the multiverse theory; what causes these universes to pop into existence? Is there some sort of universe generating machine, and if so, where did that come from, and isn't that more complex than the universes it spits out? The truth is, whether you believe in God or not, you cannot give a full account of everything—something has to exist necessarily. The disagreement is over whether that something is God or nature. As Alvin Plantinga elegantly puts it, "Explanations come to an end; for theism they come to an end in God."

When it comes to an ultimate explanation of everything, both views must appeal to some form of mystery, though it is often only the theist who is faulted for this. As we briefly discussed in chapter five, this criticism is inconsistent. In one breath, atheists fault theists for appealing to mystery when accounting for God's eternal nature, since such appeals "shut down conversation and stifle scientific inquiry." However, in the next breath, they fault theists for refusing to live with uncertainty by forcing their narrative explanations, due to their psychological need to understand everything. Demonstrating this, A. C. Grayling explains how scientists have no need for such certainty:

> *The scientific mindset, which welcomes the open-endedness of uncertainty because it is an invitation to enquiry and discovery, is the opposite of this. Notably, a religious explanation of how the*

world began, why it exists, and where we are all going to end, can be given in twenty minutes or less. It takes years to master the rudiments of physics.[45]

While atheists have no problem appealing to mystery when it comes to the issues their worldview cannot explain, they hold theists to a separate, unachievable standard. For instance, atheists see unguided natural selection as the cause for the biological complexity within nature, but realize they have no working model for the cosmological complexity seen in the universe; yet this doesn't bother them. Nevertheless, atheists like Dawkins hold out hope that some kind of naturalistic multiverse theory will do for physics what Darwinism did for biology.[46] But is this any more probable than intelligent design? I don't see how. Dawkins's argument basically boils down to, "philosophical naturalism is possible, and so therefore it is true."[47] Think back to chapter one—while it is technically possible that the universe popped into existence five seconds ago and all of our memories are fabricated, no one in their right mind is going to believe it simply because no one can disprove it. The fact is, we have no idea how to scientifically measure the probability of either unguided evolution or intelligent design, so we need something else.[48]

Weighing the Arguments

What should we conclude about intelligent design? Is it a knockdown argument against atheism? Can the theist's victory celebration begin? I don't think so. Alvin

Plantinga doesn't think so either. In his book, *Where the Conflict Really Lies*, he concludes that though the arguments for intelligent design do offer some support for theism, they offer only mild support, since all arguments for it are ultimately escapable.[49] For every argument favoring intelligent design, there is a plausible, rational, naturalistic argument to avoid its conclusions, and the same goes for arguments in favor of atheism. This means that we cannot prove one worldview to be right over the other purely by means of scientific or philosophical argument alone. This also means sweeping statements that declare atheism or theism to be completely ignorant and unjustifiable positions should be avoided. So, is that it? In the end, no one can really know, and so we should all embrace agnosticism? No, I don't think so. In the last chapter, I want to show you another way—what I believe is the only way for determining our worldview.

CHAPTER TWELVE
Believe the Better Story

> *"I believe in Christianity as I believe that the Sun has risen, not only because I see it, but because by it I see everything else."*
> — C.S. Lewis

> *"Merely having an open mind is nothing; the object of opening a mind, as of opening the mouth, is to shut it again on something solid."*
> — G. K. Chesterton

The arguments for intelligent design can be persuasive, and do indeed offer some support for theism; however, as we saw in the last chapter, they are ultimately rationally avoidable and so they cannot be used as conclusive proofs for God's existence. Yet the vast majority of people throughout history have been confident that a higher power exists. According to a PEW research study from 2015, nearly 90% of people living in the United States believe in God or a universal spirit.[1] But if God's existence cannot be proven, why do most of us continue to believe in Him anyway?

For many, belief in God is largely based upon a deeply personal spiritual encounter that has forever changed them. However, for those who haven't had this experience, these anecdotal accounts are not very compelling. Though many people truly believe they have had a religious experience, atheists often argue that psychology, not theology, offers a better explanation. For instance, as scientist Carl Sagan pointed out, there have been over one million reported UFO sightings since 1947, but as far as we know, none of them correspond to actual alien encounters. In *The End of Faith*, Sam Harris explains how we normally consider it to be mad, psychotic, or delusional to hold beliefs that have no rational justification. However, he explains, "When their beliefs are extremely common we call them 'religious'." Harris's point is, just because these beliefs are common does not mean they are rational. Theology, he claims, is little more than a "branch of human ignorance," and in fact, is "ignorance with wings."[2] Therefore, according to this thinking, even though people within every culture claim to have had some sort of supernatural or paranormal experience, human psychology (usually evolutionary psychology) is much better equipped to explain it.[3]

Common Sense

While many philosophers tend to agree that all proofs for God's existence are rationally avoidable, many theists argue that the reason most people believe in God's existence is because it is something we can't *not* know; it is a self-evident truth. If this is true, then it is just as misguided for atheists to demand proof for God's existence as it would be to demand proof for the existence of the laws of logic. As we've discussed already, at least some truths must be self-evident for anything else to be true. At least some truths must be common sense.

Have you ever been in an argument with someone who said you were wrong because "it's just common sense"? This is the *common-sense* fallacy, and it is often used as a shortcut for defending a position without having to justify it. However, not all appeals to common sense are fallacious, for true common sense doesn't actually need to be proven. As we discussed in chapter one, when we talk about self-evident truths, we are referring to the same sort of thing—the bedrock of our knowledge. Taken this way, these self-evident intuitions do not need to be proven, and to demand proof for them is actually perverse. For instance, the following are self-evident truths: belief in the past, consciousness, logic and mathematics, love is real (it is more than a simple biochemical reaction in our brain), life has objective meaning and purpose, the existence of human rights, good and evil, free will, and music and art are reflections of true beauty—they are not, as Steven Pinker once said, merely "auditory cheesecake."[4] Just as these basic intuitions are self-evidently true, Christians believe that our belief in God is also self-evidently true, and therefore it does not need to be proven.

While many atheists find this argument to be weak and see it as blind faith, from the theist's perspective, it's not anymore blind to believe in God than it is to believe in the rest of our intuitions. After all, we all have starter beliefs from which we build our worldview; the disagreement is over which beliefs are the right starter beliefs. Ultimately, whether we find evidential arguments for or against God's existence to be compelling is determined by our starter beliefs, and it is these beliefs that determine our worldview.

Trusting our Intuitions

Existentialist philosopher Jean-Paul Sartre once said, "That God does not exist, I cannot deny. That my whole being cries out for God, I cannot forget."[5] According to the Bible, our whole being cries out for God because it was made to. We were built for God, and His absence causes us to long for Him.[6] In Romans chapter one, the apostle Paul explains that God's existence is plainly known by all because His invisible qualities have been on full display since the creation of the world.[7] The book of Psalms says, "The heavens declare the glory of God, and the sky above proclaims his handiwork."[8] This would explain why spiritual awareness comes naturally for us, and why it seems to take a considerable intellectual effort to shake it. If God's existence is self-evident, then we have a rational explanation for why the vast majority of humanity has, in at least some manner, believed that God exists. However, what about those who don't believe He exists? Doesn't their disbelief prove that God's existence isn't self-evident after all?

In the book of Psalms, we find the most commonly-used verse by internet apologists in the entire Bible: "The fool says in his heart, 'There is no God.'"[9] Too often, this is incorrectly understood to say that atheists are unintelligent or stupid, which of course is not true at all. When the Bible speaks of atheists being fools, it is not a reference to their lack of knowledge, but, as Romans chapter one explains, their suppression of it.[10] In other words, atheists are not stupid; rather, they are willingly repressing what they know to be true.

Atheists strongly disagree with the Bible's diagnosis for their unbelief in God. Instead, they argue that our belief in God is a byproduct of evolution's natural selection. Belief in God exists because it made our ancestors happier, less selfish, and resulted in a better chance of survival; it is an accidental byproduct of evolutionary mechanisms that provided an adaptive advantage—the idea of *agency detection*. For example, our ancestors were constantly under threat of being eaten by wild animals, and the ones who survived were always cautious and aware of their potential threat. From an evolutionary standpoint, it is worth spending the extra energy to avoid a threat that isn't there for the occasion when one actually is. Taking the longer road home is but a minor inconvenience compared to being eaten alive by a predator. The same evolutionary traits that cause agency detection when nothing is there also causes us to believe in God when He's not there. This means, they argue, that our intuitional belief in God is a false positive resulting from our evolutionary history, and so it is not a reliable indicator that He actually exists.[11] Consequently, both theists and atheists have plausible explanations for humanity's belief in God. However, when comparing the two, we should pause to ask which theory has more explanatory power. Which theory fits best with reality as we experience it?

A naturalistic evolutionary account of human nature essentially explains away most of our intuitions. What our brains tell us about love, beauty, art, free will, consciousness, the meaning of life, human suffering, human rights, good and evil, and God's existence are nothing more than evolutionary illusions put in place to aid our survival. As we saw earlier, evolution's natural selection does not concern itself with truth content, but the survival of the host, and so, for the most part, our intuitions are untrustworthy and can be better understood by evolutionary psychology. However, as we saw in chapter eight, if our reasoning faculties center on what we need to survive and not what is true, then why should we trust them? If we cannot trust our belief-forming faculties to tell us the truth about our most basic intuitions, then we should seriously question whether we can trust them at all, especially when it comes to our power to reason. A worldview that invokes the power of reason even as it destroys it, is a worldview we should seriously question putting our faith in.[12]

Blind Faith

If you pay attention to the popular atheist writers, you'll quickly learn that faith is bad—really bad—probably even evil, if such a thing could exist.[13] Believing in God is ignorant, childish, and irrational. Why? As we've seen, all of the major arguments for God's existence do not work as conclusive proofs, so believing in His existence is equivalent to believing in fairies, unicorns, Santa Claus, or The Flying Spaghetti Monster. For belief in God to be rational, there would need to be some major, compelling scientific evidence, but since there isn't any, faith is blind.

In an interview on the Daily Show with Jon Stewart, Richard Dawkins explained that faith means to believe without evidence, and you shouldn't believe anything without evidence.[14] Unfortunately, Stewart never asked what evidence Dawkins had to support his conclusion that we shouldn't believe anything without evidence. In his book *The God Delusion*, Dawkins goes even further, saying, "Faith is the great cop-out, the great excuse to evade the need to think and evaluate evidence. Faith is belief in spite of, even perhaps because of, the lack of evidence." Or, as Mark Twain famously put it, "Faith is believing what you know ain't so."[15] The point they repeatedly make is that religious faith is blind.

While some religions pride themselves on holding to a form of blind faith (Fideism), Christian faith couldn't be further from this. Biblical faith isn't "believing what you know ain't so," rather, it's continuing to believe in what you've come to know is so. C. S. Lewis once explained how our minds are not completely ruled by reason, but instead are greatly influenced by our passions and emotions. Lewis viewed faith as the warden of our emotions that kept them in check. For instance, he explained that by his reason he was perfectly convinced by good evidence that trained surgeons understood how to use anesthetics properly before surgery. However, when he was down on the operating table his emotions would flare up and cause a child-like panic to set in, leading him to question whether the anesthetics would actually work before they began cutting. In other words, Lewis lost his faith in anesthetics. It was not his reason that was causing his loss of faith, on the contrary, his faith was based on reason. It was his imagination and emotions that caused his doubt. The battle, Lewis explained, "is between faith and reason on one side and emotion and imagination on the other."[16]

For many Christians, doubt is a recurring condition of our faith as we question and wrestle with it. Lewis confessed that as a Christian he would sometimes have moods that caused him to think that Christianity was very improbable; however, as an atheist, he had moods where Christianity looked terribly probable. Mignon McLaughlin had it right when she said, "There's something in every atheist, itching to believe, and something in every believer, itching to doubt."[17] Lewis understood the power his emotions had to influence him against his reason, and so he saw faith as the means of holding onto things that our reason has once accepted in spite of our changing moods. Our moods will always cause a rebellion against our reason, and so faith is the only weapon we have to combat the uprising. According to Lewis, without faith, we can be neither a sound Christian nor even a sound atheist, but will be a creature wavering about, with our beliefs dependent on the weather and the state of our digestion.[18] Therefore, we all, atheist and theist alike, live by faith.

Living by Faith

In *The God Argument,* A. C. Grayling rejects the claim that all beliefs are based on faith. He argues that faith is not needed in order to believe in science and the use of reason. Science, he argues, "is always open to challenge and refutation, faith is not."[19] But as we discussed in chapter one, what Grayling is really advocating is scientism, not science, as he misunderstands the fragile nature of scientific certainty. All inductive reasoning (the foundation of science) rests upon unprovable beliefs that must be taken on faith. Despite all of his confidence in the power of scientific inquiry, even a staunch Darwinist such as Richard Dawkins admits that it is possible that Darwinian Theory could be disproven if new facts come to light that overturn or alter it beyond recognition.[20] In the same way we cannot prove that God exists, neither can we prove that any scientific theory is absolutely infallible. Scientists operate by faith all the time by holding belief in a theory until it is either grounded by further evidence or replaced by a better theory. For this reason, science will always have an element of faith.[21]

Hebrews 11:1 defines faith as, "the assurance of things hoped for, the conviction of things not seen."[22] We should recognize that many of our best scientific endeavors attempt to understand what cannot be seen, and so naturally involve an element of faith. In the early 1900s,

Albert Einstein developed his theory of general relativity. However, even by 1930 one of his core predictions still had not yet been observed, rendering the theory unproven. Still, Einstein felt perfectly comfortable believing in his theory anyway, since its explanatory power and rational consistency were enough to justify it. Though it had not yet been proven, Einstein had faith that it would one day be confirmed, and so he was comfortable believing it on the basis of partial confirmation.[23]

Commenting on the close relationship between faith and science, David Berlinski writes, "We can make no sense either of daily life or the physical sciences in terms of things that are seen. The past has gone to the place where the past goes; the future has not arrived. We remember the one; we count on the other. If this is not faith, what, then, is it?"[24] C. S. Lewis once talked about faith in this way when he explained how most of what we accept as truth is based upon belief in authority. He wrote:

Do not be scared by the word authority. Believing things on authority only means believing them because you have been told them by someone you think trustworthy. Ninety-nine per cent of the things you believe are believed on authority. I believe there is such a place as New York. I have not seen it myself. I could not prove by abstract reasoning that there must be such a place. I believe it because reliable people have told me so. The ordinary man believes in the Solar System, atoms, evolution, and the circulation of the blood on authority—because the scientists say

> *so. Every historical statement in the world is believed on authority. None of us has seen the Norman Conquest or the defeat of the Armada. None of us could prove them by pure logic as you prove a thing in mathematics. We believe them simply because people who did see them have left writings that tell us about them: in fact, on authority. A man who jibbed at authority in other things as some people do in religion would have to be content to know nothing all his life.*[25]

In agreement with Lewis's basic idea, Sam Harris makes clear the misleading distinction that people commonly make between knowledge and belief. He writes:

> *While we often make a conventional distinction between "belief" and "knowledge," these categories are actually quite misleading. Knowing that George Washington was the first president of the United States and believing the statement "George Washington was the first president of the United States" amount to the same thing . . . Most of our beliefs have come to us in just this form: as statements that we accept on the assumption that their source is reliable, or because the sheer number of sources rules out any significant likelihood of error. In fact, everything we know outside of our personal experience is the result of our having encountered specific linguistic propositions—the sun is a star; Julius Caesar was a Roman emperor; broccoli is good for you—and found no reason (or means) to doubt them.*[26]

No view of God can be conclusively proven: theistic or otherwise. As we've seen, the skeptic has a plausible, reasonable, way out for the philosophical, historical, and experiential arguments for God. But the same goes for their alternative atheistic arguments. However, just as with science, the fact that something cannot be proven doesn't mean we can't place our trust in a theory without having final confirmation of its certainty. Explaining how it all comes down to faith, Alister McGrath writes:

> *When Dawkins speaks of "proof," he actually means something rather weaker, such as "good reasons for believing that something is right," while realizing that it cannot actually be proved at present. This is not a radical or controversial statement, but simply an accurate summary of the difficulties faced by the natural sciences as they seek to offer the best account of what we know about the world. It is simply not true that scientists believe theories because they have been "proved." They believe them because they represent the best explanation of what may be observed.*[27]

What then is faith? Faith is putting our trust in the best account of what we know about the world. Therefore, despite common misconceptions, biblical faith is not blind. It does not believe in things despite the evidence, but because of it.

Doubt

At this point, we should pause to examine the relationship between faith and doubt. After all, wasn't the entire point of the New Testament story of "doubting Thomas" that it is more blessed to believe without evidence than with?[28] This is a common misinterpretation and is mostly due to misunderstanding the difference between doubt and skepticism. Though "doubting Thomas" often receives a bad rap for only believing after he saw the evidence for Christ's resurrection, we sometimes forget that none of the other disciples believed either until they saw the risen Jesus. When Jesus confronts Thomas, He challenges him to believe and offers evidence to help with his unbelief. Throughout Jesus' ministry, whenever the crowds ask for signs and wonders, He sometimes provides them and sometimes withholds them. The difference in Jesus' response is due to the heart of the listeners.

In Mark chapter nine, a man brings his son before Jesus with the hope that He will heal him. The man pleads with Jesus, "Have mercy on us and help us, *if you can.*"[29] Jesus responds, "What do you mean, 'If I can'?" Jesus is God, of course He can. Jesus then tells the man that everything is possible for the one who believes. But what does the man do in response to this? Does he just muster up faith in something that violates his reason? No, that is impossible, and as atheists rightly point out, it is disingenuous anyway. Instead, the man cries out to Jesus, "I do believe, but help me overcome my unbelief!"[30] Jesus' response is remarkable. He doesn't turn to him and say, "shame on you for failing to believe in what your reason cannot accept!" Instead, Jesus turns and heals his son, which is an answer to both of the man's requests.

In this case, Jesus offered the man further evidence to help strengthen his faith. However, he doesn't always respond this way. At other times, Jesus responds in anger and refuses to give additional signs and wonders. This is precisely what occurs in Matthew 16 when the religious leaders approach Jesus demanding further proof of Him being God. Instead of signs and wonders, He gives them nothing. Why the different response? The key is the difference between doubt and willful unbelief (skepticism). We must remember that the religious leaders had already seen many signs and wonders performed by Jesus, so their doubt had hardened into skeptical (deeply biased) unbelief. Unlike the man who genuinely wanted to believe in what he sensed to be true, the religious leaders demanded more signs not because they wanted to believe, but because they wanted to continue justifying their unbelief. Willful unbelief (skepticism) is the choice to reject evidence because our heart does not want to believe it, whereas doubt is the genuine pursuit of evidences to find the truth. Therefore, doubt is not the antithesis of faith, but pride. The Bible does not condemn genuine doubt, but biased, skeptical unbelief.

Not all Christians wrestle honestly with their doubts. There are Christians who ignore their doubts, either out of laziness, apathy, or fear that it is a sin to doubt. This rightly perturbs atheists and furthers their belief that Christianity is an anti-intellectual worldview based upon blind faith. However, no matter our worldview, wrestling with our doubts is the only way to forge our beliefs into something that can endure. Tim Keller explains the importance of struggling with our doubts, saying:

A faith without some doubts is like a human body without any antibodies in it. People who blithely go through life too busy or indifferent to ask hard questions about why they believe as they do will find themselves defenseless against either the experience of tragedy or the probing questions of a smart skeptic. A person's faith can collapse almost overnight if she has failed over the years to listen patiently to her own doubts, which should only be discarded after long reflection. Believers should acknowledge and wrestle with doubts — not only their own but their friends' and neighbors'. It is no longer sufficient to hold beliefs just because you inherited them. Only if you struggle long and hard with objections to your faith will you be able to provide grounds for your beliefs to skeptics, including yourself, that are plausible rather than ridiculous or offensive. And, just as important for our current situation, such a process will lead you, even after you come to a position of strong faith, to respect and understand those who doubt.[31]

Keller is right. Both believers and skeptics need to work at being open and honest with their doubts, while seeking to understand opposing worldviews in their strongest form. When we present other people's beliefs in their weakest form, we show our bias and insecurity with our own beliefs. When we carry on this way, we show that we have little interest in truth, but only in justifying our emotions and what we want to be true.

A Circle of False Beliefs

As we've discussed, grandiose condemnations of religious belief are philosophically bankrupt. So why then do so many prominent atheist writers use arguments that have been defeated long ago? While some of this may be due to a genuine misunderstanding, many of the writers who use these defeated arguments have been educated enough to know better. Many of them even turn to ridicule and contempt for any view that differs from their own. Alvin Plantinga believes one possible reason for this is that their atheism is merely a form of carrying on adolescent rebellion. Another option he suggests (which is consistent with the first), is that they don't actually know of any good reasons or arguments for their views, so they simply resort to schoolyard tactics.[32] I think philosopher David Hume had it right when he concluded that people who behave this way are being driven by their passions, not reason.

If our natural, unchecked tendency is to be controlled by our desires and not reason, then this explains why those who have not honestly wrestled with their doubts never truly abandon weak arguments. What often happens, in my experience, is that when an argument is shown to be weak or inconclusive, they simply move onto the next argument without ever acknowledging the previous one to be weak or defeated. After this process continues on for some time, with weak argument after weak argument being dismantled, the conversation moves back to the original argument, which is yet again presented as an argument that was never defeated.[33] If people mostly determine their worldview based upon reason, then this behavior is puzzling; however, if people tend to cling to their worldview based upon their emotional desires, then this makes perfect sense. If we are honest, we must acknowledge that we are all deeply biased when it comes to views that are not our own.

If you remain unconvinced, consider what Harvard biologist Richard Lewontin, an atheist himself, had to say on the matter:

Our willingness to accept scientific claims that are against common sense is the key to an understanding of the real struggle between science and the supernatural. We take the side of science in spite of the patent absurdity of some of its constructs, in spite of its failure to fulfill many of its extravagant promises of health and life, in spite of the tolerance of the scientific community for unsubstantiated just-so stories, because we have a prior commitment, a commitment to materialism. It is not that the methods and institutions of science somehow compel us to accept a material explanation of the phenomenal world but, on the contrary, that we are forced by our [commitment] . . . to material causes to create an apparatus of investigation and a set of concepts that produce material explanations, no matter how counterintuitive, no matter how mystifying to the uninitiated. Moreover, that materialism is absolute, for we cannot allow a divine foot in the door.[34]

Notice what Lewontin is saying. He is admitting that he and those who think like him are completely selective in their skepticism. They are hostile to belief in God because it opposes the worldview they so desperately want to be true. Their skepticism only goes one way, which causes them to cling to their dogma in the face of opposing evidence even when it forces them into absurdities.³⁵

A selective skepticism that raises the bar for other beliefs well beyond the height of its own is an embrace of blind faith. This kind of selective bias not only contributes to the warfare model between science and religion, but also leads to an atmosphere of hostility and incivility that shuts down conversation and honest inquiry—the very thing that skepticism typically prides itself in supporting. Instead, skeptics should acknowledge that all beliefs (including their own) are biased, unprovable, and rationally avoidable, which would be a great step towards achieving civility in a diverse society. Only when we are able to present opposing arguments in their strongest and most compelling form will we be able to attempt to engage others responsibly and fairly.³⁶

When we come to recognize the limitations of human knowledge, it will not only lead to more humility with our own beliefs, but deeper respect for those who do not share our beliefs. This doesn't mean we shouldn't argue for what we believe is true, it simply means we must recognize the enormous difficulty we all face in approaching arguments openly, rationally, and without bias. When it comes to doubting other people's beliefs, we must hold our own beliefs to the same level of doubt.³⁷ Doing this will lead, as Alister McGrath says, to a greater humility in both religious and antireligious advocacy.³⁸ While reasoning and empirical evidence are useful, they are simply incapable of conclusively determining our worldview.³⁹ This means that the choice is not between faith and reason, but between faith and faith. The question is then, which worldview should we put our faith in?

If our worldview is largely based upon our emotional commitments, then are we doomed to believe whatever our passions dictate? I am not convinced we are. While every argument for God's existence is rationally avoidable, I believe the combined weight of theism's explanatory power can be potent.[40] Instead of seeing each individual argument as a single determining proof, their collective force can be compelling enough to rattle us. Still, reason alone isn't enough to determine which worldview we will choose, and so we must look to something else. We must look to our intuition and make an existential wager.

Pascal's Wager

The idea that we should wager belief in God, instead of belief in no God, is called Pascal's Wager, after French philosopher Blaise Pascal. The common representation of Pascal's wager usually goes something like this: when it comes to God's existence, it makes more sense to wager on belief in God. After all, if we live betting on the existence of God, we have everything to gain: eternal happiness, reward, and joy. But if there turns out to be no God, we've only missed out on enjoying some of the world's frivolous behavior. However, if we bet on God not existing and end up being wrong, then we have lost everything and face an eternity of suffering and punishment in Hell. Therefore, it is wiser to bet on God's existence over his nonexistence.

While this argument is convincing for many, as Richard Dawkins rightly points out, Pascal's Wager, when understood this way, isn't an argument for genuine belief in God, but for feigning belief in God—we cannot force ourselves to believe in something our reason cannot accept. Though we could decide to engage in religious activity, as Dawkins rightly explains, the God of the Bible is not interested in mere religious activity, but genuine belief. An omniscient God would surely be able to see right through our disingenuous behavior, thus making Pascal's Wager a useless strategy.[41]

While Dawkin's critique is reasonable, Christian apologist Ravi Zacharias argues that Dawkin's depiction of Pascal's Wager isn't fully accurate. He believes that what Pascal was really saying was that there are two tests for belief in God: the empirical test (based upon investigation) and the existential test (based upon our intuitions and the longings of our heart). Pascal believed that Christianity fully satisfies the empirical test in the person and works of Jesus Christ, as well as the existential test by providing meaning in life. However, he argued that atheism failed the existential test. Consequently, Pascal saw belief in God as the best wager, for in Christ he had found life's meaning (existential fulfillment), which could be found nowhere else.[42]

Whether Pascal's argument was originally meant this way or not, the fact remains, when it comes to determining our worldview, it must not only satisfy our intellect, but also the intuitions and longings of our heart.[43] This is why atheist journalist Katha Pollitt said that atheism alone, as the rejection of gods and the supernatural, is incapable of meeting our deepest human longings for connection and inspiration, and suggests that art can perhaps fulfill what atheism cannot.[44] The existential longings of the human heart explain why many atheists have turned to humanism to satisfy the need for deeper meaning and connection.

In *The Real American Dream: A Meditation on Hope*, Andrew Delbanco argues that for a cultural narrative (a worldview) to succeed, it must offer hope. It must help us "imagine some end to life that transcends our own tiny allotment of days and hours if we are to keep at bay the dim, back-of-the-mind suspicion that one may be adrift in an absurd world," and shake "the lurking suspicion that all our getting and spending amounts to nothing more than fidgeting while we wait for death."[45] This helps us see why Christianity has been so successful as its message is, as atheist philosopher Erik Wielenberg puts it, "fundamentally one of hope."[46] This is why I strongly believe that even if you don't believe in Christianity right now, you should want to, for only Christianity is capable of passing the empirical test, as well as the existential test of our hearts.

Believe the Better Story

Without a doubt, there are advantages to believing in a naturalistic universe. There is even a sort of Nihilistic beauty to it all, as well as a perceived sense of freedom. However, when you compare its narrative to the Christian narrative, the contrast couldn't be more clear. The narrative of naturalism tells us that the universe "has precisely the properties we should expect if there is, at bottom, no design, no purpose, no evil and no good, nothing but blind, pitiless indifference."[47] On the contrary, the book of Genesis tells us that we were created by a good and loving God, who after His work "saw everything that he had made, and indeed, it was very good."[48] The narrative of naturalism is undoubtedly bleak —so bleak that it is an unlivable worldview that cannot possibly pass the existential test.

As we've seen, naturalism tells us that most of what we intuitively believe about reality cannot actually be trusted. It tells us that life has no meaning other than the arbitrary meaning we give it, and when we die, we rot. Free will is an illusion, along with beauty, love, meaning, morality, and God, which are explained away through evolution's natural selection. However, even a naturalist cannot live this way because, deep down, we all know better.[49] We know that these basic intuitions are reliable indicators of our reality. Therefore, belief in God is a self-evident truth that we cannot prove but can't not know, for it is foundational to our existence. This is why even when we allow our mind to tell us that life is ultimately meaningless, our heart won't allow us to live this way. When we stand in the presence of great art or natural beauty, we know it is not meaningless. We know, deep down, that life is not "a tale told by an idiot, full of sound and fury, signifying nothing."[50]

The message of Christianity is ultimately one of hope. It is a love story of how the God of the universe entered into His broken creation, in the person of Jesus Christ, to rescue His lost children so that one day everything could be made new. It explains why our world is so beautiful, yet so broken. It tells us that we are not our own, but that we are His, and that we were created for a purpose that was not meant to end in the grave. It is the story of how God invites His lost sons and daughters to return home and rejoin the dance of God by becoming who we were always meant to be. For these prodigal children, suffering and death are not the end, but the beginning, as their loving Father has promised to one day make everything bad come untrue.[51]

In Matthew 11:28, Jesus offers an invitation, "Come to me, all who labor and are heavy laden, and I will give you rest."[52] Jesus isn't simply inviting tired workers who just finished a long day's work to come and rest in His home, He is saying that the God-shaped hole in our hearts can only find existential fulfillment in Him, and so He invites us in. I urge you to accept His invitation, for if you do, you'll find that Jesus is everything your heart was looking for and more—so much more. Are you struggling to believe the Christian story? Perhaps you maybe even want to believe it, but you are not totally convinced yet, and so you think you can't. I can promise you, if you are waiting until the day you are fully convinced, it will never come. No Christian has ever come to Christ because every single one of their doubts were settled. To be a Christian is to accept Jesus Christ for who He says He is—the God and Savior of this world—and to place your trust and faith in Him.

While I was in seminary, my church hosted a discussion forum where we invited non-believers and skeptics to come and study the Gospel of Mark with us. For several weeks, we broke into discussion groups consisting of Christians and their unbelieving family, friends, neighbors, and coworkers. At our last meeting, everyone was asked to write down on a scale of one to ten how confident they were that Jesus was who the Bible claimed He was. The responses were quite interesting. One elderly gentleman who was in his eighties had been a Christian for a large portion of his life, and so he quickly and boldly wrote down a ten. Some of the other Christians at our table ranged between seven and nine, while the non-believers ranged between two and six. Lastly, I revealed my number to be a six, which surprised many of them. After all, if this seminary student who was their discussion leader was only willing to put a six down for his confidence level, what does that say for the believability of Christianity? Here's what I told them.

First, I clarified my number, explaining that while some days it was a six, many days it was as high as seven or eight, depending on my mood and level of doubt. I then explained how I am naturally a doubter, and the disciple I relate with most is "doubting Thomas." However, the remarkable thing about Christianity is that it's not the strength of our faith that matters, but the object of our faith. I then shared the following illustration I had recently read, which shows us why we can put our faith in Christ while still having doubts:

Imagine you are on a high cliff and you lose your footing and begin to fall. Just beside you as you fall is a branch sticking out of the very edge of the cliff. It is your only hope and it is more than strong enough to support your weight. How can it save you? If your mind is filled with intellectual certainty that the branch can support you, but you don't actually reach out and grab it, you are lost. If your mind is instead filled with doubts and uncertainty that the branch can hold you, but you reach out and grab it anyway, you will be saved. Why? It is not the strength of your faith but the object of your faith that actually saves you. Strong faith in a weak branch is fatally inferior to weak faith in a strong branch. This means you don't have to wait for all doubts and fears to go away to take hold of Christ. Don't make the mistake of thinking that you have to banish all misgivings in order to meet God. That would turn your faith into one more way to be your own Savior. Working on the quality and purity of your commitment would become a way to merit salvation and put God in your debt. It is not the depth and purity of your heart but the work of Jesus Christ on our behalf that saves us.[53]

In *The Life of Pi*, the narrator explains how we all run on the legs of reason only so far and then we jump.[54] We don't have a choice—we all put our faith in something even if we don't realize it. The question is not "will you jump?" but "which worldview will you jump to?" If you are considering faith in Christ, it begins with that first step. Martin Luther King Jr. once advised, "Take the first step in faith. You don't have to see the whole staircase, just take the first step." Yes, taking that first step of faith requires repentance—there is no way around this. You cannot embrace Christ without embracing who He is and what He says. This means rejecting alternate beliefs and placing your faith and trust in God while walking in relationship with Him. It means believing that Christ is who He says He is and placing your trust in Him, not yourself, your good works, or even your religion to save you.

In the book of Psalms, the psalmist invites us to "Taste and see that the LORD is good." If you are interested in exploring the Christian faith, I encourage you to begin by reading the words of Jesus recorded in the book of Mark. For myself and many other Christians, there is a kind of majestic beauty that almost jumps off the pages that causes our heart to scream, "This is everything I was looking for!" In Jesus we find what beauty, art, and great music were whispering to us all along. This astounding beauty is what drew the disciples in and caused them to say, "Did not our hearts burn within us while he talked to us?"[55] At the start of this book, I said there were three reasons why I believed the Christian narrative: the philosophical, the historical, and the experiential, but that the last was the least influential for me. However, I'm not sure I was right. The last reason offers something entirely different from the others: it offers the existential answer to the longing of our heart. Jesus is what our hearts yearn for, and He alone is capable of filling the God-shaped void in our heart that continually throbs. Is your heart aching? If so, turn to Jesus, and your heart will be satisfied beyond what you ever dared to hope.

Thank you for reading this book!

If you enjoyed it, please consider leaving an Amazon review.
Indy authors depend on them. It really does make a difference.

Follow the author at:
WWW.TWITTER.COM/ZACH_BROOM
WWW.FACEBOOK.COM/ZACHARYABROOM

To be informed of future books, sign up at:
WWW.ZACHBROOM.COM

Acknowledgements

I'd like to thank my friend, Mike Brady, for our many precious conversations and for refusing to let my bad arguments slide. This book is a result of our friendship. I want to thank Dennis Wilkinson for guiding and coaching me into the world of apologetics, for introducing me to the concepts discussed in chapter twelve, as well as introducing me to the writings of Tim Keller. Also, I want to thank Chad Williams for our many conversations over coffee, which helped me better grasp and articulate the ideas in chapter one. Thank you to my good friend Dave Griffieth, who has a servant's heart—whose help, feedback, and critique especially impacted chapter nine, as well as the rest of the book through our many conversations over the years. He's the only person I know who appreciates C. S. Lewis more than I do, and that's saying something. Also, thank you to Deborah Griffieth, my editor, who worked so hard to clean up the roughest of rough drafts. She did a wonderful job balancing encouragement with directness. Thank you to my good friend Nick Zaffke, who has been a close friend of my family's ever since I can remember—his volunteer editing had an enormous impact on readability, especially in chapter one. Thank you to Craig Muri (whose passion for theology quickly became my own) for introducing me to the writings and ideas of Jonathan Edwards. Thank you to Will Butler, Sam Ingvalson, and many others from Parker's Lake Baptist Church for helping by talking through these concepts with me.

Finally, I'd like to thank my family for supporting me through this project—my father, who modeled the faith to me and never discouraged asking hard questions, and my mother for encouraging me to finish. Thank you to my mother and father-in-law, who helped and encouraged me along the way. I'd especially like to thank my wife Becky for all of her help. She patiently listened as I struggled to explain the ideas in this book, helped refine them into coherency, and spent countless hours editing and helping me word things more clearly. Without her, this book may have gotten started, but it never would have been finished.

Notes

Introduction

1. https://www.ajc.com/news/crime--law/jacob-wetterling-killer-gives-chilling-details-abducted-year-old-final-moments-alive/OQXUNMZy2wPpfGmqAfVVCM (last accessed on March 12, 2019).
2. http://www.startribune.com/danny-heinrich-confesses-to-abducting-and-killing-jacob-wetterling/392438361 (last accessed on March 12, 2019).
3. Statistics from http://arkofhopeforchildren.org/child-trafficking/child-trafficking-statistics (last accessed on May 5, 2016).
4. http://www.nbcnews.com/id/42108748/ns/us_news-crime_and_courts/t/massive-online-pedophile-ring-busted-cops/#.WZMld1F95PZ (last accessed on August 15, 2017).
5. J. Budziszewski, *What We Can't Not Know: A Guide* (Ignatius Press, 2011), p. 171.
6. https://www.barna.com/research/the-end-of-absolutes-americas-new-moral-code (last accessed on June 25, 2018).
7. C. S. Lewis, *Mere Christianity* (HarperOne, 2015), p. 8.
8. Sam Harris, *The Moral Landscape: How Science Can Determine Human Values* (Free Press, 2011), p. 83.
9. *God & Morality: Four Views* (IVP Academic, 2012), Kindle Location 545-548.
10. Romans 7:15, English Standard Version.
11. C. S. Lewis, *Mere Christianity*, p. 16.
12. Ibid., p. 7.
13. Bart Ehrman, *God's Problem: How the Bible Fails to Answer Our Most Important Question—Why We Suffer* (HarperOne, 2009), p. 21.
14. Nuremberg Trial Proceedings, Vol. 8 69th day, Wednesday, February 27th, 1946. Available at http://avalon.law.yale.edu/imt/02-27-46.asp (last accessed on March 12, 2016).
15. Viktor E. Frankl, *The Doctor and the Soul: From Psychotherapy to Logotherapy, Revised and Expanded* (Vintage; third edition, 1986), p. xxvii.
16. Albert Mohler, *The Conviction to Lead: 25 Principles for Leadership That Matters* (Bethany House Publishers, 2012), Kindle Location 614.

17. Paul A. Lombardo, *A Century of Eugenics in America: From the Indiana Experiment to the Human Genome Era* (Indiana University Press, 2011), p. 96.
18. Scott Christianson, *The Last Gasp: The Rise and Fall of the American Gas Chamber* (University of California Press, 2010), p. 32.
19. Cyprian Blamires, *World Fascism: A Historical Encyclopedia* (ABC-CLIO, 2006), p. 207.
20. William L. Shirer, *The Rise and Fall of the Third Reich: A History of Nazi Germany* (Simon & Schuster, 2011), Chapter 4.
21. Richard Dawkins, *River Out of Eden: A Darwinian View of Life* (Basic Books, 1996), p. 155.
22. Atheist philosopher J. L. Mackie recognized the connection that moral ideas have to every area of knowledge when he wrote, "Moral principles and ethical theories do not stand alone: they affect and are affected by beliefs and assumptions which belong to other fields." J. L. Mackie, *Ethics: Inventing Right and Wrong* (Penguin Books, 1991), Chapter 9.
23. https://www.cbsnews.com/news/jury-child-killer-should-die/ (last accessed on May 6, 2019).
24. Ravi Zacharias, *The End of Reason*, Kindle Location 370-373.
25. Ibid., Kindle Location 639-641.
26. Richard Dawkins, *River Out of Eden*, p. 155.

Chapter One

1. Quoted in Alvin Plantinga, *Where the Conflict Really Lies: Science, Religion, and Naturalism* (Oxford University Press, 2011), p. 267.
2. Ibid., p. 268.
3. Sam Harris, *The Moral Landscape*, p. 29.
4. Massimo Pigliucci has written an excellent article denouncing his fellow atheists for going too far into scientism. See Massimo Pigliucci, *New Atheism and the Scientific Turn in the Atheism Movement* (Midwest Studies In Philosophy, XXXVII, 2013).
5. Oxford Dictionaries, http://www.oxforddictionaries.com (last accessed on March 7, 2016).
6. Alvin Plantinga, *Where the Conflict Really Lies*, p. 299-300.
7. Ibid., p. 300.
8. Alvin Plantinga is not anti-science; he's pro-science. He writes, "Modern science is therefore a most impressive way in which humankind communally reflects the divine nature," and "modern science is an enormously impressive attempt to come to know something about ourselves and our world." Ibid., p. 5.

9. Massimo Pigliucci, *New Atheism and the Scientistic Turn in the Atheism Movement* (Midwest Studies In Philosophy, XXXVII, 2013).
10. Ibid.
11. Ibid.
12. Massimo Pigliucci, *Answers for Aristotle: How Science and Philosophy Can Lead Us to A More Meaningful Life* (Basic Books, 2012), Kindle Location 1421-1422.
13. Robert Wright, *The Moral Animal: Why We Are the Way We Are: The New Science of Evolutionary Psychology* (Vintage, 1995), p. 46.
14. David Hume pointed out the problem of induction, and later Bertrand Russell used the inductivist turkey analogy to further demonstrate it.
15. See Massimo Pigliucci, *Answers for Aristotle*, Kindle Location 1432-1437.
16. Ibid., Kindle Location 1445-1456.
17. G. K. Chesterton wrote of this problem saying: "For the sake of simplicity, it is easier to state the notion by saying that a man can believe that he is always in a dream. Now, obviously there can be no positive proof given to him that he is not in a dream, for the simple reason that no proof can be offered that might not be offered in a dream." G. K. Chesterton, *Orthodoxy* (Kindle Edition, 2017), p. 16.
18. Alvin Plantinga, Where the Conflict Really Lies, p. 43.
19. Ibid.
20. J. Budziszewski, *What We Can't Not Know: A Guide*, p. 83.
21. Sam Harris, *The Moral Landscape*, p. 37.
22. Prominent presuppositional apologists include Cornelius Van Til, Greg Bahnsen, and John Frame.
23. A. C. Grayling, *The God Argument: The Case Against Religion and for Humanism* (Bloomsbury USA, 2014), p. 91.
24. Sam Harris, *The End of Faith*, p. 183.
25. Quoted in Kenneth Boa, Robert M. Bowman Jr., *Faith Has Its Reasons: Integrative Approaches to Defending the Christian Faith*, p. 250. Also see Alvin Plantinga, *Warranted Christian Belief*, Chapter 10.
26. Francis J. Beckwith and Gregory Koukl, *Relativism: Feet Firmly Planted in Mid-Air* (Baker Books, 1998), p. 56-57.
27. C. S. Lewis, *The Abolition of Man* (Macmillan, 1955), p. 53.
28. For a helpful explanation of uniformity and induction see Alvin Plantinga, *Where the Conflict Really Lies: Science, Religion, and Naturalism*, chapter 9.
29. Aristotle, *Metaphysics*, section 1006a.
30. C. S. Lewis, *Miracles* (HarperOne, 2015), p. 166.

31. Massimo Pigliucci, *New Atheism and the Scientistic Turn in the Atheism Movement* (Midwest Studies In Philosophy, XXXVII, 2013).
32. Friedrich Nietzsche, *The Twilight of the Idols and the Anti-Christ: or How to Philosophize with a Hammer* (Penguin Classics, 1990), p. 72.
33. Quoted in Ronald H. Nash, *Faith and Reason: Searching for a Rational Faith* (HarperCollins, 1994), p. 73.
34. Sigmund Freud, *The Future of an Illusion* (W. W. Norton & Company, 1989), chapter 6.
35. Bertrand Russell, *Why I Am Not a Christian and Other Essays on Religion and Related Subjects* (Simon and Schuster, 1957), p. 54.
36. Thomas Nagel, *The Last Word* (Oxford University Press, 1997), p. 130.
37. This point is made in J. Budziszewski, *What We Can't Not Know: A Guide* (Ignatius Press, 2011), p. 68.
38. Quoted in Ravi Zacharias, *Can Man Live Without God* (Thomas Nelson Inc, 2004), p. 30.
39. Discussed and quoted in Timothy Keller, *The Reason for God: Belief in an Age of Skepticism* (Penguin Publishing Group, 2008), Kindle Edition, p. 73.
40. Alister McGrath, *The Twilight of Atheism: The Rise and Fall of Disbelief in the Modern World* (Crown Publishing Group, 2007), Kindle Location 2370-2372.
41. Timothy Keller, *The Reason for God*, p. 50.
42. Quoted in Alister McGrath, *The Twilight of Atheism*, Kindle Location 2882.
43. Jean François Revel, *The Flight from Truth: The Reign of Deceit in the Age of Information* (Random House, 1991), p. xiii.
44. This point is made in Timothy Keller, *The Reason for God*, p. 9.

Chapter Two

1. Christopher Hitchens, *God Is Not Great: How Religion Poisons Everything* (McClelland & Stewart, 2008), p. 64.
2. Bertrand Russell, *Why I Am Not a Christian*, p. 22.
3. Christopher Hitchens made this point when he wrote: "I suppose that one reason I have always detested religion is its sly tendency to insinuate the idea that the universe is designed with 'you' in mind or, even worse, that there is a divine plan into which one fits whether one knows it or not. This kind of modesty is too arrogant for me." Christopher Hitchens, *Hitch-22: A Memoir* (Grand Central Publishing, 2010), p. 332-333.

4. George Gaylord Simpson, *The Meaning of Evolution: A Study of the History of Life and of Its Significance for Man* (Yale University Press, 1967), p. 345.
5. Carl Sagan, *Pale Blue Dot: A Vision of the Human Future in Space* (Ballantine Books, 1997), p. 6.
6. Alvin Plantinga, *Where the Conflict Really Lies*.
7. Ibid., p. 266.
8. Ibid., p. 194.
9. Ibid., p. 266.
10. Ibid., p. 266.
11. According to Johannes Kepler, the great German scientist who discovered the laws of planetary motion: "Those laws are within the grasp of the human mind. God wanted us to recognize them by creating us after his own image so that we could share in his own thoughts . . . and if piety allow us to say so, our understanding is in this respect of the same kind as the divine, at least as far as we are able to grasp something of it in our mortal life." Ibid., p. 277.
12. Ibid., p. 285.
13. Quoted in Max Jammer, *Einstein and Religion* (Princeton University Press, 1999), p. 93. See also Victor J. Stenger, *Has Science Found God? The Latest Results in the Search for Purpose in the Universe* (Prometheus Books, 2003), p. 85. See also, Gregory Koukl, *Faith Is Not Wishing: 13 Essays for Christian Thinkers* (Stand to Reason, 2011), p. 51.
14. Timothy Keller provides a helpful critique and explanation of Dawkins's claim that all of the great modern scientists do not believe in God. See: Timothy Keller, *The Reason for God*, p. 85.
15. Ibid., p. 87.
16. Alister McGrath, *The Twilight of Atheism*, Kindle Location 1368-1373.
17. Alister McGrath, *The Twilight of Atheism: The Rise and Fall of Disbelief in the Modern World* (Crown Publishing Group, 2007), p. 87.
18. Ibid., p. 88.
19. Ibid.
20. Gregory Koukl, *Faith Is Not Wishing: 13 Essays for Christian Thinkers* (Stand to Reason, 2011), p. 51.
21. Point made by Greg Epstein, *Good Without God: What a Billion Nonreligious People Do Believe* (William Morrow Paperbacks, 2010), p. 10.
22. C. S. Lewis, *God in the Dock* (Wm. B. Eerdmans Publishing Co., 2014), p. 140.

23. Alvin Plantinga, *Where the Conflict Really Lies*, p. 79.
24. Alister McGrath, *The Twilight of Atheism*, Kindle Location 2743-2744.
25. Ibid., Kindle Location 1736-1738.
26. Mark W. Durm and Massimo Pigliucci, "Gould's Separate 'Magisteria': Two Views," *Skeptical Inquirer,* Nov. 1 (1999).
27. Richard Dawkins, "The Alleged Separation Between the Two Is Not So Tidy." *Free Inquiry*, March 18, 1998.
28. A. C. Grayling, *The God Argument*, p. 55.
29. Ibid., p. 74.
30. Alvin Plantinga makes a similar argument in, *Warranted Christian Belief*, p. 406. Quoted in Timothy Keller, *The Reason for God*, p. 84. He writes, "[This argument] is like the drunk who insisted on looking for his lost car keys only under the streetlight on the grounds that the light was better there. In fact, it would go the drunk one better: it would insist that because the keys would be hard to find in the dark, they must be under the light."
31. Paraphrase of Alvin Plantinga, *Where the Conflict Really Lies*, Kindle Location 132.
32. Ibid., Kindle Location 101-103, 311, 350.
33. Alister McGrath, *The Twilight of Atheism*, Kindle Location 1239-1242.
34. A. C. Grayling, *The God Argument*, chapter 14.
35. Timothy Keller, *The Reason for God*, p. 116.
36. Ibid.
37. A. C. Grayling, *The God Argument*, p. 161.
38. This point is made in Timothy Keller, *The Reason for God*, p.11.
39. A. C. Grayling, *The God Argument*, p. 68.
40. Alvin Plantinga, "A Defense of Religious Exclusivism," in *The Analytic Theist*, ed. James F. Sennett (Eerdmans, 1998), p. 205. Quoted in Timothy Keller, *The Reason for God*, p. 244.
41. Gregory Koukl, *Faith Is Not Wishing*, p. 16.
42. This kind of argument is the logical fallacy known as Bulverism, a term coined by C. S. Lewis. See C. S. Lewis, *God in the Dock*, p. 301.
43. Richard Dawkins, *The God Delusion* (Houghton Mifflin Harcourt, 2008), p. 354.
44. Ibid., p. 356.
45. Ibid., p. 358.
46. Ibid., p. 365-367.
47. This point is made by J. Budziszewski, *What We Can't Not Know: A Guide*, p. 174-175.
48. See Alvin Plantinga, *Where the Conflict Really Lies*.

49. Plantinga writes: "But suppose you are a naturalist: you think that there is no such person as God, and that we and our cognitive faculties have been cobbled together by natural selection. Can you then sensibly think that our cognitive faculties are for the most part reliable? I say you can't." Ibid., p. 113.
50. Ibid., p. 315-316.
51. Ibid., p. 315.
52. Many scientists and philosophers hopefully look to string theory and quantum mechanics to save them from determinism.
53. C. S. Lewis, *God in the Dock* (Wm. B. Eerdmans Publishing, 2014), p. 144
54. C. S. Lewis, *God in the Dock*, p. 21.
55. C. S. Lewis, *Miracles*, p. 22.
56. Plantinga writes: "In this chapter, we've seen that theistic religion gives us reason to expect our cognitive capacities to match the world in such a way as to make modern science possible. Naturalism gives us no reason at all to expect this sort of match; from the point of view of naturalism, it would be an overwhelming piece of cosmic serendipity if there were such a match." Alvin Plantinga, *Where the Conflict Really Lies*, p. 304.
57. Ibid., See preface.
58. http://www.independent.co.uk/news/science/stephen-hawking-admits-the-biggest-blunder-of-his-scientific-career-early-belief-that-everything-8568418.html (last accessed on May 10, 2016).
59. Charles Darwin, *On the Origin of Species By Means of Natural Selection, or, the Preservation of Favoured Races in the Struggle for Life* (FQ Books, 2010), p. 131.
60. Alister McGrath, *The Twilight of Atheism*, Kindle Location 1520-1531.
61. Michael Shermer, *Why People Believe Weird Things: Pseudoscience, Superstition, and Other Confusions of Our Time* (Holt Paperbacks, 2002), p. 124.
62. Massimo Pigliucci, *Answers for Aristotle*, p. 258.

Chapter Three

1. UMass Amherst, "UMass Amherst Researcher Finds Most People Lie in Everyday Conversation" https://www.umass.edu/newsoffice/article/umass-amherst-researcher-finds-most-people-lie-everyday-conversation (last accessed on May 12, 2016).
2. Hume argued that morality came from our passions, and could be considered a non-cognitivist himself.

3. Massimo Pigliucci, *Answers for Aristotle*, Kindle Location 781.
4. Pigliucci provides a clear definition of morality (metaethics) and ethics: "This is the territory of so-called metaethics—the discipline that examines the rational justifications for adopting any moral system at all (as opposed to ethics, the branch of philosophy that debates the relative merits of different views of morality and how they apply to individual cases)." Ibid., Kindle Location 391-397.
5. A. C. Grayling, *The God Argument*, p. 187.
6. Timothy Keller provides a helpful distinction between moral feelings and moral obligations in *The Reason for God*, p. 144-145.
7. Sam Harris, *Letter to a Christian Nation* (Vintage, 2008), p. 51.
8. A. C. Grayling, *The God Argument*, p. 132.
9. Ibid., 133.
10. Ravi Zacharias, *The End of Reason*, Kindle Location 440-443.
11. Huxley rightly understood the limits of human epistemology.
12. Bertrand Russel, John G. Slater, Peter Köllner, *Last Philosophical Testament: 1943-68* (Psychology Press, 1997), p. 91.
13. This idea is from William Lane Craig: http://www.reasonablefaith.org/definition-of-atheism (last accessed, May 11, 2016).
14. Alister McGrath, *The Twilight of Atheism*, Kindle Location 2639-2641.
15. Ibid., Kindle Location 2647-2657.
16. William Lane Craig, http://www.reasonablefaith.org/definition-of-atheism (last accessed, May 11, 2016).
17. A. C. Grayling, *The God Argument*, p. 132.
18. Greg Epstein, *Good Without God: What a Billion Nonreligious People Do Believe*, p. 190.
19. Ibid., p. 19.
20. A. C. Grayling, *The God Argument*, p. 138, 152.
21. Ibid., p. 149.
22. Greg Epstein, *Good Without God*, p. 10.
23. A. C. Grayling, *The God Argument*, p. 132.
24. English Standard Version.
25. Analects 15:23.
26. Nicocles, 3.60.
27. Mahabharata 5:1517.
28. Victor J. Stenger, *God: The Failed Hypothesis: How Science Shows That God Does Not Exist* (Prometheus Books, 2010), p. 198-199.
29. Richard Dawkins, *The God Delusion*, p. 287.
30. Ibid., p. 287-288.
31. Ibid., p. 292.
32. English Standard Version.

33. Matthew 5:43-44.
34. Exodus 23:4-5.
35. Leviticus 19:33-34.
36. See Luke 10.
37. Genesis 18:18, 22:18.
38. Galatians 6:10.
39. Francis Schaeffer, *True Spirituality* (Tyndale House Publishers, 2012), p. 138.
40. Greg Epstein, *Good Without God*, p. 115. Also, Peter Singer wrote: "Consistently with the idea of taking the point of view of the universe, the major ethical traditions all accept, in some form or other, a version of the Golden Rule that encourages equal consideration of interests." Peter Singer, *How Are We to Live?: Ethics in an Age of Self-Interest* (Prometheus Books, 1995), p. 273.
41. Greg Epstein, *Good Without God*, p. 137.
42. Ibid.
43. Walter Sinnott-Armstrong, *Morality Without God?* (Oxford University Press, 2011), p. 13.
44. Victor J. Stenger, *God: The Failed Hypothesis*, p. 210.
45. Sam Harris, *Letter to a Christian Nation*, p. 39. Victor J. Stenger, *God: The Failed Hypothesis*, p. 194.
46. William Lane Craig, http://www.reasonablefaith.org/can-we-be-good-without-god (last accessed, May 11, 2016).
47. Greg Epstein, *Good Without God*, p. 120. Richard Dawkins, *The God Delusion*, p. 298-299.

Chapter Four

1. This information can be found in the following Sixty Minutes report: https://www.abc.net.au/mediawatch/transcripts/ep3260m.pdf (last accessed August 16, 2019).
2. Mackie describes the history of objective moral values in *Ethics: Inventing Right and Wrong*, Kindle Location 245-251.
3. Paraphrased from Ravi Zacharias, *The End of Reason*, Kindle Location 495-500.
4. Alister McGrath makes this point about Dostoevsky in, *The Twilight of Atheism*, Kindle Location 2282-2292.
5. Jean-Paul Sartre, *The Philosophy of Existentialism: Selected Essays* (Philosophical Library/Open Road, 2012), Kindle Location 568-571.
6. Alister McGrath, *The Twilight of Atheism*, Kindle Location 2245-2248.

7. Mackie writes: "Moral properties constitute so odd a cluster of properties and relations that they are most unlikely to have arisen in the ordinary course of events without an all-powerful god to create them. J. L. Mackie, *The Miracle of Theism: Arguments For and Against the Existence of God* (Oxford University Press; First Edition, 1983), p. 115
8. J. L. Mackie, *Ethics: Inventing Right and Wrong*, Kindle Location, 239-241, 1490-1494, 3482-3488.
9. Michael Ruse, "Evolutionary Theory and Christian Ethics," *In The Darwinian Paradigm* (London: Routledge, 1989), pp. 262, 268-269.
10. A. C. Grayling, *The God Argument*, p. 187.
11. Greg Epstein, *Good Without God*, p. 36.
12. English Standard Version.
13. Timothy Keller, *The Reason for God*, p. 14.
14. Paul Copan, *Loving Wisdom: Christian Philosophy of Religion* (Chalice Press, 2012), p. 91.
15. Ravi Zacharias, *Deliver Us From Evil: Restoring the Soul in a Disintegrating Culture* (Thomas Nelson, 1998), p. 113-115.
16. This is a summary of what Mackie wrote in, *Ethics: Inventing Right and Wrong*, Kindle Location 2173-2180.
17. Sam Harris, *The End of Faith: Religion, Terror, and the Future of Reason* (W. W. Norton, 2005), p. 179.
18. Concept in Timothy Keller, *The Reason for God*, p. 45.
19. Keller writes: "The inconsistency of working against oppression when you refuse to admit there is such a thing as truth is the reason that postmodern "theory" and "deconstruction" is perhaps on the wane." *The Reason for God*, p. 36.
20. G. K. Chesterton, *Orthodoxy*, p. 33-34.
21. Idea is from Timothy Keller, *The Reason for God*, p. 145.
22. I was introduced to this idea from C. S. Lewis's and Timothy Keller's various writings.
23. Timothy Keller makes this point in, *Encounters with Jesus: Unexpected Answers to Life's Biggest Questions* (Penguin Books, 2013), p. 13-14.
24. The Declaration of Independence.
25. J. L. Mackie, *Ethics: Inventing Right and Wrong*, Kindle Location 2589-2591.
26. Summarized from Timothy Keller, *The Reason for God*, p. 149.
27. Michael J. Perry, *Toward a Theory of Human Rights*, p. xi. Quoted in Timothy Keller, *The Reason for God*, p. 150.
28. See Alister McGrath, *The Twilight of Atheism*, Kindle Location 2044-2056
29. Ibid., Kindle Location 2042-2049.

30. Ibid., Kindle Location 3967-3973.
31. A. C. Grayling, *The God Argument*, p. 182.
32. Idea from Timothy Keller, *The Reason for God*, p. 151.
33. Idea and quoted from, Ibid., p. 152.

Chapter Five

1. Ravi Zacharias, *Has Christianity Failed You?* (Zondervan, 2010), p. 48. See Mark D. Linville's critique of naturalistic moral realism in, *God and Morality: Four Views*, Kindle Location 468-477.
2. This was said in a debate between William Lane Craig and Sam Harris, University of Notre Dame, Indiana, United States, April 2011.
3. William J. Wainwright "Morality and Religion," The Continuum Companion to Ethics (London: Continuum, 2010), p.119-142.
4. William Wainwright explains why objective morality is a simpler explanation, Ibid.
5. These ideas are from William Lane Craig's article "Can We Be Good Without God," http://www.reasonablefaith.org/can-we-be-good-without-god (last accessed May 5, 2016).
6. Robert Merrihew Adams, *Finite and Infinite Goods: A Framework for Ethics* (Oxford University Press, 2002), p. 15-49.
7. If goodness originates in God, then this means that He is the very standard of goodness and the perfect exemplar of it. Any being like this is worthy of our worship, devotion, and obedience. William Wainwright writes: "God is both Goodness's perfect exemplar and its standard." "Morality and Religion," The Continuum Companion to Ethics (London: Continuum, 2010), p. 119-142.
8. See Erik Wielenberg's explanation of Euthyphro's Dilemma in, *Value and Virtue in a Godless Universe* (Cambridge University Press, 2005), p. 64-67.
9. This point is made in, *God & Morality: Four Views*, Kindle Location 1034-1048.
10. David Berlinski summarizes this problem clearly in, *The Devil's Delusion: Atheism and its Scientific Pretensions*, p. 40.
11. Gottfried Wilhelm Freiherr von Leibniz, *Discourse on Metaphysics and Other Essays* (Hackett Publishing, 1989), p. 2.
12. *God & Morality: Four Views*, Kindle Location 726-728. See also, Bertrand Russell, *Why I Am Not a Christian*, p. 12.
13. Greg Epstein, *Good Without God*, p. 33.
14. John Stuart Mill, *An Examination of Sir William Hamilton's Philosophy* (Cosimo, Inc., 2009), p. 129.

15. C. S. Lewis, *The Problem of Pain* (Zondervan, 2001), p. 28.
16. Erik Wielenberg, Value and Virtue in a Godless Universe, p. 32.
17. Ibid., p. 64-67. Massimo Pigliucci, *Answers for Aristotle*, 269.
18. Epstein writes: "In either case Euthyphro drives home the point that mere belief in God can't make us good, and it can't point the way to "timeless values" that we humans aren't equally capable of arriving at on our own terms. Gods don't—can't—create values. Humans can, and so we must do so wisely." Greg Epstein, *Good Without God*, p. 32.
19. See Keith E. Yandell's account of moral essentialism in chapter three of *God & Morality: Four Views*, Kindle Location 991-992. Yandell lists several different options that Euthyphro's Dilemma does not account for, thus showing that it is a false dilemma.
20. Mark D. Linville writes: "we may think of God's commands, which are constitutive of moral obligation for us, as issuing from God's essential goodness. The commands are thus anything but arbitrary, and God's moral authority in issuing them is grounded in the essential goodness of his character. That moral goodness, in turn, supervenes upon certain of God's essential characteristics, such as justice, mercy and love." *God & Morality: Four Views*, Kindle Location 1605-1607.
21. See Genesis 18:14, Numbers 11:23, 1 Samuel 14:6, Job 42:1-2, Jeremiah 32:17, Jeremiah 32:27, Matthew 19:26, Mark 10:27, Luke 1:37, Luke 18:27, Revelation 19:6, Isaiah 6:3.
22. 1 Peter 1:16, Titus 1:2, Hebrews 6:18, Psalm 111:7–8, Psalm 119:160, Luke 16:17, Galatians 6:7–8, Jeremiah 31:3, Isaiah 40:28.
23. C. S. Lewis, *A Grief Observed* (HarperOne, 2001), p. 81.
24. I am aware there are many other examples skeptics use to argue that the God of the Bible is not immutable, but for the sake of brevity, I only addressed this example, since it's more common.
25. Earl S. Kalland, "Deuteronomy," in *The Expositor's Bible Commentary: Deuteronomy, Joshua, Judges, Ruth, 1 & 2 Samuel*, ed. Frank E. Gaebelein, Vol. 3 (Grand Rapids, MI: Zondervan Publishing House, 1992), p. 57.
26. Romans 13.
27. Genesis 9:6.
28. Windsor Mann, *The Quotable Hitchens: From Alcohol to Zionism — The Very Best of Christopher Hitchens* (Da Capo Press, 2011), p. 237. Also, in Elizabeth Anderson's section of *The Portable Atheist*, titled "If God Is Dead, Is Everything Permitted?" she argues that the moral argument is a defeater of theism not atheism. Christopher Hitchens, *The Portable Atheist: Essential Readings for the Nonbeliever* (Da Capo Press, 2007), p. 248.

29. It is the logical fallacy of *argumentum ad populum* to say that consensus is required for truth. Even if everyone believed that the world was flat this wouldn't make it true.
30. Ralph G. Nichols and Thomas R. Lewis, *Listening and Speaking: A Guide to Effective Oral Communication* (W.C. Brown, 1954), p. 74.
31. Sam Harris argues against consensus when defending his moral position. Sam Harris, *The Moral Landscape: How Science Can Determine Human Values* (Free Press, 2011), p. 31.
32. George Orwell, 1984 (Signet Classic, 1961), p. 217.
33. A. C. Grayling, *The God Argument*, p. 25.
34. A. C. Grayling, *The God Argument*, p. 257. See also, Greg Epstein, *Good Without God*, p. 28.
35. Massimo Pigliucci, *Answers for Aristotle*, p. 286.
36. Alvin Plantinga, *Where the Conflict Really Lies*, p. 5.
37. This is one of the pillars of Sam Harris's moral position in The Moral Landscape. Harris recognizes that moral systems do not need to be complete nor perfect. In reality, all human knowledge functions this way. Sam Harris, *The Moral Landscape*, p. 67.
38. Steven Pinker, *The Better Angels of Our Nature: Why Violence Has Declined* (Penguin Books, 2012), p. 11. See also, Walter Sinnott-Armstrong, *Morality without God?*, p. 109. A. C. Grayling writes: "Technically speaking, Christian punishment for blasphemy should be the same as in Pakistan. Leviticus 24:16 says that the blasphemer is to be put to death, and Luke 12:10 says that blaspheming against the Holy Spirit is unforgivable, a claim supported by Mark 3:29 where it is deemed an 'eternal sin'." A. C. Grayling, *The God Argument*, p. 244.
39. Richard Dawkins, *The God Delusion*, p. 51. See also, Christopher Hitchens, *The Portable Atheist: Essential Readings for the Nonbeliever* (Da Capo Press, 2007), p. 338.
40. Stenger writes: "no one of conscience today would think it moral to kill everyone captured in battle, saving only the virgin girls for their pleasure. Few modern Christians take the commands of the Bible literally. While they claim to appeal to scriptures and the teachings of the great founders and leaders of their faiths, they pick and choose what to follow—guided by some personal inner light. And this is the same inner light that guides nonbelievers." Victor J. Stenger, *God: The Failed Hypothesis*, p. 207-208.
41. Richard Dawkins, *The God Delusion*, p. 269. Also, see Christopher Hitchens, *God Is Not Great: How Religion Poisons Everything*, p. 211.
42. A. C. Grayling, *The God Argument*, p. 4.
43. See Matthew 5:17-18, 2 Corinthians 1:20, Romans 10:4.
44. See Hebrews 10.

45. See Hebrews 7:23-24.
46. See 1 Corinthians 3:16; John 4:21-23.
47. See Mark 7:18-19.
48. Martin Luther King Jr., "Letter from Birmingham Jail." p. 5. http://www.uscrossier.org/pullias/wp-content/uploads/2012/06/king.pdf (last accessed March 16, 2016).
49. Alister McGrath, *The Twilight of Atheism*, Kindle Location 4206-4210.
50. Ravi Zacharias, *The End of Reason*, Kindle Location 529-532.
51. C. S. Lewis, Mere Christianity, p. 40.
52. A. C. Grayling, *The God Argument*, p. 35-36.
53. Ibid., p. 36.
54. Ibid., p. 36-37.
55. Ibid., p. 127, 135.
56. C. S. Lewis, *Surprised by Joy* (Harcourt, Brace, Jovanovich, 1966), p. 207-208.
57. J. I. Packer, *Doing Theology in Today's World: Essays in Honor of Kenneth S. Kantzer* (Zondervan Publishing House, 1994), p. 21.
58. Owen Barfield, *History in English Words* (Lindisfarne Books, 2002), p. 169.
59. Owen Barfield, *Worlds Apart* (Barfield Press UK, 2010), p. 13-14.
60. Jeffrey Burton Russell, "The Myth of the Flat Earth" http://www.asa3.org/ASA/topics/history/1997Russell.html?iframe=true&width=100%&height=100% (last accessed May 5, 2016).
61. Stephen Jay Gould, *Rocks of Ages: Science and Religion in the Fullness of Life* (Random House Publishing Group, 2011), Kindle Location 1123-1267.
62. Ibid.
63. Massimo Pigliucci, *Denying Evolution: Creationism, Scientism, and the Nature of Science* (Sinauer Associates, 2002), p. 38.
64. Stephen Jay Gould, *Rocks of Ages*, Kindle Location 1123-1267.
65. Nearly every Christian scholar aside from Lactantius and Cosmas Indicopleustes believed in a round Earth. Ibid.
66. Jeffrey Burton Russell writes: "Nor did this situation change with the advent of Christianity. A few—at least two and at most five—early Christian fathers denied the sphericity of Earth by mistakenly taking passages such as Ps. 104:2-3 as geographical rather than metaphorical statements. On the other side tens of thousands of Christian theologians, poets, artists, and scientists took the spherical view throughout the early, medieval, and modern church. The point is that no educated person believed otherwise." "The Myth of the Flat Earth" http://www.asa3.org/

ASA/topics/history/1997Russell.html?iframe=true&width=100%&height=100% (last accessed May 5, 2016).
67. Ibid.
68. Ibid. The same is true of the myth that the Crusades were about Christian aggression, riches, and spoils. See Rodney Stark, *God's Battalions: The Case for the Crusades* (HarperOne, 2010).
69. John Newton, John Cecil, *The Works of Rev. John Newton* (Uriah Hunt, 1831), p. 89.
70. Richard Dawkins, *The God Delusion*, p. 259.
71. Ibid.
72. Daniel C. Dennett, *Breaking the Spell: Religion as a Natural Phenomenon* (Penguin, 2006), p. 307.
73. Grayling writes: "For the humanist it matters to ask this: if interest in and concern for one's fellows is a reason for being moral, what relevance does the existence of a deity have? Why cannot we accept that we are prompted to the ethical life by these natural human feelings? The existence of a god adds nothing, other than as an invisible policeman who sees what we do always and everywhere, even when alone in the dark, and who rewards and punishes accordingly." A. C. Grayling, *The God Argument: The Case Against Religion and for Humanism*, p. 242.
74. Walter Sinnott-Armstrong, *Morality Without God?*, p. 107.
75. J. Budziszewski, *What We Can't Not Know*, p. 106.
76. Wielenberg recognizes this when he writes: "The idea seems to be that unless you will be punished for doing what you ought not to do and rewarded for doing what you ought to do, there is no reason to give a damn about the differencebetween the two. But this is false and, indeed, indicates a childish view of morality. Grown-ups recognize that the fact that a given action is morally obligatory is itself an overriding reason for performing that action. A morally obligatory action is an action that one has to do whether one wants to do it or not. Rewards and punishments may provide additional reasons for doing what we morally ought to do, but they do not constitute the only reasons for doing so." Erik Wielenberg, *Value and Virtue in a Godless Universe*, p. 80.
77. J. Budziszewski writes: "The civil penalty instructs him that the act is wrong and provides a further motive—if he needs one over and above the sheer wrong of it—for avoiding it." J. Budziszewski, *What We Can't Not Know*, p. 102-103.
78. See the New York City blackout of 1977 which resulted in mass looting and vandalism.

79. For a helpful resource for understanding how peer acceptance greatly influences our moral choices, see Malcom Gladwell's book, *The Tipping Point: How Little Things Can Make a Big Difference*.
80. Richard Wurmbrand, *Tortured for Christ* (Hodder & Stoughton, 1967), p. 34.
81. Walter Sinnott-Armstrong makes this argument in *Morality Without God?*, p. 101.

Chapter Six

1. Non-overlapping magisteria.
2. Sam Harris, *The Moral Landscape: How Science Can Determine Human Values* (Free Press, 2011), p. 31.
3. Ibid., p. 28.
4. Ibid., p. 39.
5. Ibid., p. 11.
6. Ibid., p. 13, 28, 122.
7. Thomas Nagel, "The Facts Fetish," *The New Republic*, November 11, 2010, p. 30-32.
8. Massimo Pigliucci, *Answers for Aristotle*, p. 24.
9. Ibid., p. 62.
10. Ibid., p. 63.
11. Massimo Pigliucci, *New Atheism and the Scientistic Turn in the Atheism Movement* (Midwest Studies In Philosophy, XXXVII, 2013).
12. Thomas Nagel writes: "He needs to resist the objection that moral judgments do not come from reason at all but are emotional responses, and that the reasons people offer for their moral beliefs are after-the-fact rationalizations rather than true explanations." Thomas Nagel, "The Facts Fetish," *The New Republic*, November 11, 2010, p. 30-32.
13. Pigliucci writes: "Hume was a keen observer of human nature, and he realized that we do things because we have motivations, but that motivations come out of "passions" (emotional drives), not reason." Massimo Pigliucci, *Answers for Aristotle*, p. 150.
14. Explanation derived from Massimo Pigliucci, *Answers for Aristotle*, p. 220-222, and William J. Wainwright "Morality and Religion," The Continuum Companion to Ethics (London: Continuum, 2010), p.119-142.
15. Pigliucci makes this argument, saying: "An atheist or a member of a different religious sect would be happy to engage the Christian in debates about abortion based on neutral concepts such as the protection of innocent lives, personhood, and the like. But she would have nothing to say to someone who claims that abortion is

immoral on the sole ground that (their particular) God says so." Massimo Pigliucci, *Answers for Aristotle*, p. 224.
16. Epstein writes: "But we Humanists do not seek to impose our view on the secular moral and legal systems. Rather, we see our views as no better and no worse than anyone else's when it comes to whether they should become secular law. We need to build consensus with other groups in order to find solutions that work for all people." Greg Epstein, *Good Without God*, p. 160-161. Also, Timothy Keller describes this concept in *The Reason for God*, p. 12-14.
17. Keller writes: "Although many continue to call for the exclusion of religious views from the public square, increasing numbers of thinkers, both religious and secular, are admitting that such a call is itself religious." *The Reason for God*, p. 16.
18. J. Budziszewski, *What We Can't Not Know*, p. 55.
19. Ibid.
20. Massimo Pigliucci, *Answers for Aristotle*, p. 151.
21. Walter Sinnott-Armstrong, *Morality Without God?* (Philosophy in Action, 2009), p. 77.
22. Ibid., p. 63.
23. Christopher Hitchens, *God Is Not Great*, p. 150.
24. Sam Harris, *Letter to a Christian Nation*, p. 24.
25. David Berlinski, *The Devil's Delusion*, p. 34
26. Sam Harris, *The Moral Landscape*, p. 74.
27. Sam Harris's moral approach is an attempt to bridge the gap between morality being discovered and morality being created. By his view there can be different and competing moral systems that equally promote human flourishing. This has the potential benefit of retaining diversity while, ideally, preventing the allowance of horrific brutality.
28. Atheist philosopher Walter Sinnott-Armstrong argues that he does not need to be able to solve every single moral dilemma, and he's right; however, if his moral philosophy cannot handle even the most basic ethical dilemmas, then his moral philosophy is in serious trouble. *Morality without God?*, p. 73-74.
29. Millard J. Erickson, *Christian Theology* (Baker Academic; second edition, 2007), p. 450.
30. Ibid., 41.
31. Sam Harris, *The Moral Landscape*, p. 11, 36.
32. *God & Morality: Four Views*, Kindle Location 102-103.
33. Ibid., Kindle Location 116.
34. J. L. Mackie, *Ethics: Inventing Right and Wrong*, p. 51.

35. William Lane Craig said this in a debate with Walter Sinnott-Armstrong. "Do Suffering and Evil Disprove God?" April 1, 2000, Wooddale Church, Eden Prairie, MN.
36. Walter Sinnott-Armstrong, *Morality Without God?*, p. 70.
37. Erik J. Wielenberg, *Robust Ethics: The Metaphysics and Epistemology of Godless Normative Realism* (Oxford University Press, 2014), p. 52.
38. While Sam Harris acknowledges that his system is based on first principles (self-evident truth), he doesn't defend it philosophically. Why? Because he is bored by it. He writes: "I am convinced that every appearance of terms like "metaethics," "deontology," "noncognitivism," "antirealism," "emotivism," etc., directly increase the amount of boredom in the universe." Sam Harris, *The Moral Landscape*, p. 213. Harris's intentions are to reach a broader audience than he could if using these terms; however, one could argue this can be done without dismissing the entire field in a footnote.
39. This is Wielenberg's view, who writes: "Another possibility is a view like mine, according to which all (non-brute) ethical facts rest at least in part on a set of basic ethical facts. Such basic ethical facts are the axioms of morality and, as such, do not have an external foundation. Rather, they are the foundation of morality." Erik J. Wielenberg, "In Defense of Non-Natural, Non-Theistic Moral Realism," *Faith and Philosophy*, Vol. 26 No. 1 January 2009, p. 36.
40. Wielenberg writes: "For what it is worth, the ethical claim that pain is intrinsically bad seems to me not to cry out for further explanation; indeed, I find it less in need of explanation than the existence of a perfect person who created the universe." Ibid. He also writes, "Pain, for example, seems to be an intrinsic evil. It is evil in and of itself; its badness is part of its intrinsic nature and is not bestowed upon it from some external source." Erik J. Wielenberg, *Value and Virtue in a Godless Universe*, p. 50.
41. Point made by Wielenberg in "In Defense of Non-Natural, Non-Theistic Moral Realism," *Faith and Philosophy*, Vol. 26 No. 1 January 2009.
42. Craig responds: "aren't we presupposing morality in trying to ground morality? We're saying that an action is morally unjustified if it causes harm that is morally unjustified—no duh!" Quoted in Erik J. Wielenberg, "In Defense of Non-Natural, Non-Theistic Moral Realism," *Faith and Philosophy*, Vol. 26 No. 1 January 2009, p. 37.
43. William Lane Craig, "Reply to Objections," in *Does God Exist?* The Craig-Flew Debate, ed. Stan Wallace (Burlington, VT: Ashgate, 2003), pp. 157, 162–163. Quoted in Erik J. Wielenberg, "In Defense

of Non-Natural, Non-Theistic Moral Realism," *Faith and Philosophy*, Vol. 26 No1 January 2009, p. 38.
44. Ibid., p. 37. Similarly, Thomas Nagel writes: "And that assumption in turn leads to the conclusion that a value judgment could be true only if it were made true by something like a physical fact. That, of course, is nonsense." Thomas Nagel, "The Facts Fetish," *The New Republic*, November 11, 2010, p. 30-32.
45. Wielenberg writes: "The ethical shopping list of Adams, Craig, and Moreland contains items like this: (a) there is a being that is worthy of worship, (b) if the Good commands you to do something, then you are morally obligated to do it, and (c) the better the character of the commander, the more reason there is to obey his or her commands." Erik J. Wielenberg, "In Defense of Non-Natural, Non-Theistic Moral Realism," *Faith and Philosophy*, Vol. 26 No. 1 January 2009, p. 37-40.
46. Ibid., 38-39.
47. Wielenberg writes: "It turns out that Adams, Craig, Moreland, and I are all committed to the existence of basic ethical facts. If this is right, then none of us can reasonably criticize the approach of the other on the grounds that it posits values with no external foundation." Ibid., 34.
48. Walter Sinnott-Armstrong, *Morality Without God?*, p. 98-99.
49. William Lane Craig, *Reasonable Faith: Christian Truth and Apologetics* (Crossway, 2008), p. 178.
50. Erik Wielenberg vs Robert Morey, "Absolute Morality Without God?" *Reasonable Doubts*.
51. Erik J. Wielenberg, *Value and Virtue in a Godless Universe*, p. 67.
52. William Lane Craig, *Reasonable Faith*, p. 178.
53. Wainwright explains: "The fact that so many modern ethical theorists reject moral realism strongly suggests that the existence of basic moral facts, on the other hand, is not self-explanatory or intrinsically intelligible." Ibid.

Chapter Seven

1. Paraphrased from Huffington Post, Chris Martine, "The Day That Botany Took on Bobby Jindal by Just Being Itself." http://www.huffingtonpost.com/dr-chris-martine/the-day-that-botany-took-_b_3703257.html (last accessed on May 12, 2016).
2. Richard Dawkins, *The Blind Watchmaker: Why the Evidence of Evolution Reveals a Universe without Design* (W. W. Norton & Company, 1996), p. 9.

3. Darwin wrote: "I have called this principle, by which each slight variation, if useful, is preserved, by the term Natural Selection." Charles Darwin, *Origin of Species by Means of Natural Selection, Or the Preservation of Favored Races in the Struggle for Life* (P.F. Collier & Son, 1902), p. 99.
4. Alvin Plantinga, *Where the Conflict Really Lies*, p. 319. Darwin wrote: "This preservation of favourable variations and the destruction of injurious variations, I call Natural Selection, or the Survival of the Fittest. Variations neither useful nor injurious would not be affected by natural selection and would be left a fluctuating element." Charles Darwin, *The Origin of Species*, p. 121.
5. Robert Wright, *The Moral Animal*, p. 28. See also, page 25. Though Charles Darwin didn't believe that Natural Selection was the exclusive means of modification, most evolutionists today believe it is. Darwin wrote: "I am convinced that natural selection has been the main but not the exclusive means of modification." *The Origin of Species*, p. 303.
6. Robert Wright explains: "No human behavior affects the transmission of genes more obviously than sex. So no parts of human psychology are clearer candidates for evolutionary explanation than the states of mind that lead to sex." *The Moral Animal*, p. 28.
7. Described in Peter Singer, *How Are We to Live?*, p. 92.
8. Pigliucci explains: "Natural selection, the argument goes, would favor any behavior that maximizes the chances of passing your genes to the next generation, regardless of whether those genes are actually inside you or in one of your relatives. It is Hamilton's ideas about kin selection that were popularized by science writer Richard Dawkins with his metaphor of 'selfish genes.'" Massimo Pigliucci, *Answers for Aristotle*, p. 49.
9. John Stuart Mill, "On Nature." https://www.lancaster.ac.uk/users/philosophy/texts/mill_on.htm (last accessed on February 8, 2019).
10. Sigmund Freud, *Civilization and Its Discontents* (Hogarth Press, 1995), p. 85.
11. Massimo Pigliucci writes of virtue in a naturalistic world, saying: "In a sense, to be virtuous means to rise above one's weaknesses to do the right thing, both for ourselves and for others. That is the way toward human flourishing." Massimo Pigliucci, *Answers for Aristotle*, p. 6.
12. Robert Wright, *The Moral Animal*, p. 336.
13. Greg Epstein, *Good Without God*, p. 21-25.

14. Michael Ruse writes: "Why are we moral? Because humans who are moral tend to do better than those who are not and are thus more likely to leave offspring." *God & Morality: Four Views*, Kindle Location 311-312.
15. A. C. Grayling, *The God Argument*, p. 193.
16. Wright explains why we should be moral in a naturalistic universe, saying: "Perhaps the best answer to this question is a sheerly practical one: thanks to our old friend non-zero-sumness, everyone's happiness can, in principle, go up if everyone treats everyone else nicely. You refrain from cheating or mistreating me, I refrain from cheating or mistreating you; we're both better off than we would be in a world without morality." Robert Wright, *The Moral Animal*, p. 335.
17. Greg Epstein, *Good Without God*, p. 87.
18. Plato, *The Dialogues of Plato, Volume 1* (Random House, 1920), p. 623-624.
19. David Hume, *An Enquiry Concerning the Principles of Morals* (A. Millar, 1751), p. 194-195.
20. In agreement with Hume's view, Peter Singer writes: "If asked why anyone should act morally or ethically, I can give a bolder and more positive response than I did in my earlier thesis. I can point to people who have chosen to live an ethical life, and have been able to make an impact on the world. In doing so they have invested their lives with a significance that many despair of ever finding. They find, as a result, that their own lives are richer, more fulfilling, more exciting even, than they were before they made that choice." Peter Singer, *How Are We to Live?*, p. x.
21. Mark Rowlands, *The Philosopher and the Wolf: Lessons from the Wild on Love, Death, and Happiness* (Pegasus, 2010), p. 125.
22. Singer denies this inference believing that we are not tied to our evolutionary strings. He writes: "Maybe 'nice' behaviour is advantageous, but if so, aren't those who are being nice merely more enlightened egoists? This objection makes a mistake that is similar to the misunderstanding I mentioned in Chapter 5 in connection with altruism towards kin. Our feelings of love towards our brothers and sisters are no less genuine because we can explain how such feelings evolved: it is still true that we help our siblings because we care about them, not because of the degree of genetic overlap between us. Similarly, the fact that co-operation is the best policy does not mean that those who are co-operative are necessarily being co-operative because they desire to gain an advantage." Peter Singer, *How Are We to Live?*, p. x.
23. Sam Harris, *The End of Faith*, p. 191-192.

24. Ibid., p. 187.
25. Robert Wright, *The Moral Animal*, p. 337.
26. Michael Shermer, *Why People Believe Weird Things* (Holt Paperbacks, 2002), p. 123.
27. Michael Shermer, *The Believing Brain: From Ghosts and Gods to Politics and Conspiracies—How We Construct Beliefs and Reinforce Them as Truths* (St. Martin's Griffin, 2012), p. 34.
28. Michael Shermer, *Why People Believe Weird Things*, p. 124.
29. Robert Wright, *The Moral Animal*, p. 102. For an explanation of how different societies hold different subjective moral beliefs, see Steven Pinker, *The Better Angels of Our Nature*, p. 632.
30. Peter Singer explains the "right side of history" idea in, *How Are We to Live?*, p. 223.
31. Richard Dawkins, *The God Delusion*, p. 304-305.
32. Ibid., p. 307.
33. Ibid., p. 307.
34. Ibid., p. 308-309.
35. C. S. Lewis, *God in the Dock*, p. 4.
36. C. S. Lewis, *Mere Christianity*, p. 14.
37. G. K. Chesterton, *Orthodoxy*, p. 86.
38. Michael Ruse writes: "If the evolutionary process is nonprogressive in any meaningfully moral way, and I think this is so, then we could as easily have evolved a completely different moral system from that which we have. Instead of thinking that we ought to love our neighbors, we might well think that we should hate our neighbors. Indeed, something like this is perfectly possible." *God & Morality: Four Views*, Kindle Location 646-649.
39. Ibid., Kindle Location 871-876.
40. Biologist George Williams (1926–2010) wrote in a technical journal of philosophy in 1988: "I account for morality as an accidental capability produced, in its boundless stupidity, by a biological process that is normally opposed to the expression of such a capability." Quoted in Massimo Pigliucci, *Answers for Aristotle*, p. 47.
41. Charles Darwin, *The Descent of Man and Selection in Relation to Sex*, Volume 1 (D. Appleton, 1896), p. 99.
42. Robert Wright, *The Moral Animal*, p. 327-328.
43. Ibid., p. 328-329.
44. Ibid., p. 328.
45. *God & Morality: Four Views*, Kindle Location 697-698.
46. Daniel C. Dennett, *Darwin's Dangerous Idea: Evolution and the Meanings of Life* (Simon & Schuster, 1996), p. 507.
47. Emphasis mine.

48. *God & Morality: Four Views*, Kindle Location 684-687. Ruse explains: "When I say "killing is wrong," I don't just mean that I feel that killing is wrong. I mean that killing truly is absolutely, objectively wrong. That is why I believe it myself, but also why I think I have the right and obligation to say this to you. I'm not just telling you about my own emotions or feelings, I'm telling you what I think holds for us all. Note the important qualification that I am speaking at what I have just called the "phenomenological" level. If I am right philosophically, then there is no absolute, objective basis to morality. I am talking about how we feel and what we mean. In other words, I am talking about our psychology, if you like. My position is exactly that of David Hume when he claimed that his philosophical inquiries led him to skepticism, but that after a while back in the real world (playing backgammon and so forth) his psychology took over and he didn't bother about the skepticism." Ibid., Kindle Location 678-683.
49. Ibid.
50. *God & Morality: Four Views*, Kindle Location 311-312. An evolutionary naturalistic worldview sees all human behavior through the lens of reproductive success. Take divorce for an example; even though people divorce for emotional reasons like a dull and nagging wife, a mid-life crisis, an abusive or indifferent husband, or because they were lured away by a sensitive and caring man, these emotional reasons are, as Robert Wright calls them, simply "evolution's executioners." He goes to explain: "Beneath all the thoughts and feelings and temperamental differences that marriage counselors spend their time sensitively assessing are the stratagems of the genes—cold, hard equations composed of simple variables: social status, age of spouse, number of children, their ages, outside opportunities, and so on. Is the wife really duller and more nagging than she was twenty years ago? Possibly, but it's also possible that the husband's tolerance for nagging has dropped now that she's forty-five and has no reproductive future." Robert Wright, *The Moral Animal*, p. 86.
51. Patricia Churchland, Journal of Philosophy LXXXIV (October 1987), p. 548. Quoted in Alvin Plantinga, *Where the Conflict Really Lies*, p. 315.
52. Richard Dawkins, *The God Delusion*, p. 199-207.
53. Epstein writes: "We evolved over millions of years to look for causes, whether they exist or not, because if we hadn't, the world would look even more confusing to us than it does now." Greg Epstein, *Good Without God*, p. 27.
54. Ibid., 169-170.

55. Massimo Pigliucci acknowledges this in, *New Atheism and the Scientistic Turn in the Atheism Movement* (Midwest Studies In Philosophy, XXXVII, 2013). See also, Alvin Plantinga's critique of this in, *Where the Conflict Really Lies*, p. 141.
56. C. S. Lewis, *God in the Dock*, 274.
57. Sam Harris writes: "Many scientists and philosophers realized long ago that free will could not be squared with our growing understanding of the physical world." Sam Harris, *The Moral Landscape*, p. 103.
58. Richard Dawkins, *River Out of Eden*, p. 133.
59. Sam Harris, *Free Will* (Free Press, 2012), p. 7-8, 25-26. In *The Moral Landscape* Harris writes: "I no more initiate events in executive regions of my prefrontal cortex than I cause the creaturely outbursts of my limbic system. The truth seems inescapable: I, as the subject of my experience, cannot know what I will next think or do until a thought or intention arises; and thoughts and intentions are caused by physical events and mental stirrings of which I am not aware . . . From the perspective of your conscious mind, you are no more responsible for the next thing you think (and therefore do) than you are for the fact that you were born into this world." Sam Harris, *The Moral Landscape*, p. 103.
60. Robert Wright, *The Moral Animal*, p. 355.
61. Wright explains: "we must get used to the idea of holding robots responsible for their malfunctions—so long, at least, as this accountability will do some good." Ibid.
62. Harris writes; "Our system of justice should reflect our understanding that each of us could have been dealt a very different hand in life. In fact, it seems immoral not to recognize just how much luck is involved in morality itself." Sam Harris, *Free Will*, p. 4. See also, Sam Harris, *The Moral Landscape*, p. 109.
63. Daniel Dennett, "Reflections on Free Will", *Naturalism: Nature is Enough*, January 24, 2014. Available at http://www.naturalism.org/resources/book-reviews/reflections-on-free-will (last accessed on May 17, 2016).
64. Ibid.
65. Massimo Pigliucci, *Answers for Aristotle*, p. 138.
66. J. L. Mackie, *Ethics: Inventing Right and Wrong*, p. 228.
67. Sam Harris comments: "More than in any other area of academic philosophy, the result resembles theology." Sam Harris, *Free Will*, p. 18.
68. Richard Dawkins, *River Out of Eden*, p. 155.
69. Kai Nielsen, "Why Should I Be Moral?" *American Philosophical Quarterly*, 21) (1984): p. 90.

* * *

Chapter Eight

1. Steven Weinberg, *The First Three Minutes: A Modern View Of The Origin Of The Universe* (Basic Books, 1993), p. 154.
2. Leo Tolstoy, *The Spiritual Works of Leo Tolstoy: A Confession, The Kingdom of God is Within You, What I Believe, Christianity and Patriotism, Reason and Religion, The Gospel in Brief and More* (e-artnow, 2016), Kindle Location 11388-11389.
3. David Friend, *The Meaning of Life: Reflections in Words and Pictures on Why We Are Here* (Little, Brown, 1991), p. 33. Quoted in Timothy Keller, The Reason for God, p. 250.
4. This point is made by J. Budziszewski, *What We Can't Not Know: A Guide* (Ignatius Press, 2011), p. 130.
5. See Romans 1:18-24.
6. Richard Dawkins, *The God Delusion*, p. 405.
7. Alfie Kohn, *No Contest: The Case Against Competition* (Houghton Mifflin Harcourt, 2013), p. 112-113.
8. Drawing from Soren Kierkegaard, Tim Keller makes this point in *The Reason for God*, p. 160.
9. Timothy Keller, *Walking with God through Pain and Suffering*, p. 70-71.
10. Greg Epstein, *Good Without God*, p. 83. He goes to say: "happiness as the standard for a meaningful life is too egocentric, too nebulous, or both." Ibid., p. 84.
11. J. L. Mackie, *Ethics: Inventing Right and Wrong* (Penguin Books, 1991), p. 142-143.
12. Erik J. Wielenberg, Value and Virtue in a Godless Universe, p. 30.
13. Ibid., p. 34.
14. Bertrand Russell, *A Free Man's Worship, and Other Essays* (Unwin Paperbacks, 1976), p. 10.
15. Tim Keller makes this point in, *The Reason for God*, p. 131.
16. Point made by William Lane Craig, "The Absurdity of Life Without God." Quoted in Erik J. Wielenberg, *Value and Virtue in a Godless Universe*, p. 162.
17. Walter Sinnott-Armstrong, *Morality Without God?*, p. 128. Peter Singer argues this point, saying: "Most important of all, you will know that you have not lived and died for nothing, because you will have become part of the great tradition of those who have responded to the amount of pain and suffering in the universe by trying to make the world a better place." Peter Singer, *How Are We to Live?*, p. 235. See pages 230-235 for his more detailed explanation.

18. Ibid., p. 146.
19. Cormac McCarthy, *Sunset Limited: A Novel in Dramatic Form* (Dramatists Play Service, 2006), p. 52. In "The Sunset Limited," dir. Tommy Lee Jones (HBO Studios, 2012, DVD).
20. Ibid.
21. Richard Dawkins, *River Out of Eden*, p. 155.
22. Ibid.
23. Erik J. Wielenberg, *Value and Virtue in a Godless Universe*, p. 23.
24. This paragraph is paraphrased from Alister McGrath, *The Twilight of Atheism*, p. 155-156.
25. Idea described in Greg Epstein, *Good Without God*, p. 70.
26. Thomas Nagel, *What Does It All Mean?: A Very Short Introduction to Philosophy* (Oxford University Press, 1987), p. 100-101.
27. Ibid., 101.
28. Erik J. Wielenberg, *Value and Virtue in a Godless Universe*, p. 125.
29. Ibid., p. 150.
30. See Tim Keller, *The Reason for God*, p. 149.
31. Robert Wright, *The Moral Animal*, p. 378.
32. C. S. Lewis, *Miracles*, p. 58.
33. Massimo Pigliucci, *Answers for Aristotle*, p. 26.
34. Steven Pinker, *The Blank Slate: The Modern Denial of Human Nature* (Penguin Books, 2003), p. 53-54
35. Sam Harris, *The Moral Landscape*, p. 14.
36. Ibid., p. 101.
37. Thomas Nagel, "The Facts Fetish," *The New Republic*, November 11, 2010, p. 30-32.
38. Richard Dawkins, *The Selfish Gene: 30th Anniversary Edition* (Oxford University Press, 2006), p. 3.
39. Richard Taylor, *Ethics, Faith, and Reason* (Prentice-Hall, 1985), p. 2-3. Quoted in William Lane Craig, http://www.reasonablefaith.org/definition-of-atheism (last accessed, May 18, 2016).
40. Quoted in Ravi Zacharias, *The End of Reason*, p. 23.

Chapter Nine

1. Paraphrase of Timothy Keller, *The Reason for God*, p. 211.
2. See Genesis Chapter 1.
3. 1 John 4:8b.
4. Timothy Keller, *The Reason for God*, p. 214.
5. This concept of the trinity is from C. S. Lewis, *Mere Christianity*, p. 175-176, which is further expanded upon by Timothy Keller in, *The Reason for God*, p. 211-220.
6. J. L. Mackie, Ethics: Inventing Right and Wrong, p. 198.

7. Timothy Keller has a helpful sermon from 2008 titled "In the Image of God." See transcript from: http://baylyblog.com/blog/2009/01/tim-keller-addresses-abortion (last accessed on May 18, 2016).
8. This point is developed in J. Budziszewski's, *What We Can't Not Know*, p. 75.
9. C. S. Lewis, *Mere Christianity*, p. 136.
10. Greg Epstein, *Good Without God*, p. 121.
11. See the ontological argument put forth by Anselm, Archbishop of Canterbury first set forth the Ontological Argument in the eleventh century. See also, J. Budziszewski, *What We Can't Not Know*, p. 31-32.
12. Bart Ehrman, *God's Problem: How the Bible Fails to Answer Our Most Important Question—Why We Suffer* (HarperOne, 2009), p. 128.
13. H. P. Lovecraft, *Against Religion: The Atheist Writings of H.P. Lovecraft* (Lulu.com, 2010), p. 108.
14. http://www.wsj.com/articles/SB122178211966454607 (last accessed on May 18, 2016).
15. Story of David Foster Wallace described in Timothy Keller, *Encounters with Jesus*, p. 30.
16. *God & Morality: Four Views*, Kindle Location 729-732.
17. See C. S. Lewis's analogy of a fleet of ships sailing in formation. C. S. Lewis, *Mere Christianity*, p. 72.
18. Timothy Keller compares this to a fish's aquatic nature in, *The Reason for God*, p. 44.
19. G. K. Chesterton, *Orthodoxy*, p. 32.
20. Quoted in Ravi Zacharias, *The End of Reason*, p. 68.
21. Ravi Zacharias, *Why Suffering?: Finding Meaning and Comfort When Life Doesn't Make Sense* (FaithWords, 2015), p. 62.
22. Concept from Timothy Keller, *Jesus the King: Understanding the Life and Death of the Son of God* (Penguin Books, 2013), p. 71-72. Also, Timothy Keller, *Encounters with Jesus*, p. 67.
23. Christopher Hitchens, *God Is Not Great*, p. 64.
24. Timothy Keller, *Preaching: Communicating Faith in an Age of Skepticism* (Penguin Group, 2015), p. 83.
25. Ibid., p. 75.
26. Ibid., p. 74. I owe much to Keller for his explanations of sin and evil.
27. Ideas from Timothy Keller, *The Reason for God*, p. 160-163.
28. Quoted in Peter Singer, *How Are We to Live?*, p. 205.
29. Quoted in Erik J. Wielenberg, *Value and Virtue in a Godless Universe*, p. 27.

30. See Timothy Keller, *Every Good Endeavor: Connecting Your Work to God's Work* (Penguin Group, 2012), p. 132.
31. Jonathan Edwards, "The Works of President Edwards in Four Volumes: A Reprint of the Worcester Edition, with Valuable Additions and a Copious General Index," Volume 4 (Leavitt, Trow, & Company, 1844), p. 578.
32. C. S. Lewis, *Mere Christianity*, p. 45.
33. Sam Harris, *Letter to a Christian Nation*, p. 26.
34. PZ Myers, *The Happy Atheist* (Knopf Doubleday Publishing Group, 2013), p. 52.
35. Dan Barker, *Life Driven Purpose: How an Atheist Finds Meaning* (Pitchstone Publishing, 2015), Kindle Location 199-202.
36. A. C. Grayling, *The God Argument*, p. 44.
37. Richard Dawkins, *The God Delusion*, p. 285-286.
38. Russell wrote: "There is one very serious defect to my mind in Christ's moral character, and that is that He believed in hell. I do not myself feel that any person that is really profoundly humane can believe in everlasting punishment. Christ certainly as depicted in the Gospels did believe in everlasting punishment, and one does find repeatedly a vindictive fury against those people who would not listen to His preaching—an attitude which is not uncommon with preachers, but which does somewhat detract from superlative excellence." Bertrand Russell, *Why I Am Not a Christian*, p. 17.
39. See Timothy Keller, *The Reason for God*, p. 71.
40. Rebecca Pippert, *Hope Has Its Reasons* (IVP Books, 2009), Chapter 6, "What Kind of God Gets Angry?" Also discussed in Timothy Keller, *The Reason for God*, p. 71.
41. Rebecca Pippert, *Hope Has Its Reasons* (IVP Books, 2009), Chapter 6, "What Kind of God Gets Angry?"
42. Described in Timothy Keller, *Jesus the King*, p. 175.
43. Timothy Keller, *The Reason for God*, p. 73.
44. C. S. Lewis, *The Problem of Pain*, p. 75.
45. C. S. Lewis, *Mere Christianity*, p. 92.
46. English Standard Version.
47. Richard Dawkins makes this point in *The God Delusion*, p. 118.
48. Christopher Hitchens, *God Is Not Great*, p. 115.
49. Richard Dawkins, *The God Delusion*, p. 118. Hitchens also makes this point in, *God Is Not Great*, p. 111.
50. 1 Corinthians 15:3-5, New International Version.
51. Richard Dawkins, *The God Delusion*, p. 121.
52. Ibid.
53. Ibid., p. 122.

54. See Timothy Keller, *The Reason for God*, p. 100-102.
55. For a helpful list of further reading on textual criticism see, Ibid., 262.
56. William Lane Craig vs. Bart D. Ehrman, "Is There Historical Evidence for the Resurrection of Jesus?" Reasonable Faith http://www.reasonablefaith.org/is-there-historical-evidence-for-the-resurrection-of-jesus-the-craig-ehrman#ixzz3TSC2C2Ok (last accessed on April 27, 2019).
57. Ibid.
58. Ibid., William Lane Craig points out that even though one might be able to argue that methodologically historians can't conclude that Jesus was supernaturally resurrected from the dead, people shouldn't limit themselves to this constraint when exploring who Jesus was. It would be a tragedy and a shame if we were to miss the truth about Jesus simply because of some methodological constraint.
59. C. S. Lewis interacted with this same argument in his day. See, C. S. Lewis, *Miracles*, p. 160-162.
60. Point made in Timothy Keller, *The Reason for God*, p. 203.
61. See 1 Corinthians 15:19.
62. C. S. Lewis, *God in the Dock*, p. 101-102.
63. Timothy Keller, *The Reason for God*, p. 263.
64. Those who are seriously considering Christianity should begin by reading the Gospel of Mark. Once you've read that, read *The Reason for God*, by Timothy Keller, and *Mere Christianity* by C. S. Lewis. These books have impacted my own faith tremendously and I owe a great debt to the authors.
65. Concept described in Timothy Keller, *The Reason for God*, p. 175.
66. Ibid., p. 232.
67. Ibid.
68. Ibid., p. 29.
69. See Romans 5.
70. See Romans 8 and Revelation 21:3-4.
71. C. S. Lewis, *The Last Battle* (HarperCollins, 2002), p. 228.

Chapter Ten

1. https://ourworldindata.org/child-mortality (last accessed on October 31, 2018).
2. Statistics from Timothy Keller, *Walking with God through Pain and Suffering* (Penguin Books, 2013), p. 1. For more similar statistics see www.wfp.org. (last accessed on May 18, 2016).
3. Timothy Keller, *The Reason for God*, p. 20.

4. Bart Ehrman, *God's Problem*, p. 1.
5. Alister McGrath, *The Twilight of Atheism*, Kindle Location 1652.
6. Sam Harris writes: "The problem of vindicating an omnipotent and omniscient God in the face of evil (this is traditionally called the problem of theodicy) is insurmountable. Those who claim to have surmounted it, by recourse to notions of free will and other incoherencies, have merely heaped bad philosophy onto bad ethics." Sam Harris, *The End of the Faith*, p. 173. See also, A. C. Grayling, *The God Argument*, p. 25-26. Mackie writes: "the problem of evil constitutes an insuperable difficulty for any orthodox theism," J. L. Mackie, *Ethics: Inventing Right and Wrong*, p. 232.
7. Greg Epstein, *Good Without God*, p. 66.
8. Variations of the free will theodicy have been espoused by theologians such as Thomas Aquinas, Søren Kierkegaard, Alvin Plantinga, and C. S. Lewis.
9. C. S. Lewis, *Mere Christianity*, p. 93.
10. Keller explains our natural draw to this view, saying: "The free will theodicy has become very popular, but it may be so partially because our culture inclines us to find it appealing. It sounds plausible to people in Western civilization, where we have been taught to think of freedom and choice as something almost sacred." Timothy Keller, *Walking with God through Pain and Suffering*, p. 91.
11. This issue is the crux of the debate on God's sovereignty in regard to human salvation. Arminianism is naturally libertarian in its view, believing that God cannot affect our decisions without violating human freedom. Calvinism believes that, though humanity makes choices, we always choose sin, and so are unable to choose God without Him choosing us. Compatibilism teaches that God is completely sovereign, not despite our choices, but through them.
12. God cannot change (James 1:17); He is Righteous (Psalm 11:7); He cannot lie (Titus 1:2); He is holy, or without sin (Isaiah 6:3, 1 Peter 1:16); He cannot be tempted by evil (James 1:13); He cannot be unfaithful (2 Timothy 2:13).
13. Bart Ehrman, *God's Problem*, p. 120.
14. See Timothy Keller, *Walking with God through Pain and Suffering*, p. 140.
15. Biblical passages discussed in Ibid., p. 141-142.
16. See Acts 27 where Paul is on his way to Rome. Also, Keller provides several instances in the Bible where this paradox is in play, Ibid., p. 142-144.
17. Romans 8:28a, English Standard Version.

Endnotes

18. See Revelation 13:8, 1 Peter 1:18-20, Ephesians 1:4-5.
19. See Psalm 145:20, Revelation 20:15, Romans 2:6-10, Matthew 10:28, 2 Thessalonians 1:9, John 5:29, Acts 17:31, Revelation 20:11-15, 2 Corinthians 5:1, Romans 5:12.
20. Discussed in Bart Ehrman, *God's Problem*, p. 52.
21. The text does not mean that Job was perfect. See the following: "Perfection, integrity, or blamelessness referred to the absence of certain observable sinful acts. Job, his friends, and the author of the book were thinking of honesty, marital fidelity, just treatment of servants, generosity to the poor, and the avoidance of idolatry. Job denied wrongdoing in all these areas." Robert L. Alden, *Job, Vol. 11, The New American Commentary* (Broadman & Holman Publishers, 1993), p. 47–48.
22. Job 1:21, English Standard Version.
23. Job 1:22, English Standard Version.
24. Job 2:9, English Standard Version.
25. In the discourse between God and Satan we see that Job's suffering is actually provoked and permitted by God; it isn't Satan who brings up Job in the first place, it's God.
26. Job asks, "Why do the wicked prosper, growing old and powerful?" and, "Why doesn't the Almighty bring the wicked to judgment? Why must the godly wait for him in vain?" Job 21:7, Job 24:1, New Living Translation.
27. See Job 4-5.
28. See Job 8, 18, and 25.
29. See Job 11.
30. Job responds: "You are miserable comforters, all of you!" (Job 16:2).
31. Christian Smith, Melina Lundquist Denton, *Soul Searching: The Religious and Spiritual Lives of American Teenagers* (Oxford University Press, 2005), p. 162-163.
32. Ibid.
33. Job 38:2-3, New Living Translation.
34. Job 40:4-5, New International Version.
35. Romans 9:20, English Standard Version.
36. In Luke chapter 13 Jesus speaks of the tower in Siloam that fell on eighteen people and killed them and explains that they were no guiltier than the others living in Jerusalem.
37. See Hebrews 12:5-11.
38. C. S. Lewis, *The Problem of Pain*, p. 92.
39. For a description of the many different reasons that God allows suffering, see Robert L. Alden, *Job, Vol. 11*, The New American

Commentary (Broadman & Holman Publishers, 1993), p. 40–41. Timothy Keller, *Walking with God through Pain and Suffering*, (p. 47).
40. Richard Dawkins, *The God Delusion*, p. 398-399.
41. Ibid.
42. John 11:4, New International Version.
43. John 11:14-15, New International Version.
44. John 11:35, New International Version.
45. John 11:38a. English Standard Version.
46. Timothy Keller, *Encounters with Jesus*, p. 53.
47. This contrast of worldviews is paraphrased from Timothy Keller, *Walking with God through Pain and Suffering*, p. 30.
48. Instead of being indifferent, Christians are to groan from pain and suffering, but not in a hopeless way. See 1 Thessalonians 4:13 and 2 Corinthians 4:8-9.
49. Bart Ehrman, *God's Problem*, p. 5.
50. Ibid., p. 27-28.
51. Lewis wrote: "Omnipotence means power to do all that is intrinsically possible, not to do the intrinsically impossible. You may attribute miracles to Him, but not nonsense. There is no limit to His power." C. S. Lewis, *The Problem of Pain*, p. 19.
52. Ibid.
53. Richard Swinburne, *The Coherence of Theism* (Clarendon Press, 1993), p. 153.
54. This point is made in Timothy Keller, *Walking with God through Pain and Suffering*, p. 123-124.
55. This concept is derived from the various writings of C. S. Lewis and Timothy Keller. However, for a direct example of this, see Ibid., p. 117.
56. Alvin Plantinga, *Where the Conflict Really Lies*, p. 59. Also see page 101 for more explanation of God's intervening in human history.
57. Quoted in Greg Epstein, *Good Without God*, p. 120.
58. Charles Darwin, *The Life and Letters of Charles Darwin: Including an Autobiographical Chapter*, Volume 1 (D. Appleton, 1901), p. 282.
59. A. C. Grayling, *The God Argument*, p. 226.
60. Epstein writes: "Humanism's basic focus is different—it is about engaging with life, acknowledging the reality of aging, sickness, death, and other problems so that we can learn to most fully appreciate the time, health, and life we have." Greg Epstein, *Good Without God*, p. 107.
61. Epictetus, *Discourses III*, 24, 84–88. Quoted in Timothy Keller, *Walking with God through Pain and Suffering*, p. 328.
62. Quoted in Alister McGrath, *The Twilight of Atheism*, Kindle Location 2808-2814.

63. Fyodor Dostoevsky, *The Brothers Karamazov: A Novel in Four Parts With Epilogue* (Farrar, Straus and Giroux, 2002), p. 245.
64. New International Version.
65. Concept from Timothy Keller, *The Reason for God*, p. 28.
66. Quoted in Alister E. McGrath, *Mere Apologetics: How to Help Seekers and Skeptics Find Faith* (Baker Books, 2012), p. 164.
67. See Romans 5:8.
68. See Ephesians 2:1-10.
69. Christopher Hitchens, *The Portable Atheist: Essential Readings for the Nonbeliever* (Da Capo Press, 2007), p. 339. Dawkins asks the same question in Richard Dawkins, *The God Delusion*, p. 287.
70. Timothy Keller's written works are saturated with this kind of language and comparisons. For example, see Timothy Keller, *The Reason for God*, p. 191.
71. Ibid., p. 30.
72. Romans 8:38-39 says, "For I am convinced that neither death nor life, neither angels nor demons, neither the present nor the future, nor any powers, neither height nor depth, nor anything else in all creation, will be able to separate us from the love of God that is in Christ Jesus our Lord." New International Version.
73. For a helpful explanation of this see Alister McGrath, The Twilight of Atheism, Kindle Location 2793-2814. Also, Timothy Keller, *Walking with God through Pain and Suffering*, p. 102-103.
74. New International Version.
75. Described in Timothy Keller, *The Reason for God*, p. 226.
76. C. S. Lewis, *Mere Christianity*, p. 147.
77. Psalm 73:25-26, English Standard Version.

Chapter Eleven

1. Christopher Hitchens, *The Portable Atheist*, p. 84.
2. Greg Epstein, *Good Without God*, p. 11-12.
3. William Paley, *Natural Theology: Or, Evidences of the Existence and Attributes of the Deity*, 12th ed. (London: J. Faulder, 1809), p. 1–2.
4. Described in Alister McGrath, *The Twilight of Atheism*, Kindle Location 1588-1595.
5. Richard Dawkins, *The Blind Watchmaker* (W. W. Norton & Company, 2015), p. 4-9.
6. Quoted in Alvin Plantinga, *Where the Conflict Really Lies*, p. 257.
7. See Behe's works, *Darwin's Black Box*, and *The Edge of Evolution*.
8. Michael Behe describes irreducible complexity saying: "By irreducibly complex I mean a single system composed of several well-matched, interacting parts that contribute to the basic

function, wherein the removal of any one of the parts causes the system to effectively cease functioning." Michael Behe, *Darwin's Black Box: The Biochemical Challenge to Evolution* (Free Press, 2006), p. 39.
9. For an overview, see Alvin Plantinga, *Where the Conflict Really Lies*, p. 225.
10. Richard Dawkins, *The Blind Watchmaker*, p. 9.
11. Paley saw the eye as a clear example of design. See William Paley, *Natural Theology*, p. 2.
12. Explanation of the eye from, American Optometric Association. http://www.aoa.org/patients-and-public/resources-for-teachers/how-your-eyes-work?sso=y (last accessed on May 18, 2016).
13. While it is argued that natural selection allows some neutral genetic modifications to be preserved that do not provide a direct evolutionary advantaging, I choose not to discuss this for sake of brevity, since it does not effect the force of the argument.
14. See Charles Darwin, *The Origin of Species*, Chapter 6.
15. Richard Dawkins. *The Blind Watchmaker*, p. 81.
16. Ibid., p. 81.
17. Alvin Plantinga, *Where the Conflict Really Lies*, p. 18.
18. Richard Dawkins, *The Bind Watchmaker*, p. 79.
19. Critique of Dawkins's view in Alvin Plantinga, *Where the Conflict Really Lies*, p. 22.
20. Paul Draper, "Irreducible Complexity and Darwinian Gradualism: a Reply to Michael J. Behe," *Faith and Philosophy* 22 (2002), p. 26. Quoted in Alvin Plantinga, *Where the Conflict Really Lies*, p. 231.
21. Ibid.
22. Ibid., p. 231-232, 235-236.
23. Christopher Hitchens, *The Portable Atheist*, p. 231-232.
24. http://www.salon.com/2006/08/07/collins_6/ (last accessed on May 24, 2016). Quoted in Timothy Keller, *The Reason for God*, p. 128.
25. http://www.theguardian.com/commentisfree/2007/jun/26/spaceexploration.comment (last accessed on May 24, 2016).
26. Ibid.
27. Paul Davies, BBC Horizon documentary, "The Anthropic Principle," 1987.
28. See Plantinga for a detailed explanation of this in, *Where the Conflict Really Lies*, p. 195.
29. Richard Dawkins, *The God Delusion*, p. 169.
30. Fred Hoyle, "The Universe: Past and Present Reflections." *Engineering and Science*, November, 1981, p. 8–12
31. Alvin Plantinga, *Where the Conflict Really Lies*, p.199.

32. Richard Dawkins, *The God Delusion*, p. 173.
33. Timothy Keller, *The Reason for God*, p. 129.
34. Richard Dawkins, *The God Delusion*, p. 174.
35. http://amestrib.com/news/biologist-dawkins-discusses-illusion-design-stephens#sthash.cla26khe.dpuf (last accessed on January 20, 2016).
36. Richard Dawkins, *The God Delusion*, Chapter 4.
37. Ibid., p. 178.
38. Dawkins writes: "The key difference between the genuinely extravagant God hypothesis and the apparently extravagant multiverse hypothesis is one of statistical improbability. The multiverse, for all that it is extravagant, is simple. God, or any intelligent, decision-taking, calculating agent, would have to be highly improbable in the very same statistical sense as the entities he is supposed to explain." Ibid., p. 175.
39. Alvin Plantinga, *Where the Conflict Really Lies*, p. 29.
40. Ibid.
41. See Plantinga's explanation and space tractor analogy in Ibid., p. 27.
42. A. C. Grayling, *The God Argument*, p. 115.
43. See Dawkins discuss this in Richard Dawkins, *The God Delusion*, p. 136.
44. A. C. Grayling, *The God Argument*, p. 77.
45. Ibid., p. 96.
46. Dawkins writes: "We don't yet have an equivalent crane for physics. Some kind of multiverse theory could in principle do for physics the same explanatory work as Darwinism does for biology." Richard Dawkins, *The God Delusion*, p. 188.
47. Ibid., p. 25.
48. See Ibid., p. 235.
49. Alvin Plantinga, *Where the Conflict Really Lies*, p. 224, 258.

Chapter Twelve

1. http://www.pewresearch.org/fact-tank/2015/11/04/americans-faith-in-god-may-be-eroding/ (last accessed on March 2, 2016).
2. Sam Harris, *The End of Faith*, p. 173. While Harris admits that religious people are not insane per say, he argues that their religious beliefs absolutely are.
3. Christopher Hitchens, *The Portable Atheist*, p. 235.
4. Idea suggested in Steven Pinker, *How the Mind Works* (W. W. Norton & Company, 2009), p. 534.

5. Jean Paul Sartre, *Essays in Aesthetics* (Open Road Media, 2012), preface.
6. Ecclesiastes 3:11.
7. See Romans 1:18-20.
8. Psalm 19:1, English Standard Version.
9. See Psalm 14:1 and Psalm 53:1.
10. See Romans 1:18.
11. Timothy Keller, *The Reason for God*, p. 134.
12. See http://www.nytimes.com/2006/02/19/books/review/19wieseltier.html?pagewanted=print (last accessed on March 9, 2014).
13. Dawkins writes: "Faith is an evil precisely because it requires no justification and brooks no argument. Teaching children that unquestioned faith is a virtue primes them—given certain other ingredients that are not hard to come by—to grow up into potentially lethal weapons for future jihads or crusades." Richard Dawkins, *The God Delusion*, p. 347-348.
14. http://www.cc.com/shows/the-daily-show-with-trevor-noah/interviews/i6jzgw/exclusive-richard-dawkins-extended-interview (last access on May 25, 2016).
15. Mark Twain, *Following the Equator: A Journey Around the World* (Twain Press, 2011), p. 63.
16. C. S. Lewis, *The Complete C. S. Lewis Signature Classics* (Zondervan, 2007), p. 116.
17. Mignon McLaughlin, *The Second Neurotic's Notebook*, 1966
18. C. S. Lewis, *The Complete C. S. Lewis Signature Classics*, p. 117.
19. A. C. Grayling, *The God Argument*, p. 150.
20. Richard Dawkins, *A Devil's Chaplain: Reflections on Hope, Lies, Science, and Love* (Houghton Mifflin Harcourt, 2004), p. 81. Quoted in Timothy Keller, *The Reason for God*, p. 119.
21. Paraphrased in Alister McGrath, *The Twilight of Atheism*, p. 98.
22. Hebrews 11:1, English Standard Version.
23. Ibid., p. 96-97.
24. David Berlinski, *The Devil's Delusion*, p. 45.
25. C. S. Lewis, *Mere Christianity*, p. 63.
26. Sam Harris, *The Moral Landscape*, p. 115-116.
27. Alister McGrath, *The Twilight of Atheism*, p. 97.
28. Grayling argues this, saying: "the point of the Doubting Thomas story in the New Testament is that it is more blessed to believe without evidence than with." A. C. Grayling, *The God Argument*, p. 149. In John 20:29, after Thomas believes, Jesus responds saying: "Have you believed because you have seen me? Blessed are those

who have not seen and yet have believed." English Standard Version.
29. Emphasis mine.
30. Mark 9, New Living Translation.
31. Timothy Keller, *The Reason for God*, p. 98.
32. Alvin Plantinga, *Where the Conflict Really Lies*, Kindle Location 114.
33. This is a tautology, as it merely repeats the same arguments over and over in different ways.
34. Richard C. Lewontin, "Billions and Billions of Demons." *The New York Review of Books*, January 9, 1997. Available at http://www.nybooks.com/articles/1997/01/09/billions-and-billions-of-demons/ (last accessed on May 26, 2016).
35. This analysis of Lewontin is paraphrased from J. Budziszewski, *What We Can't Not Know*, p. 67.
36. See Timothy Keller, *The Reason for God*, p. 220.
37. Ibid., p. 216.
38. Alister McGrath, *The Twilight of Atheism*, p. 220.
39. Michael Shermer writes: "So it really does come down to some ultimate unknown? Yes, it does." Michael Shermer, *The Believing Brain*, p. 35.
40. Keller makes this point in Timothy Keller, *The Reason for God*, p. 139.
41. Richard Dawkins, *The God Delusion*, p. 130.
42. For this explanation of Pascal's wager, see Ravi Zacharias, *The End of Reason*, p. 79-80.
43. See 1 Corinthians 15:12-19. While the existential test is important, if Christ did not rise from the dead, then Christianity fails the empirical test and is worthless.
44. See Greg Epstein, *Good Without God*, p. 189.
45. Andrew Delbanco, *The Real American Dream: A Meditation on Hope* (Harvard University Press, 1999), p. 1-2. Quoted in Timothy Keller, *Walking with God through Pain and Suffering*, p. 75.
46. Erik J. Wielenberg, *Value and Virtue in a Godless Universe*, p. 121.
47. Richard Dawkins, *River Out of Eden*, p. 155.
48. Genesis 1:31.
49. As mentioned earlier, Lewis explains: "Holding a philosophy which excludes humanity, they yet remain human. At the sight of injustice they throw all their Naturalism to the winds and speak like men and like men of genius. They know far better than they think they know." C. S. Lewis, *Miracles*, p. 58.
50. Macbeth.
51. J. R. R. Tolkien, *The Return of the King*. See Ibid.
52. English Standard Version.

53. Timothy Keller, *The Reason for God*, p. 232
54. Yann Martel, *Life of Pi (Illustrated): Deluxe Illustrated Edition* (Houghton Mifflin Harcourt, 2007), p. 28.
55. Luke 24:32a, English Standard Version.

Made in the USA
Coppell, TX
26 November 2019